Addressing the
State of the Union

Addressing the
State of
the Union

The Evolution and Impact of
the President's Big Speech

Donna R. Hoffman
Alison D. Howard

LYNNE
RIENNER
PUBLISHERS

BOULDER
LONDON

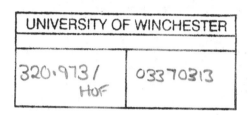
Published in the United States of America in 2006 by
Lynne Rienner Publishers, Inc.
1800 30th Street, Boulder, Colorado 80301
www.rienner.com

and in the United Kingdom by
Lynne Rienner Publishers, Inc.
3 Henrietta Street, Covent Garden, London WC2E 8LU

Library of Congress Cataloging-in-Publication Data
Hoffman, Donna R., 1969–
    Addressing the state of the union : the evolution and impact of the
president's big speech / Donna R. Hoffman, Alison D. Howard.
        p. cm.
    Includes bibliographical references and index.
    ISBN-13: 978-1-58826-451-0 (hardcover : alk. paper)
    ISBN-10: 1-58826-451-3 (hardcover : alk. paper)
    1. Presidents—United States—Messages. 2. Political oratory—United
States. 3. Speechwriting—United States. 4. United States—Politics and
government. I. Howard, Alison D., 1970– II. Title.
JK587.H65 2006
352.23'840973—dc22

                                                              2006004033

British Cataloguing in Publication Data
A Cataloguing in Publication record for this book
is available from the British Library.

Printed and bound in the United States of America

The paper used in this publication meets the requirements
∞ of the American National Standard for Permanence of
Paper for Printed Library Materials Z39.48-1992.

  5   4   3   2   1

Contents

Tables and Figures

Tables

Figures

Acknowledgments

There are many who deserve a heartfelt thank-you for assisting us with this project. One phase of our research was supported by a summer research grant from the College of Social and Behavioral Sciences, University of Northern Iowa. Meg Taylor and Brandi Halverson provided many hours of valuable research assistance.

We wish to thank Leanne Anderson at Lynne Rienner Publishers for her enthusiasm, encouragement, and help along the path to completing this project. Sonia Smith and Shena Redmond at Lynne Rienner were invaluable at the end of the project and exceeded our expectations in the final editing process.

Our sincere gratitude is extended to the three anonymous reviewers who provided insightful, constructive, and thoughtful comments that reinforced our ideas and writing, yet managed to make the manuscript stronger. In addition, various pieces of our concept, research, and drafts were helpfully commented on by Gary Copeland and Keith Gaddie.

Finally, our families embraced our efforts throughout this project. This book is dedicated to our encouraging, loving, and supportive husbands, Mike and Lyman, and to Donna's son, Nathan. We thank you for your patience and tolerance throughout this endeavor.

—*Donna R. Hoffman and*
Alison D. Howard

1

Donning the Hat
of Chief Legislator

Presidential communications occur at multiple levels and in multiple formats. Communications are aimed at the media, who will report the president's words to the public. A president may hold a press conference, take questions from the press while meeting with a foreign head of state, or answer a question from the press on the way to Marine One. Presidents communicate with executive agencies through an executive order or a cabinet meeting. They give numerous speeches to different audiences. Presidents may address an interest group, employees of a factory they are visiting, members of their party, or the larger public with a televised address from the Oval Office in a time of crisis. There are communications with Congress in the form of veto messages, legislative proposals, and meetings with congressional leadership. Presidents also communicate without saying a word. The famous picture of George W. Bush atop the World Trade Towers' rubble with a bullhorn and flag in hand communicated national resolve and a call to action in the days following September 11, 2001. These examples of presidential communications are not exhaustive, and virtually every utterance and every action of the president is scrutinized for what it communicates.

Just as there are multiple avenues of presidential communication, there are multiple jobs that presidents must undertake. One job of the president, or "hats" that the president wears, is that of chief legislator.[1] Presidents have many others that they may don, among them chief executive, chief diplomat, and commander-in-chief. Acting in the role of chief legislator, the president is no ordinary legislator. Presidents play a role at the very beginning of the legislative process through their powers to recommend measures to Congress, and they command a large policy staff to assist them in devising legislative strategies and priorities. They play a role at the end of the

1

legislative process because they must accept or reject legislation before it can become law. In between, they can use all of the considerable powers of their office to persuade, bargain, pressure, and lobby as they attempt to get what they want out of Congress. Furthermore, presidents are the one elected official who have a national constituency, and they possess the "bully pulpit" from which they command the attention of that constituency. These things give the chief legislator a distinct advantage over regular legislators. Yet, presidents cannot introduce bills, participate in committee hearings or mark-ups, or debate and vote on the floor of either chamber.

Just as the president as chief legislator is not an ordinary legislator, the State of the Union address (SUA) is no ordinary presidential communication. The speech itself was instrumental in the development of the president's role as chief legislator, a role not ascribed to presidents in the nineteenth century. The SUA is one of the things that gives presidents the ability to be the extraordinary legislators that they are. Two constitutional provisions are at the root of the modern SUA, and both of them rest in Article II, Section 3. These two provisions dictate the president "from time to time give to the Congress information on the State of the Union, and recommend to their Consideration such Measures as he shall judge necessary and expedient." The Constitution does not dictate how, or even when, a president should give information on the state of the Union. It is silent on how the president should go about recommending "necessary and expedient" measures. As a result, there has been variation in the way presidents have carried out these functions. For much of the nineteenth century, the SUA was typically a long, and often tedious, written document presidents sent to Congress. The contemporary SUA, however, delivered in person before Congress and transmitted to the world, represents an opportunity for presidents. One common question asked by those who seek to evaluate presidents is, "Did the president make the most of his opportunities?"[2] The SUA offers an opportunity for presidents to communicate, with both Congress and the public, where they want to lead the country. In the American system of government, both Congress and the president must participate in what Woodrow Wilson termed "the dance of legislation."[3] Even though it takes two to tango, so to speak, the American public now looks to the president, not Congress, to provide legislative leadership, guidance, and initiative.

The use of SUAs has both aided and reflected the expansion of the president's role in the legislative process. The speech is the ultimate communication of the president acting as chief legislator. An examination of SUAs, therefore, gives an important insight into the relationship between presidents and the Congresses they seek to lead. To this end, we examine how successful presidents are in communicating and accomplishing their legislative goals outlined in an SUA. Throughout the course of the book, we ask five main questions.

- How did what we now know as the State of the Union address evolve?
- What is the nature of the communication that takes place in the SUA?
- For what purposes do chief legislators use the SUA?
- Does Congress follow where a president leads with the SUA?
- What is the ultimate result of the presidential communication that takes place in the SUA?

Why Study State of the Union Addresses?

Within the "modern presidency" that dates from Franklin Roosevelt to the present day, presidents have generally chosen to make formal speeches to joint sessions of Congress that have come to be known as State of the Union addresses. Often these speeches are delivered in the evening, so presidents can capture the attention of a large portion of their secondary audience, the American public, who can dial their radio, tune their television, or direct their Web browser to a source carrying the president's address. Within the confines of the SUA, a president's multiple hats will be on display. The very act of appearing before a joint session of Congress exemplifies the president as head of state. During the address, presidents will report on executive actions they have taken in their role as chief executive, and may even discuss future executive actions they will take. As commander-in-chief, they will talk about the state of the armed forces. Wearing their diplomatic hat, presidents will address relations with foreign nations. What we are primarily concerned with in this book, however, is when presidents put on their chief legislator hat in the SUA. The SUA's oral delivery, reinstituted by Woodrow Wilson, is linked to the emergence of the president's chief legislator role. With this change in the speech's format, it developed into a significant power for presidents to utilize. Much of the speech, through the legislative actions presidents request, is aimed at providing congressional leadership. These same requests also tell the public what actions the president wants from Congress.

The emergence of the chief legislator role was not a development anticipated by the Founders. The men at the constitutional convention in Philadelphia were concerned about the proper balance between the executive and legislative branches. Giving the title of "chief legislator" to the one person they were deeming to be commander-in-chief, as well as chief magistrate, would not have boded well for the ratification struggle in which one criticism of the new constitution was a too-powerful, single executive. In *Federalist 73,* Alexander Hamilton addresses executive-legislative relations and particularly the president's major legislative power, the qualified veto. He states, "But the Convention *have pursued a mean* in this business; which will both facilitate the exercise of the power vested in this respect in the executive magistrate, and make its efficacy to depend on the sense of a considerable part of the legislative body."[4] In pursuing a mean, they sought to check both the legislative powers of the executive, as well as the powers of the legislature to encroach on the executive. The evolution of the president into chief legislator, therefore, could potentially upset the carefully balanced powers of the executive and legislative branches.

A major aspect of the chief legislator's power is rhetorical and exemplified in the contemporary SUA. Rhetoric, going back to ancient Greece, has been viewed as a potentially dangerous art that could lead to demagoguery. As presidential scholar Jeffrey Tulis has pointed out, "The founders . . . feared provision for popular leadership because they expected that, as an institutional practice, statesmanship would quickly degenerate into demagoguery, which might raise anew the great divisions of class, section, or constitutive principle."[5] As the presidency changed, the president did become a popular leader, using rhetoric to appeal to the public, and what Tulis has termed the *rhetorical presidency* emerged.[6] One scholar of presidential rhetoric has asserted,

> Because the president of the United States can now assault both the eyes and the ears (and hence the hearts and minds) of the American people whenever he chooses to do so, the political and economic forces that supposedly keep him in check are themselves confronted by a powerful social force in the person of the president. The age of the mass media, in short, has substantially altered traditional political compacts, and the president of the United States has been the primary beneficiary of such alterations.[7]

There is, thus, a fear that the constitutional balance has been altered in such a way that gives the president more power than the Founders intended. Presidential rhetoric is a key component of the change in presidential power in the twentieth century. The history of the SUA reflects the evolution of the presidency itself, where one finds a progression of power prompted by key individual innovations in practice. Because presidents have become chief legislators, it is vital to understand the nature of the role, the rhetorical power they have, and the role the SUA played in the evolution of the chief legislator power. The SUA provides the president with the ultimate "bully pulpit" and we argue that the SUA is now a significant power contemporary presidents have. The nature of this power, however, is important. Is this power that chief legislators have with the modern SUA a weapon to wield, coercing the acceptance of their wishes, or is it merely a tool that aids them in the pursuit of their goals?

State of the Union Addresses as a Source of Data

Studies of presidential speeches can be classified in multiple ways. First, there is the way different disciplines approach the topic. As Martin Medhurst explains, political scientists tend to study the rhetorical presidency, while communications scholars tend to study presidential rhetoric. Political scientists are inclined to approach the subject from an institutional angle, while communications scholars mainly approach the subject by way of rhetorical criticism.[8] Second, within both approaches SUAs are sometimes treated as a distinct entity, sometimes combined with others as one component of major speeches, in other instances simply included as part of the entire corpus of presidential speech, and occasionally excluded altogether.

In 1968, Gerald Pomper first published his influential *Elections in America*, a portion of which was devoted to examining how often parties fulfill pledges they make in party platforms. Much as Pomper discussed how the conventional wisdom on party platforms was that they were useless,[9] SUAs as a source of data have been somewhat maligned as well. They have sometimes been marginalized, disparaged, and occasionally ignored as a source of data. John Kingdon calls them a "classic garbage can"; a whole host of things are dumped into them.[10] They have been cited, somewhat disparagingly, for their inclusion of "laundry lists."[11] George Edwards and Dan Wood are critical of using SUAs as a data source for presidential priorities.[12] Some studies of presidential rhetoric specifically exclude SUAs as a source of data because of their broad nature[13] or because their timing is nondiscretionary.[14] Studying SUAs in their own right as a form of political communication with Congress has received little attention.

A number of studies do utilize SUAs as the primary, or a major, source of data, and they tend to be of four types. One type analyzes the substance of the address, or what policies and issues are discussed. Historian Seymour Fersh examined annual messages and SUAs from 1790 to 1959 and discerned the way the message evolved over time from a simple reporting document to a written summary of cabinet reports to an agenda-setting device.[15] John Kessel utilized computerized content analysis of SUAs to study presidential behavior.[16] Both Kingdon and Paul Light utilized SUAs in their works on agenda setting, although they incorporated additional data also.[17] More recently, Andrew Rudalevige has utilized SUA data for inclusion into his investigation of the president's legislative program, which he conceived as being broader than the presidential agenda.[18] A more narrowly focused study of agenda setting by Matthew Moen analyzed the content of Ronald Reagan's messages.[19]

A second type of study seeks to investigate the public's connection to what the president says using SUAs in conjunction with survey data. Jeffrey Cohen used data from SUAs to examine whether presidential mentions of policy influenced the public's agenda,[20] as well as the responsiveness of presidential SUAs to public opinion.[21] William Oliver, in a narrowly focused study, examined presidential mentions of crime in SUAs and the public's reaction.[22] Kim Quaile Hill looked at the reciprocal influence of the public and the president on SUA content.[23]

A third area of SUA research has examined media reactions to the president's SUA,[24] while the final type of study, done primarily by communications scholars, examines how presidents communicate through their rhetoric, or how they say what they say.[25] We should add that there are other broader studies of presidential rhetoric and speeches that utilize SUAs but as a part of a larger corpus of presidential communications.[26]

We seek to bring together the two approaches to studying presidential speech, the institutionally oriented rhetorical presidency approach with the presidential rhetoric approach of communication studies, and specifically study the one type of presidential speech, the SUA, that illustrates most clearly and comprehensively, the president acting as chief legislator. We are interested in the SUA as a genre.[27] We do not study presidential agenda setting, and we are not studying the effect of the SUA on public opinion, or the media. We seek to examine what the chief legislator says in the SUA, how he says it, and what this tells us about the role of the chief legislator and his communications with both his constituents and the legislators he seeks to lead. We are interested not only in what chief legislators say, specifically, about policy in the SUA, but also how they say it.

Our contention is that, as a form of political communication, SUAs deserve more study as a medium of passing information between the president and Congress. The SUA is not just any speech; it is a communication formally given by one institution of the US government to another. It is more than that, however, because other audiences listen, particularly the public, whom both the president and Congress represent.

SUAs possess characteristics that make them imminently suitable for study. Several qualities make them useful as a data source. First, a requirement to report on the state of the Union is a constitutional provision. All presidents must, in some form, undertake this task. How this provision has been carried out has varied over time. The major portion of our examination will be isolated to the 1965–2002 time period. During this period, the format has almost exclusively taken oral form, and we confine ourselves to an examination of the oral addresses. Furthermore, the speeches all occur in the same setting, the House chamber, with the same institutional audiences in attendance. In addition, the public audience has been maximized with evening delivery of the speech, and advances in electronic technology have enabled widespread dissemination over radio, television, and the Internet.

We begin the major portion of our analysis with 1965 because that is the year Lyndon Johnson moved the delivery of the SUA to the evening, a tradition generally followed since, in order to capture the attention of the prime-time television viewing audience. The two primary audiences for the speech, Congress and the public, therefore, remain a constant factor during this period.

Another important factor is that SUAs occur with regularity and at the same point in the congressional calendar, near the beginning of each session. Finally, the SUAs tell us what policy areas the president believes are important and has chosen to highlight rhetorically to the public and Congress. The media anticipate the speech in their reporting and cover it immediately afterward. They typically use it as a reference point during the congressional session to assess the progress of key pieces of the president's priorities.

Events, personalities, skill, previous administrations, partisanship, and many other factors influence presidencies. Presidents use various communications to different degrees. Some presidents veto rarely. Others veto more frequently. Some presidents preside over great national crises brought on by international or economic events while others preside during times of relative peace and prosperity. What makes SUAs useful as a source of data is that they are a constant in an institution buffeted so much by events, circumstances, and individual actions. Importantly, SUAs offer a view of the contemporary presidency and individual presidents through the same lens. There is much variability in the presidency. One sees it over time through the evolution of the office. One sees it between presidents with different styles and personalities. One even sees it within a presidency, such as when external events arise that influence presidential actions and outlooks. SUAs have value because they allow us to view one aspect of the presidency in a constant fashion, enabling comparisons that allow for the emergence of similarities, and also differences, between presidents and within presidencies regarding the way presidents communicate as chief legislator.

Plan of the Book

We begin Chapter 2 by examining the two constitutional provisions on which annual messages and SUAs are based that charge the president with reporting and recommending measures to Congress.[28] A brief history of the message is given as we trace the evolution of the document over time. Nineteenth-century annual messages were typically viewed as a duty presidents had to fulfill. As time passed and views of the presidency as an institution changed, the SUA afforded an opportunity for the president to act as chief legislator. Looking at SUAs over time evinces the changes in the institution of the presidency and illustrates the emergence of the chief legislator role. In the twentieth century, as oral SUAs became the rule, the SUA evolved from being a presidential duty to being a presidential power. Presidents took advantage of the oral format to act as chief legislator. The speech's communicative powers were also expanded as technology enabled the public to have access to the president's words.

After taking a historical look at annual messages and SUAs, we confine the rest of our analysis to more recent presidents and their SUAs from 1965 to 2002. Chapter 3 begins with an examination of the structure of the SUA and how presidents utilize the SUA as a form of political communication. The chief legislator is the only nationally elected official, and as such, must communicate his policy goals to both Congress and the public. SUAs are a valuable form of communication for the chief legislator, and all SUAs utilize the same form or structure in which they address policy dilemmas and propose policy solutions.[29] As a part of this policymaking rhetoric, the chief legislator engages in activities that attempt to convince Congress and the public that his legislative requests are worth enacting. The policymaking rhetoric presidents use will convey policy substance as well as employ symbolic images, examples, and language in order to persuade his audiences to follow his policy prescriptions. Even though all presidents include these elements in their SUAs, each president puts his own individual stamp on the speech. For chief legislators, the SUA has become a speech that is both tactical and reactive as they attempt to maximize the likelihood of advancing their legislative requests with Congress.

We turn our attention in Chapter 4 to the chief legislator's behavior as evidenced by the substantive rhetoric presidents use in their SUAs. As presidents gained the role of chief legislator, they began to play a more active role at the beginning and middle of the legislative process, in addition to their traditional role at the end. The public came to judge presidents on whether or not they accomplished their policy initiatives. Chief legislators and regular legislators share some of the same goals, such as a desire to make public policy, and for first-term presidents, a desire to be reelected. At the same time, presidents want to procure for themselves a positive legacy. For chief legislators, these goals are mutually reinforcing. Because the role of chief legislator has become firmly rooted in the presidency, the SUA has developed into an important tool for presidents to use in the pursuit of their goals. Just as they share some goals with regular legislators, chief legislators also engage in similar activities that help them further their goals. Like regular legislators, chief legislators claim credit for accomplishments and take positions, and the annual SUA provides an ideal forum in which to engage in these activities. They will do so with their substantive rhetoric in which they claim credit for accomplishments and take positions by urging congressional action. The levels of position taking and credit claiming presidents engage in varies depending upon the type of SUA, but all presidents engage in these activities in their SUAs.

SUAs can be categorized into various types that hinge on the political circumstances presidents confront at the time of the speech. When they confront crises, all presidents seek to use the SUA to rally their audiences, although the object they seek to rally people around will vary depending on the nature of the crisis. When faced with similar circumstances—such as in an inaugural year, the second and third years, reelection years, lame duck status, or their second term—presidents tend to behave similarly in their SUAs. Thus, there is a kind of life cycle of SUAs, lending another element of commonality across presidencies.

Contemporary presidents are expected, by both Congress and the public, to lead on policy issues. The SUA provides presidents with a platform from which to communicate and highlight what their major policy proposals for the coming year will be; the policymaking rhetoric contained in the SUA is structured to facilitate policy leadership. Are presidents successful in getting Congress to enact the policies they ask for in the SUA? Does Congress follow where the president leads? This is the major question we address in Chapter 5. Overall, we find that contemporary presidents receive, in full or part, about two in five of the legislative requests they make of Congress in the year following their request. Successes vary greatly from president to president, as well as within a presidency.

Four case studies allow for further analysis of the SUA requests presidents make of Congress. Presidents have many roles to fulfill and these roles are not as distinct as the hat metaphor might imply. Roles overlap. Just within the realm of domestic policy, presidents pursue multiple issues acting in multiple roles simultaneously. The president does not just contend with members of Congress, but also a gaggle of interest groups, the media, his own White House staff, the public, and people within executive agencies. Policymaking does not exist in a vacuum, but rather in a complex environment. The case studies allow a look at this environment and offer a way to assess the role the SUA played in the outcome of the president's request, as well as what the president's chief motivations likely were for the request.

Each of our four cases has a different outcome. One case we examine is a presidential request of Congress that was not successful, one is a request that was fully successful, another is a request that was partially successful, and finally we examine a request multiple presidents made in multiple SUAs that was eventually successful. Each case study details the particular request, traces its outcome, and assesses the role the SUA played in the outcome. Johnson's request for Congress to propose a constitutional amendment that would increase House terms to four years offers an example of a chief legislator being successful in convincing Congress to advance a languishing issue, but ultimately failing in terms of seeing the policy come to fruition. Reagan's success in convincing Congress to fund the manned space station shows how interest from the president and attention in the SUA can add the needed element for a request to be successful. Jimmy Carter's civil service reform in 1978 illustrates nicely a presidential initiative from the SUA on which the president had to lobby persistently and compromise in order to get most, but not everything, he wanted. Finally, multiple presidents in multiple SUAs asked Congress for the line-item veto. Eventually, Congress complied. In each case, the SUA played an integral role in the outcome.

Our examination of SUAs illustrates one way in which the institution of the presidency has changed over time. Furthermore, we see the relationships that contemporary presidents have with Congress and the public change across presidencies, and also within a presidency. While these are not new insights, keeping the presidency in proper perspective is important. One should not be alarmed about the rhetorical powers presidents have gained, because they still must operate in a political system where separate institutions share power.[30] As presidents gained the new role of chief legislator, they began to utilize two constitutional provisions in a way that contributed to this new role. The SUA itself became a power, but it is still a limited power. It is a tool for chief legislators to utilize; it is not a weapon with which they can cudgel Congress into accepting their policies. The SUA facilitates, but does not guarantee, successful presidential leadership of Congress. Our research on the president's use of the SUA reminds us of the limitations of the office. Even as the president gained a significant new role, that of chief legislator, the change did not upend the balance of legislative power between the president and Congress.

There is, however, another issue to consider. Whereas one should not be alarmed about presidential rhetoric, neither should one be complacent about it. Ultimately, the way presidents utilize the contemporary SUA can raise expectations on the part of constituents that the president has the solution to policy dilemmas. In the SUA, presidents will talk about problems in a simplified fashion, often with sweeping rhetoric, and they offer solutions in a way that encourages acceptance. A member of Congress might do the same thing in addressing his or her own constituents, but when nothing happens, the member can conveniently blame the institution of Congress itself for a lack of action. Constituents, therefore, can continue to approve of their individual congressperson.[31] The *chief* legislator, however, is expected to deliver. The public expects action. When presidents fail to get Congress to act on their requests, as will often happen, a gap results in what the public expects the president to do and what the president can actually deliver. This *expectations gap*, as it is called, can cause public cynicism about government to increase. The chief legislator's actual power is limited, but the public's perception of the power the president holds is out of kilter. The SUA is an important factor in fostering this perception of a presidency-centered government. By examining the way the president uses the SUA to communicate, and the results of his efforts to lead Congress, one is reminded of the limits on the legislative powers presidents have.

Notes

1. Clinton Rossiter, *The American Presidency* (New York: Harcourt, Brace, 1956). Rossiter does not use the term *hats,* but details the various roles, or tasks, that presidents perform. Rossiter, 4–25. The first reference to presidential roles as "hats" appears to come from Neustadt. Richard E. Neustadt, *Presidential Power and the Modern Presidents*, Rev. ed. (New York: Free Press, 1990), xxi. There is a danger in overusing the hat metaphor, which we shall endeavor not to do. One should recognize that presidential roles are not as separate as might be implied when talking about "hats." Rossiter cautions that the presidency "is a wonderful stew whose unique flavor cannot be accounted for simply by making a list of its ingredients. . . . The President is not one kind of official one part of the day, another kind in another part—king in the morning, legislator at lunch, administrator in the afternoon, commander before dinner and politician at odd moments that come his weary way. He is all these things all the time, and any one of his functions feeds upon and into all the others" (p. 25).

2. Erwin Hargrove, *The President as Leader: Appealing to the Better Angels of Our Nature* (Lawrence: University of Kansas Press, 1998), 162.

3. Quoted in Eric Redman, *The Dance of Legislation* (New York: Simon and Schuster, 1973), 15.

4. Emphasis added. Alexander Hamilton, James Madison, and John Jay, *The Federalist Papers,* ed. Garry Wills (New York: Bantam, 1982), 375.

5. Jeffrey K. Tulis, *The Rhetorical Presidency* (Princeton: Princeton University Press, 1987), 111.

6. Ibid., 4.

7. Roderick P. Hart, *The Sound of Leadership: Presidential Communication in the Modern Age* (Chicago: University of Chicago Press, 1987), 213.

8. Martin J. Medhurst, "A Tale of Two Constructs: The Rhetorical Presidency Versus Presidential Rhetoric," introd. in *Beyond the Rhetorical Presidency*, ed. Martin J. Medhurst (College Station: Texas A&M University Press, 1996), xi–xxv.

9. Gerald M. Pomper, with Susan S. Lederman, *Elections in America*, 2nd ed. (New York: Longman, 1980), 129.

10. John W. Kingdon, *Agendas, Alternatives, and Public Policies,* 2nd ed. (New York: Harper Collins, 1995), 188.

11. Paul C. Light, *The President's Agenda: Domestic Policy Choice from Kennedy to Clinton,* 3rd ed. (Baltimore: Johns Hopkins University Press, 1999), 6.

12. George C. Edwards, III, and B. Dan Wood, "Who Influences Whom? The President, Congress, and the Media," *American Political Science Review* 93 (1999):330.

13. David Lewis, "The Two Rhetorical Presidencies: An Analysis of Televised Presidential Speeches, 1947–1991," *American Politics Quarterly* 25 (July 1997):380–395; Jeffrey E. Cohen and John A. Hamman, "The Polls: Can Presidential Rhetoric Affect the Public's Economic Perceptions?" *Presidential*

Studies Quarterly 33 (June 2003):408–422; Lydia Andrade and Garry Young, "Presidential Agenda Setting: Influences on the Emphasis of Foreign Policy," *Political Research Quarterly* 49 (1996):591–605.

14. Lyn Ragsdale, "The Politics of Presidential Speechmaking, 1949–1980," *American Political Science Review* 78 (December 1984):971–984.

15. Seymour H. Fersh, *The View from the White House: A Study of the Presidential State of the Union Messages* (Washington, DC: Public Affairs Press, 1961).

16. John H. Kessel, "The Parameters of Presidential Politics," *Social Science Quarterly* 55 (1974):8–24; "The Seasons of Presidential Politics," *Social Science Quarterly* 58 (1977):418–435.

17. Kingdon, *Agendas;* Light, *The President's Agenda.*

18. Andrew Rudalevige, *Managing the President's Program: Presidential Leadership and Legislative Policy Formation,* (Princeton, NJ: Princeton University Press, 2002).

19. Matthew C. Moen, "The Political Agenda of Ronald Reagan: A Content Analysis of the State of the Union Messages," *Presidential Studies Quarterly* 18 (1988):775–785.

20. Jeffrey E. Cohen, "Presidential Rhetoric and the Public Agenda," *American Journal of Political Science* 39 (1995):87–107.

21. Cohen, *Presidential Responsiveness and Public Policy-Making: The Public and the Policies that Presidents Choose* (Ann Arbor: University of Michigan Press, 1997).

22. Willard M. Oliver, "The Pied Piper of Crime in America: An Analysis of the Presidents' and Public's Agenda on Crime," *Criminal Justice Policy Review* 13 (2002):139–155.

23. Kim Quaile Hill, "The Policy Agendas of the President and the Mass Public: A Research Validation and Extension," *American Journal of Political Science* 42 (1998):1328–1335.

24. Wayne Wanta, et al., "How President's State of the Union Talk Influenced News Media Agendas," *Journalism Quarterly* 66 (1989):537–541; Sheldon Gilberg, et al., "The State of the Union Address and the Press Agenda," *Journalism Quarterly* 57 (1980):584–588.

25. James W. Prothro, "Verbal Shifts in the American Presidency: A Content Analysis," *American Political Science Review* 50 (September 1956):726–739; Craig Allen Smith and Kathy B. Smith, "Presidential Values and Public Priorities: Recurrent Patterns in Addresses to the Nation, 1963–1984," *Presidential Studies Quarterly* 15 (1985):743–753; Karlyn Kohrs Campbell and Kathleen Hall Jamieson, *Deeds Done in Words: Presidential Rhetoric and the Genres of Governance,* (Chicago: University of Chicago Press, 1990); Barbara Hinckley, *The Symbolic Presidency: How Presidents Portray Themselves,* (New York: Routledge, 1990); Elvin Lim, "Five Trends in Presidential Rhetoric: An Analysis of Rhetoric from George Washington to Bill Clinton," *Presidential Studies Quarterly* 32 (2002):328–366; Ryan L. Teten, "Evolution of the Modern Rhetorical Presidency: Presidential Presentation and Development of the State of the Union Addresses," *Presidential Studies Quarterly* 33 (2003):333–346; Vanessa B. Beasley, *You, the People: American National Identity in Presidential Rhetoric* (College Station: Texas A&M University Press, 2004).

26. James W. Ceaser, et al., "The Rise of the Rhetorical Presidency," *Presidential Studies Quarterly* 11 (Spring 1981):158–171; Tulis, *The Rhetorical Presidency*; Hart, *The Sound of Leadership*; Samuel Kernell, *Going Public: New*

Strategies of Presidential Leadership, 3rd ed. (Washington, DC: CQ Press, 1997); Brandice Canes-Wrone, "The President's Legislative Influence from Public Appeals," *American Journal of Political Science* 45 (April 2001):313–329; Andrew W. Barrett, "Gone Public: The Impact of Going Public on Presidential Legislative Success," *American Politics Research* 32 (May 2004):338–370.

27. Campbell and Jamieson established the SUA as a genre of presidential communication. See Chapter 4, *Deeds Done in Words.*

28. From George Washington to Herbert Hoover, what we now refer to as the State of the Union address (if oral), or message (if written), was simply referred to as the annual message. See Thomas H. Neale, "The President's State of the Union Message: Frequently Asked Questions," *CRS Report for Congress* (Washington, DC: Congressional Research Service, Library of Congress, 2003).

29. Campbell and Jamieson, *Deeds Done in Words,* 74.

30. Neustadt, *Presidential Power,* 29.

31. Richard F. Fenno Jr., *Home Style: House Members in Their Districts* (Boston: Little, Brown, 1978).

2

The State of the Union Address Through Time

The Constitution directs that the president "shall from time to time give to the Congress Information of the State of the Union, and recommend to their Consideration such Measures as he shall judge necessary and expedient."[1] When the Framers of the Constitution penned these two particular provisions, they were not specific as to when the president was to give this information, the manner in which this information was to be given, or even a time frame as to how often the information should be delivered. Nor was it clear exactly what the second provision might mean in terms of the president's role in the legislative process. Were these two provisions merely *duties,* or were they presidential *powers*? Over time, and as a consequence of this ambiguity, presidents have determined for themselves when to give information, what to recommend, and the mode of delivery of both these constitutional provisions. The history of what was first called the annual message, and later the State of the Union address, is an evolving one.[2] Through a broad consideration of significant changes in the format and practice of SUAs, we highlight not just the evolution of this form of political communication, which was initially interpreted as a duty and later came to be seen as a power, but also how it spurred and reflected changes in the institution of the presidency.

SUAs have always been about presidents giving information to Congress; in this regard, the concept has changed but little. Presidents have sometimes delivered their message to Congress orally and in person; other times it has been a written document delivered to the Congress. Over time the audience for this information has enlarged beyond just Congress to encompass the American public and the rest of the world as advances in various technological media enabled much greater dissemination of the president's message, and the position of the United States as an important

15

actor on the world stage grew. How presidents have treated the provision charging them with making recommendations to Congress has varied tremendously from president to president. Some gave vague generalities, while others recommended very specific actions. Some offered few recommendations, while others offered many.

Origins of the Powers

It is important to recognize that giving information to Congress and recommending measures to Congress are two different things. Both can, however, be accomplished at the same time and routinely are. Although the two Constitutional provisions are separate, they became connected very early. In *Federalist 69,* when Alexander Hamilton explains the powers of the executive in light of Anti-Federalist criticism, he refers to the recommending provision as one of the president's powers but does not mention the provision charging the president with giving information, thereby reflecting their separate nature.[3] Later, writing in *Federalist 77,* Hamilton treats both provisions as separate *powers.*[4] George Washington's first inaugural address, which was delivered to the House and the Senate in the manner of his later annual messages, spoke of the second provision, recommending measures to Congress, but not the first, giving information, indicating they are separate provisions.[5] By the time Washington delivered what is known as his first annual message in 1790, the provisions are linked together. It is not the case that Washington saw either provision as a power. He specifically refers to the recommending provision as a *duty* in the first inaugural.[6] Later, in his first annual message, Washington again refers to the information provision as a duty.[7] Hamilton and Washington viewed both provisions as separate—Hamilton viewing them as separate powers, and Washington viewing them as separate duties. In the earliest annual messages of Washington and John Adams, they first gave information and then made recommendations to Congress to focus attention on the matters they deemed important, setting the standard that an annual message would encompass both provisions. Washington's view of these provisions as constitutional duties would become the precedent.

There is very little guidance given by the Founders as to what the two provisions of Article II, Section 3 entail. The act of giving information to the Congress would seem to be fairly straightforward in its intent, if rather vague in its specific application. The recommendation provision, however, gives rise to questions as to its intent.

Hamilton, in detailing the powers of the executive in *Federalist 77,* contends that neither the information giving nor recommending provisions (as well as the others contained in Section 3) are controversial powers.

> The only remaining powers of the Executive are comprehended in giving information to Congress of the state of the Union; in recommending to their consideration such measures as he shall judge expedient; in convening them, or either branch, upon extraordinary occasions; in adjourning them when they cannot themselves agree upon the time of adjournment; in receiving ambassadors and other public ministers; in faithfully executing the laws; and in commissioning all the officers of the United States.
>
> Except some cavils about the power of convening *either* house of the legislature, and that of receiving ambassadors, no objection has been made to this class of authorities; nor could they possibly admit of any.[8]

Indeed, it appears that the major critics of the Constitution, the Anti-Federalists, did not raise objections to either provision. It is not clear, however, how active a role the Framers of the Constitution intended the president to assume in recommending measures to Congress.

Writing in *Federalist 69*, Hamilton undertakes a comparison of the proposed president's powers with those of both the governor of New York and the British monarch. Hamilton specifically mentions the president's power "to recommend to the consideration of Congress such measures as he shall judge necessary and expedient."[9] No further elaboration is given because, as Hamilton writes of this particular power, "the power of the President will resemble equally that of the King of Great-Britain and of the Governor of New-York."[10] Hamilton does not expand any further. His audience would have been familiar with the powers of both the king and the New York governor. At this time in Great Britain, King George III was presiding over a system that gave the king substantial power in the area of recommending policies.

> English government [by the time of King George III] has ceased to be, strictly speaking, either a royal or a parliamentary government, and has become a cabinet government, — blending the executive and legislative, by taking authority derived from the ancient representatives of each, and exercising it through a body having relation to both.[11]

The state of New York, furthermore, was the only state to give its governor a role in initiating legislation.[12] In fact, the constitution of New York that was in effect from 1777 to 1801 contains wording that obviously served as a model for the federal Constitution's language regarding this grant of power to the federal executive.

> That it shall be the duty of the governor to inform the legislature, at every session, of the condition of the State, so far as may respect his department; to recommend such matters to their consideration as shall appear to him to concern its good government, welfare, and prosperity.[13]

The lack of discussion of the federal Constitution's reporting and recommending provisions during the debate over ratification, however, leaves considerable ambiguity as to what the Founders intended for the president with this grant of power.

In addition, the placement of these two provisions in Article II, rather than Article I, is also significant. One of the concerns of the Anti-Federalists regarding the executive power was that it would tend toward despotism. In regard to the president, they were especially concerned that there was not sufficient separation of the executive power with that of the legislative power. The Anti-Federalist writing under the pseudonym Cato voiced this concern by writing,

> [The president] is a constituent part of the legislative power; for every bill which shall pass the house of representatives and senate, is to be presented to him for approbation; if he approves of it, he is to sign it, if he disapproves, he is to return it with objections, which in many cases will amount to a complete negative; and in this view he will have a great share in the power of making peace, coining money, etc. and all the various objects of legislation, expressed or implied in this Constitution.[14]

In answering this particular criticism of the Constitution's critics, *Federalist 69* stresses the qualified nature of the veto.[15] Both chambers of Congress by a two-thirds vote may override a president's veto; Hamilton stresses it is not the absolute veto of the British monarchy. Note that the concern of the Anti-Federalists is wholly about the president's role at the *end* of the legislative process where he may negate legislation. The Anti-Federalists do not voice any qualms about the potential role the president would play at the *beginning* of the legislative process by recommending measures to Congress. As a result, Hamilton does not address precisely how this particular power might function in any detail. In addition, the veto power of the president is found in Article I, Section 7 of the Constitution, the article that details the legislative powers of the new government. The provision giving the president the power to suggest necessary and expedient measures to Congress, and presumably giving him some power at the beginning of the legislative process, is actually found in Article II, which details the executive, not legislative, powers. It was apparently not controversial that this provision be a part of the executive's powers; it would have been in keeping with the accepted practice in both New York and Great Britain as mentioned by Hamilton in *Federalist 69*. Because there is a lack of discussion of this provision in the Anti-Federalists' criticisms of the executive (and they were very concerned with the executive's power vis-à-vis the legislative branch), it must not have been viewed by the Anti-Federalists as entailing too much power on the part of the executive or encroaching too much into the legislative sphere. Hamilton does not feel the need to elaborate on the power this particular clause bestows beyond the bare mentions in *Federalist 69* and *77*.

Hamilton favored a strong executive, and his treatment of this power in *Federalist 69* suggests executive strength. Despite Hamilton's comparison of this power to that of the British monarch's, it does not attract the attention, or criticism, of the Anti-Federalist writers.[16] Whatever the precise intent, because of the vagueness of this provision, as well as the provision charging the president to give information, it was left to presidents to shape and mold these two powers of informing Congress and recommending measures to them.

Early Presidential Use of the Annual Message

As with many aspects of the presidency, it fell to Washington to establish precedent for the new office. Washington delivered what came to be known as the first annual message on January 8, 1790, in the Senate chamber in New York City.[17] Washington began the practice, continued by John Adams, of delivering oral addresses on the state of the Union to a joint meeting of the two chambers. These addresses occurred roughly every year, even though the Constitution did not specify a time frame. In the State of New York, in whose constitution this provision seems to have originated, it was specifically dictated that the governor would inform the legislature "at every session."[18] The federal Constitution's time frame was much more general, dictating only that this take place "from time to time."[19] President Washington established the precedent of giving the Congress information through an address once a session. Washington's inaugural address in April 1789, given near the beginning of the First Session of the First Congress, actually refers to the recommendation provision of the Constitution.

> By the article establishing the executive department, it is made the duty of the President "to recommend to your consideration such measures as he shall judge necessary and expedient." The circumstances under which I now meet you will acquit me from entering into that subject, further than to refer to the great constitutional charter under which you are assembled, and which, in defining your powers, designates the objects to which your attention is to be given. It will be more consistent with those circumstances, and far more congenial with the feelings which actuate me, to substitute, in place of a recommendation of particular measures, the tribute that is due to the talents, the rectitude, and the patriotism, which adorn the characters selected to devise and adopt them.[20]

Washington chose not to recommend any policy measures in his inaugural address, although he obviously could have, and he makes reference to this fact. It is not until the beginning of the Second Session of the First Congress that Washington gives what has become known as the First Annual Address on January 8, 1790. The Second Annual Address follows eleven months later, but was given at the beginning of the Third Session of the First Congress. These three speeches are evidence that the New York constitution's stipulation of the governor delivering a message once a session was not only a model for this provision in the Federal Constitution, but also served as a guide to Washington in establishing the practice of addressing Congress at the beginning of their new congressional session. These early speeches were called *annual messages,* and this name continued to be used even after their oral delivery ceased with Thomas Jefferson.

In the early annual messages, presidents both gave information and recommended policies. Information was given to Congress with respect to various executive actions. Washington was careful with his messages, however, and his "constitutional duty to make recommendations was approached gingerly."[21] This is further substantiated by the fact that Washington, in the first speech he gave to the First Congress, his inaugural address, chose not to make recommendations, though he referred to that power. In his annual messages, Washington did not establish a precedent of mandating specific legislative actions; he did, however, seek to focus Congress's attention on various legislative matters.

Washington's annual message format was the same for each of the eight that he delivered to Congress. The president would first inform the Congress of executive actions that had been taken in the past year. Most of these related to the president's foreign policy powers but also included information on executions of congressional legislation and other actions pertaining to the executive branch. Washington then proceeded to focus Congress's attention on certain matters that he deemed required action. These mentions generally were lacking in much detail. For example, in his second annual message, Washington stated, "The establishment of the militia, of a mint, of standards of weights and measures, of the post office and post roads are subjects which (I presume) you will resume of course, and which are abundantly urged by their own importance."[22] Occasionally, Washington's reminders to Congress were more pointed, as in this example from his eighth, and final, annual message.

> I have heretofore proposed to the consideration of Congress the expediency of establishing a national university and also a military academy. The desirableness of both these institutions has so constantly increased with every new view I have taken of the subject that I can not omit the opportunity of once for all recalling your attention to them. The assembly to which I address myself is too enlightened not to be fully sensible how much a

flourishing state of the arts and sciences contributes to national prosperity and reputation.[23]

Washington continued with this same subject for several paragraphs, indicating the importance he placed on the formation of these two particular institutions. This request Washington makes of Congress specifically refers to a policy matter that Washington has urged Congress to take up before and continues to be of importance to him—so much so that he devotes a considerable amount of space to this subject. In addition, Washington explains to the Congress why his policy proposal is necessary. This type of rhetoric, what we will call policymaking rhetoric, is often employed in State of the Union addresses. Campbell and Jamieson identify it as the overall form of SUAs, where the speaker/author frames a problem and proposes a solution in such a way that will encourage action.[24]

The final portion of Washington's messages would contain a section specifically directed to the "Gentlemen of the House of Representatives" and would give information and recommendations on revenue matters, which the Constitution stipulates must originate in the House. Finally, Washington would address the "Gentlemen of the Senate and House of Representatives" with items that had not been previously mentioned. The four annual messages of John Adams continued the same format as that of his predecessor.

These early addresses first gave information, especially in regard to foreign policy and executive actions. Second, the messages directed the attention of Congress to certain policy matters that the president felt needed to be addressed. Both Washington and Adams approached Congress with conciliatory language, and the emphasis was focusing the attention of Congress to particular policy issues. These speeches were not about dictating to Congress what they must do, but recommending what the president deemed necessary and expedient. Flattery was not eschewed, as is evident in the passage above, and cooperation was repeatedly stressed in these earliest of addresses as the presidents strove to lead the early congresses and put into practice the powers granted them by the Constitution.

The Era of the Written Message

At the end of Adams's tenure in office and for more than 100 years following, presidents would no longer make a trip down Pennsylvania Avenue at the beginning of a congressional session to address Congress. Reporting on the state of the Union and recommending measures did not cease, but was simply done in another format; it became a written message. Relieved from having to make a speech, presidents' annual messages grew in length and detail and were generally treated as a duty of presidents, not an opportunity, or power, during this time period. The nineteenth century is an era of strong congresses and relatively deferential presidents who, constrained by the view of separation of powers, did not assert themselves in the legislative process.[25] There are exceptions to this generalization, as we will discuss. Most interestingly, it is evident from reading the annual messages of this period which presidents broke out of the nineteenth-century mold and attempted assertive leadership of Congress; their views of presidential leadership are reflected in annual messages.

Jefferson's view of the power relationship between the president and the Congress was different from that of his predecessors. As Stephen Skowronek aptly points out, "it is not simply that Jefferson dominated the Congress as no president before or since but that he did so while pointedly abandoning the presumptuous formalities of executive leadership that had made Federalism look like a monarchical plot."[26] Influenced heavily by his time in France and a different view of democracy than the Federalists, Jefferson deemed the practice of delivering oral annual messages to Congress too monarchical and instituted the practice of sending written messages to Congress.[27] Seymour Fersh has also speculated that Jefferson may have changed the mode of delivery because he did not have strong rhetorical abilities, or even because "it was found that Pennsylvania Avenue was no better than a quagmire which it was dangerous to life and limb to traverse by carriage."[28] In a letter accompanying his first annual message on December 8, 1801, President Jefferson explains his reasoning to the Congress.

> Sir: The circumstances under which we find ourselves at this place rendering inconvenient the mode heretofore practised [sic], of making by personal address the first communications between the Legislative and Executive branches, I have adopted that by Message, as used on all subsequent occasions through the session. In doing this I have had principal regard to the convenience of the Legislature, to the economy of their time, to their relief from the embarrassment of immediate answers, on subjects not yet fully before them, and to the benefits thence resulting in public affairs.[29]

Jefferson thus changed the precedent set by Washington and continued by Adams to one where the president would send a written annual message to the Congress. It would be read by clerks rather than delivered orally by the president. All presidents from Jefferson until Woodrow Wilson would follow this new precedent by Jefferson regarding the annual message.

Jefferson's annual message format resembles that of Washington and Adams in that there is information given first on foreign policy actions and executive actions. Details of the finances of the government are also given. Jefferson's messages do include mentions of items that he holds up for the consideration and attention of Congress, but there are fewer of these than in the messages of Washington and Adams. The annual messages of Jefferson have a heavy emphasis on giving information to Congress and much less toward recommending measures. Sending written messages does afford Jefferson more space and an opportunity for more detail. As a whole, there is more detail in Jefferson's messages, but it relates to the discussion of executive actions, not to legislative recommendations. Much of the space is taken up by his reporting of the state of relations between the United States and various foreign powers, as well as Native American tribes. When Jefferson does refer the attention of Congress to particular policies, he speaks in generalities. For example, in his final annual message in 1808, Jefferson asks Congress to consider what they would do with a budget surplus.

> The probable accumulation of the surplusses [sic] of revenue beyond what can be applied to the payment of the public debt, whenever the freedom and safety of our commerce shall be restored, merits the consideration of Congress. Shall it lie unproductive in the public vaults? Shall the revenue be reduced? Or, shall it not rather be appropriated to the improvements of roads, canals, rivers, education, and other great foundations of prosperity and union, under the powers which Congress may already possess, or such amendment to the Constitution as may be approved by the States? While uncertain of the course of things, the time may be advantageously employed in obtaining the powers necessary for a system of improvement, should that be thought best.[30]

Jefferson suggests that Congress may need to amend the Constitution in order to have the powers necessary to undertake infrastructure improvements. He generally viewed Congress's powers as being limited to the enumerated ones in the Constitution.[31] Extra funds, he suggests, might be used in three different ways, but he offers no specifics and is deferential to the Congress. It is clear he disapproves of one option (being kept "unproductive") and favors attention to infrastructure, but he asks Congress to be anticipatory and forward-looking in this matter.

Jefferson's deference is a repeated pattern when he does choose to address legislative policy matters in his annual messages. Jefferson does not attempt forceful legislative leadership of Congress within the confines of these documents. This does not mean, however, that Jefferson was not involved in the legislative process. As Skowronek notes, "he filled the leadership vacuum in Congress by formally deferring to congressional independence and informally indicating his preferences to legislative spokesmen of his own selection."[32] In addition, we see an example of his rhetorical leadership of Congress in his annual messages when he asks them to anticipate the future; in general, he provides broad outlines and sets forward a vision for the country in his annual messages. Finally, Jefferson was an active executive, especially in the realm of foreign affairs, and this does come through each and every time he informs Congress of the actions he has taken since the last annual message. Perhaps the best example of this is from Jefferson's third annual message in which he discusses the Louisiana Purchase.

> We had not been unaware of the danger to which our peace would be perpetually exposed whilst so important a key to the commerce of the Western country remained under foreign Power. Difficulties too were presenting themselves as to the navigation of other streams, which arising within our territories, pass through those adjacent. Propositions had therefore been authorized for obtaining on fair conditions, the sovereignty of New Orleans, and of other possessions in that quarter, interesting to our quiet, to such extent as was deemed practicable; and the provisional appropriation of two millions of dollars, to be applied and accounted for by the President of the United States, intended as part of the price, was considered as conveying the sanction of Congress to the acquisition proposed. The enlightened Government of France saw with just discernment the importance to both nations of such liberal arrangements as might best and permanently promote the peace, friendship, and interests of both; and the property and sovereignty of all Louisiana, which had been restored to them, has, on certain conditions, been transferred to the United States, by instruments bearing date the 30th of April last. When these shall have received the constitutional sanction of the Senate, they will, without delay, be communicated to the Representatives also for the exercise of their functions, as to those conditions which are within the powers vested by the Constitution in Congress.[33]

The move to written delivery of the annual message also corresponded to a change in the way the executive and Congress interacted. Jefferson's style of congressional leadership, however, did not last. After the Jefferson presidency, Congress became ascendant and presidential leadership of that body was generally weak. Few annual messages in the nineteenth century presented a vision for Congress or the country; instead they simply became listings of executive details, summaries of executive reports, and policies that were neither inspiring nor interesting, just "more itemized and dull."[34] This, perhaps, should not be surprising given that the messages had ceased to be speeches, but were now written reports; concern for language, cadence, and prioritization that would be evident in the transcript of an oral address was replaced by concern for detail and comprehensiveness. "Presidential messages [in the nineteenth century] tended to be innocuous scissors-and-paste assemblages of departmental reports to the President constituting poorly integrated miscellanies."[35] In the era of the written annual message, this constitutional power of the executive was viewed generally as a duty, not as an opportunity for communicating vision, or a tool presidents could use to lead Congress. Rather, presidents began reporting to Congress factual information in long and often tedious documents.

A good example of the detail evident in many of these messages comes from President James Monroe's seventh annual message.

> There is established by law eighty-eight thousand six hundred miles of post roads, on which the mail is now transported eighty-five thousand seven hundred miles; and contracts have been made for its transportation on all the established routes, with one or two exceptions. There are five thousand two hundred and forty post offices in the Union, and as many postmasters. The gross amount of postage which accrued from the first of July, one thousand eight hundred and twenty-two, to the first of July, one thousand eight hundred and twenty-three, was one million one hundred and fourteen thousand three hundred and forty-five dollars and twelve cents. During the same period, the expenditures of the Post Office Department amounted to one million one hundred and sixty-nine thousand eight hundred and eighty-five dollars and fifty-one cents; and consisted of the following items.[36]

Monroe's detail on the postal department actually continues on another three and a half paragraphs. Similar detail, not found in the oral annual messages of Washington and Adams, is standard in written annual messages.

While the emphasis in most nineteenth-century annual messages was on providing information rather than recommending specific policies, on occasion there were important policies introduced in a president's annual message. From the same message that contained the above specifics on the postal service, Monroe also gives a first accounting of the policy that would come to be known as the Monroe Doctrine.

> We owe it, therefore, to candor and to the amicable relations existing between the United States and those Powers, to declare, that we should consider any attempt on their part to extend their system to any portion of this hemisphere, as dangerous to our peace and safety. With the existing colonies or dependencies of any European Power, we have not interfered, and shall not interfere. But, with the Governments who have declared their independence, and maintained it, and whose independence we have, on great consideration, and on just principles, acknowledged, we could not view any interposition for the purpose of oppressing them, or controlling, in any other manner, their destiny, by any European Power in any other light than as the manifestation of an unfriendly disposition toward the United States.[37]

The Public Is Recognized

A subtle change in the content and use of annual messages would occur with the presidency of Andrew Jackson. In many respects, this is reflective of the larger changes occurring within the presidency and the country as a whole. The era of Jacksonian democracy signals a move to popular and mass-based politics in the United States. With Jackson, one begins to see the annual message utilized as a vehicle with which presidents could assert themselves in the policymaking process. Fersh writes that Jackson "fashioned [the annual message] into a national platform from which he gave exposition to his policies and appealed for support over the heads of the lawmakers to the public at large."[38] While Jackson still continued the tradition of sending written messages to Capitol Hill, and they were still addressed to "Fellow-citizens of the Senate and of the House of Representatives," several of Jackson's recommendations were couched in such a way as to garner popular appeal and to remind Congress to reflect the wishes of the majority. In addition, by 1829, the House and Senate were requiring that 14,500 copies of the presidential message be printed for use in their respective bodies.[39] Dissemination of the president's message would certainly have occurred through the senators and representatives across the United States. The press was also growing during this era. "The number of papers increased from 359 to 852 between 1810 and 1828, and the number of copies tripled during this period."[40] The penny press also emerged in the 1830s, allowing the dissemination of news cheaply, and to more people.[41]

In essence, Jackson's annual messages are early examples of a variation on the theme of presidents seeking to "go public," a term coined by Samuel Kernell that involves a president trying to obtain public support for policies in hopes that the public will put pressure on Congress to act.[42] Kernell meant for the concept to be applied to modern presidents. There is, in fact, a difference in how one sees public opinion as a factor in these nineteenth-century messages and the going-public activities of modern presidents. What is notable, especially in Jackson's and later Abraham Lincoln's annual messages, is that these presidents are not appealing to the public to put pressure on Congress, but reminding Congress of the popular will and majority opinion.[43]

One of Jackson's recommendations that he couched in such a way as to appeal to the masses pertained to presidential elections. In his initial annual message in 1829, the first recommendation that he makes to Congress after giving the standard information on foreign affairs and executive actions is a desire to change the method of electing the president. Jackson had lost the presidency in 1824 despite having more electoral votes (though not a majority) and more popular votes than his opponents, although not all states at this time employed the popular vote. The House, nonetheless, picked John Quincy Adams to be president. Vindicated by his victory in the next election, as president, Jackson recommended to Congress a change in presidential elections.

> I consider it one of the most urgent of my duties to bring to your attention the propriety of amending that part of our Constitution which relates to the election of President and Vice-President. Our system of government was,

by its framers, deemed an experiment; and they, therefore, consistently provided a mode of remedying its defects. . . . In this, as in all other matters of public concern, policy requires that as few impediments as possible should exist to the free operation of the public will. Let us, then, endeavor so to amend our system, as that the office of Chief Magistrate may not be conferred upon any citizen but in pursuance of a fair expression of the will of the majority.[44]

Jackson included many recommendations for legislative action in his very lengthy messages and Congress was not always pleased with his suggestions. One member of Congress felt that all his committee was doing during Jackson's administration "was going through the form of approving the laws which [Jackson] prepared and handed down to them for acceptance."[45] Jackson's language was not as conciliatory toward Congress as many of his predecessors. In his second annual message, Jackson addressed, at length, his use of the veto. The precedent before Jackson had been that presidents used the veto rarely and only on items that they deemed to be unconstitutional. Jackson vetoed more measures than all of his predecessors combined[46] and did not apply the same standard of constitutionality as a reason for its use. After detailing at some length why he had vetoed a particular appropriations bill, Jackson further explained his unique use of the veto to the Congress.

It is due to candor, as well as to my own feelings, that I should express the reluctance and anxiety which I must at all times experience in exercising the undoubted right of the Executive to withhold his assent from bills on other grounds than their constitutionality. That this right should not be exercised on slight occasions, all will admit. It is only in matters of deep interest, when the principle involved may be justly regarded as next in importance to infractions of the Constitution itself, that such a step can be expected to meet with the approbation of the people. Such an occasion do I conscientiously believe the present to be.[47]

Jackson was a strong president who sought to provide strong leadership of Congress. His annual messages are reflective of this.

After Jackson, many nineteenth-century presidents did not use their annual messages as vigorously as he did to promote specific policy proposals for Congress. Presidents did, however, continue to use their annual messages to inform Congress of happenings and actions, summarize the reports of executive departments, as well as address concerns and ask for the attention of Congress to certain issues and topics.

Lincoln is another notable exception to the standard pattern of nineteenth-century annual messages. Upon the inauguration of Lincoln, the country was in for a change in terms of the relations between the executive and the legislature. He would significantly adapt the annual message to his own style and the times. He focused less on factual reports and more on giving his view of the current situation in the country and the policy proposals of his administration. The annual messages of Lincoln are generally shorter and certainly more eloquent (and thus more readable) than those of his predecessors.

In his first annual message, Lincoln dispensed with the usual format of the document. As the Union was enmeshed in a civil war, Lincoln paid less attention to foreign affairs, which traditionally dominated annual messages of this era. Lincoln explains his departure from this precedent:

> It is not my purpose to review our discussions with foreign states, because, whatever might be their wishes or dispositions, the integrity of our country and the stability of our Government mainly depend not upon them, but on the loyalty, virtue, patriotism, and intelligence of the American people.[48]

Lincoln also is much more forceful and specific with his recommendations to Congress. In the first message alone, Lincoln calls for Congress to act on railroad construction, forming a department or bureau of agriculture, reforming the judicial system, and consolidating statutes, among other things. Unlike most other presidents of this period, Lincoln is very specific in what he is recommending to Congress. He does not just mention that Congress should attend to constructing railroads, but he suggests specific routes to be considered.[49] In his second annual message, Lincoln gives a detailed proposal for the compensated emancipation of slaves, the text of a proposed constitutional amendment pertaining to it, as well as a discussion of its justification.[50]

The rocky times in which Lincoln presided required public support if he was going to be able to exercise leadership. As a result, Lincoln used his annual messages not only to communicate with Congress, but also to reach the public. Thus, "a constitutional 'duty,' once again as with Jackson, became a welcome opportunity for a strong willed President to address the nation. A message presumably addressed to Congress was used instead as a loudspeaker by which the President secured an audience rating which could not be matched by any congressional document."[51] Lincoln, in several instances, refers to public opinion in his messages to Congress. In his fourth and final annual message, Lincoln reminds Congress of public opinion as he discerned it from election results.

> At the last session of Congress a proposed amendment of the Constitution, abolishing slavery throughout the United States, passed the Senate, but failed for lack of the requisite two-thirds vote in the House of Representatives. Although the present is the same Congress, and nearly the same members, and without questioning the wisdom or patriotism of those who stood in opposition, I venture to recommend the reconsideration and

passage of the measure at the present session. Of course the abstract question is not changed; but an intervening election shows, almost certainly, that the next Congress will pass the measure if this does not. Hence there is only a question of time as to when the proposed amendment will go to the States for their action. And as it is to so go, at all events, may we not agree that the sooner the better? It is not claimed that the election has imposed a duty on members to change their views or their votes, any further than, as an additional element to be considered, their judgment may be affected by it. It is the voice of the people now, for the first time, heard upon the question. In a great national crisis like ours, unanimity of action among those seeking a common end is very desirable—almost indispensable. And yet no approach to such unanimity is attainable unless some deference shall be paid to the will of the majority simply because it is the will of the majority. In this case the common end is the maintenance of the Union; and, among the means to secure that end, such will, through the election, is most clearly declared in favor of such constitutional amendment.[52]

In his third annual message, Lincoln refers to both international and domestic public opinion.

Of those who were slaves at the beginning of the rebellion, full one hundred thousand are now in the United States military service, about one half of which number actually bear arms in the ranks; thus giving the double advantage of taking so much labor from the insurgent cause, and supplying the places which otherwise must be filled with so many white men. So far as tested, it is difficult to say they are not as good soldiers as any. No servile insurrection, or tendency to violence or cruelty, has marked the measures of emancipation and arming the blacks. These measures have been much discussed in foreign countries, and contemporary with such discussion the tone of public sentiment there is much improved. At home the same measures have been fully discussed, supported, criticised [sic], and denounced, and the annual elections following are highly encouraging to those whose official duty it is to bear the country through this great trial. Thus we have the new reckoning. The crisis which threatened to divide the friends of the Union is past.[53]

It was important for Lincoln's policies to point out and remind Congress what the state of public opinion was should they not be paying sufficient attention or see things in the same manner that he did.

Finally, Lincoln's annual messages were forward-looking and visionary unlike many annual messages in the nineteenth century. Perhaps because of the Civil War, Lincoln was inclined to include a focus on the larger view of the country's situation. To conclude his first annual address, Lincoln notes,

There are already among us those who, if the Union be preserved, will live to see it contain two hundred and fifty millions. The struggle *of* to-day is not altogether *for* to-day—it is for a vast future also. With a reliance on

Providence, all the more firm and earnest, let us proceed in the great task which events have devolved upon us.[54]

In addition, Lincoln's messages would also incorporate theoretical discussions that were included both to educate and to justify his views. In his first message, Lincoln entered into a lengthy explanation of the relationship between labor and capital and its application to the American case.[55]

Upon Lincoln's assassination, Andrew Johnson became president, and there ensued a mighty struggle between the executive and legislative branches that would eventually result in the impeachment of the president. Johnson used his annual messages to explain, educate, and justify his positions. In his first annual message, he states,

> To fulfill my trust I need the support and confidence of all who are associated with me in the various departments of Government and the support and confidence of the people. There is but one way in which I can hope to gain their necessary aid. It is to state with frankness the principles which guide my conduct, and their application to the present state of affairs, well aware that the efficiency of my labors will in a great measure depend on your and their undivided approbation.[56]

Congress would not prove to be particularly receptive to Johnson's leadership. He did seek to be specific in his guidance of Congress, especially over matters of reconstruction, and this is evident in his annual messages. On the matter of the representation of the states of the former Confederacy, for example, Johnson seeks to move Congress to action.

> I deem it a subject of profound regret that Congress has thus far failed to admit to seats loyal Senators and Representatives from the other States whose inhabitants, with those of Tennessee, had engaged in the rebellion. Ten States—more than one-fourth of the whole number—remain without representation; the seats of fifty members in the House of Representatives and of twenty members in the Senate are yet vacant, not by their own consent, not by a failure of election, but by the refusal of Congress to accept their credentials. . . .The Constitution of the United States makes it the duty of the President to recommend to the consideration of Congress "such measures as he shall judge necessary and expedient." I know of no measure more imperatively demanded by every consideration of national interest, sound policy, and equal justice than the admission of loyal members from the now unrepresented States.[57]

At some length, Johnson explains his rationale for the prompt inclusion of the states' representatives into Congress. His attempts at leadership of Congress, however, would not prove successful, and articles of impeachment would be voted by the House in 1868, although Johnson would be acquitted by the Senate.

After Lincoln's assassination and the impeachment of President Johnson, there ensued another period of time in which Congress became the dominant actor and annual messages reverted back to the standard pattern of the nineteenth century. They once again were composed mostly of summaries of foreign affairs and executive actions. The president's recommendations of policies to Congress tended to lack specifics and simply asked for Congress's attention to particular policy areas. Congress, however, did not expect, nor want, legislative proposals to emanate from the presidency. After Lincoln, "most successful political initiatives emanated from within the Congress. Presidents could muster little support for their proposals. As a consequence, their recommendations to Congress became almost perfunctory and tended to have little impact. Limitations placed on the exercise of executive power worked to discourage presidential requests."[58]

The Coming of the Modern Presidency

The modern presidency is delineated as beginning with the election of Franklin D. Roosevelt (FDR) in 1932. Presidents Theodore (Teddy) Roosevelt and Woodrow Wilson, however, are significant twentieth-century presidents who came before FDR in that they foreshadow certain characteristics associated with the modern presidency. In both, we see glimpses of the changes that would take place in presidential actions, powers, and the office's relationship with both Congress and the public. Both exerted a profound influence on FDR, who synthesized the key elements of both these noble foes. From a study of the annual messages, we see how these two presidents broke out of the mold that had shaped nineteenth-century presidents.

When Teddy Roosevelt became president at the turn of the century upon the assassination of William McKinley, he would foreshadow, in many respects, the future of the institution. Many of the characteristics that are common in modern presidents first were seen in Teddy Roosevelt's presidency. Roosevelt sought to be an assertive leader of both the Congress and the American public. He viewed the presidency as possessing the "bully pulpit"—*bully* in this context meaning excellent. The president's position in the political system as the only elected official who has a national constituency, presents the president, as Roosevelt saw it, with a wonderful position from which to command the attention of the nation and focus it on issues and policies of the president's choosing. Congress lacks such a podium. Even though they continued to be written, Roosevelt's eight annual messages were affected by his view of the presidency and the "bully pulpit." For Roosevelt, they were less a duty and more of an opportunity. He sent to Congress some of the longest annual messages, and the policymaking nature of his rhetoric is easily identifiable. His annual messages were

"addressed to Congress in form only, [Roosevelt] more than any of his predecessors aimed his report at the American and world audience."[59] Many
issues and subjects, both foreign and domestic, were addressed by
Roosevelt in his messages. He took the opportunity to inform both Congress
and the public and to introduce proposals to Congress as a first step in
achieving his policy goals. Roosevelt was a "pioneer in initiating the twentieth century trend of Presidential leadership in legislation."[60] The annual
message was a natural outlet for the exercise of executive leadership (both
of Congress and of public opinion) that Roosevelt so deeply believed was
his duty.

Teddy Roosevelt departed from the standard format of previous annual
messages and discussed domestic politics first and foreign affairs last. This
is significant in that it shows the annual message's potential for strategic
use in the hands of skillful presidents paying attention to congressional,
domestic, and foreign opinion. In his third annual message, Roosevelt opens
with the statement, "With a nation as with a man the most important things
are those of the household," and in all of his annual messages he first
attended to business at home before business abroad.[61] Perhaps he saw this
as a more appropriate format for approaching a Congress and public dominated by feelings of isolation, even as he steered US foreign policy on a
more internationalist course. In his fourth annual message, he would
announce an important corollary to the Monroe Doctrine that would provide
for intervention into the domestic affairs of countries in the hemisphere.

> It is not true that the United States feels any land hunger or entertains any
> projects as regards the other nations of the Western Hemisphere save such
> as are for their welfare. All that this country desires is to see the neighbor-
> ing countries stable, orderly, and prosperous. Any country whose people
> conduct themselves well can count upon our hearty friendship. If a nation
> shows that it knows how to act with reasonable efficiency and decency in
> social and political matters, if it keeps order and pays its obligations, it
> need fear no interference from the United States. Chronic wrongdoing, or
> an impotence which results in a general loosening of the ties of civilized
> society, may in America, as elsewhere, ultimately require intervention by
> some civilized nation, and in the Western Hemisphere the adherence of the
> United States to the Monroe Doctrine may force the United States, howev-
> er reluctantly, in flagrant cases of such wrongdoing or impotence, to the
> exercise of an international police power.[62]

Yet, this important statement of US foreign policy occurs near the end of the
message. By placing it here, Roosevelt can signal to Congress and the public
that he is primarily concerned with domestic issues, as are they. By devoting
as much space as he does to this discussion, he still utilizes the message to
inform Congress and educate the public about his foreign policy vision.

As an example of the way Teddy Roosevelt utilized his annual messages with regard to domestic policy, his discussion of trusts from 1901 is instructive. At length, Roosevelt details the current state of affairs in the United States concerning industrialization, and he is careful to laud capitalism: "The captains of industry who have driven the railway systems across this continent, who have built up our commerce, who have developed our manufactures, have on the whole done great good to our people. Without them the material development of which we are so justly proud could never have taken place."[63] However, he states that

> There is a widespread conviction in the minds of the American people that the great corporations known as trusts are in certain of their features and tendencies hurtful to the general welfare. This springs from no spirit of envy or uncharitableness, nor lack of pride in the great industrial achievements that have placed this country at the head of the nations struggling for commercial supremacy. It does not rest upon a lack of intelligent appreciation of the necessity of meeting changing and changed conditions of trade with new methods, nor upon ignorance of the fact that combination of capital in the effort to accomplish great things is necessary when the world's progress demands that great things be done. It is based upon sincere conviction that combination and concentration should be, not prohibited, but supervised and within reasonable limits controlled; and in my judgment this conviction is right.[64]

Roosevelt refers to the state of public opinion, notes that it is sincere and correct, and in so doing, he associates himself with it. Roosevelt is well known for his view of the president as one who discerns public opinion. Whereas Jackson and Lincoln earlier were shown to have reminded Congress in their annual messages of the public will as divined through election results, Roosevelt does not use such a link. Having discerned what the public thinks, he stands on public opinion to propose specific solutions to what he sees as the problems with industry in the United States. He recommends to Congress provisions that would enable the federal government to have access to corporations' information and to engage in regulation, as well as proposing the formation of a department of commerce. With Teddy Roosevelt, the promise of the president's annual message for presidential policy leadership of Congress based on his view of public opinion is realized in the way he utilizes policymaking rhetoric.

While Teddy Roosevelt in his annual messages never uses rhetoric that directly addresses the American people and his messages remain written documents, the public is recognized as an audience. An example of both how the public is a secondary audience and how Roosevelt used policymaking rhetoric to explain, educate, and then propose solutions occurs in his final message. He explains how organized labor had recently pushed for legislation that "represented a course of policy which, if carried out, would mean the enthronement of class privilege in its crudest and most brutal form, and the destruction of one of the most essential functions of the judiciary in all civilized lands."[65] Roosevelt further adds, "The violence of the crusade for this legislation, and its complete failure, illustrate two truths which *it is essential our people should learn.*"[66] He then proceeds for many paragraphs to explain the dangers of class warfare before he gets to his policy recommendation for Congress in this area.

Roosevelt's successor, William Howard Taft, did not have the same beliefs about the office of the president as did his predecessor. He did not agree with the expansive vision Roosevelt had of presidential powers. As a result, Congress again would take the initiative with legislative proposals. Taft's annual messages revert back to the less-than-inspiring format of most nineteenth-century messages. They also become very segmented; foreign policy is divided and delineated by region, and domestic policy is delineated by executive departments or specific topics. This format precludes any kind of overarching theme to Taft's messages. More important, Taft's messages do not retain the focus Roosevelt had on audiences beyond Congress. In his first two annual messages, the standard format of detailing foreign relations first and domestic issues next returns. His final two annual messages, however, were both a series of messages sent to the Congress over the month of December. They were divided up by topic area in the manner of his first two, but they became more extensive. Annual messages had been growing in length, and separating the content by topic made them more digestible. Taft explains this change in format in his third message.

> The amount of information to be communicated as to the operations of the Government, the number of important subjects calling for comment by the Executive, and the transmission to Congress of exhaustive reports of special commissions, make it impossible to include in one message of a reasonable length a discussion of the topics that ought to be brought to the attention of the National Legislature at its first regular session.[67]

On Taft's heels, Woodrow Wilson would alter the format of the annual message, as well as the presidency.[68] He would once again, like Teddy Roosevelt, usher in an era of presidential initiative in the legislative process, and he would return to the tradition of Washington and Adams by delivering the annual message as an oral address delivered in the presence of a joint meeting of Congress. This practice would transform the nature of the annual message and what would come to be called the State of the Union address. As a result, "the extraordinary significance of the State of the Union message today owes much to the imagination and initiative of [Wilson]."[69]

A Return to the Oral Address

Wilson believed that reinstituting the original practice of delivering a speech would allow the executive and legislative branches to work more closely with one another. This was of fundamental importance to the way Wilson viewed the presidency. His approach was an attempt to move the United States toward a more parliamentary system of government.[70] In this view, the executive and legislative branches would function more as one unit rather than two separate units, with the executive providing strong leadership. Even the language that Wilson used in his SUAs indicates his view in this regard. For example, in his second address he states, *"Our program of legislation* with regard to the regulation of business is now virtually complete. It has been put forth, as *we* intended, as a whole, and leaves no conjecture as to what is to follow."[71] Another example comes from his third SUA.

> Many conditions about which *we have repeatedly legislated* are being altered from decade to decade, it is evident, under our very eyes, and are likely to change even more rapidly and more radically in the days immediately ahead of us, when peace has returned to the world and the nations of Europe once more take up their tasks of commerce and industry with the energy of those who must bestir themselves to build anew.[72]

In both of these examples, Wilson speaks as if he were a member of the legislature by using inclusive language, very much in keeping with his preference for parliamentary government.[73] Wilson could also use forceful language with Congress in his SUAs as he sought to lead like few before him had by exhorting them to action.

> To speak plainly, we have grossly erred in the way in which we have stunted and hindered the development of our merchant marine. And now, when we need ships, we have not got them. We have year after year debated, without end or conclusion, the best policy to pursue with regard to the use of the ores and forests and water powers of our national domain in the rich States of the West, when we should have acted; and they are still locked up.[74]

In addition, public opinion played an important role for Wilson; in his view, it was the president who was to "sift through the multifarious currents of opinion to find a core of issues that he believed reflected majority will even if the majority was not yet fully aware of it."[75] To exemplify this view of Wilson's, consider the following from his second SUA: "But my point is that the people of the United States do not wish to curtail the activities of this Government; they wish, rather, to enlarge them; and with every enlargement, with the mere growth, indeed, of the country itself, there must come, of course, the inevitable increase of expense."[76] Wilson's tenure is the beginning of what Tulis terms the "rhetorical presidency," a key aspect of the modern presidency.[77] Important to this conception is the role that rhetoric plays in presidents' providing popular leadership. With the reinstitution of the oral delivery of the SUA coupled with its dissemination through mass media, it became a tool that presidents could use to educate and appeal to the public unlike ever before. It also became a tool that could provide presidents with an enlarged ability to guide and be the leader in initiating and advocating legislation.

In departing from the precedent of the written annual message and reverting back to the older format of oral delivery, Wilson comments to the Congress,

> I shall ask your indulgence if I venture to depart in some degree from the usual custom of setting before you in formal review the many matters which have engaged the attention and called for the action of the several departments of the Government or which look to them for early treatment in the future, because the list is long, very long, and would suffer in the abbreviation to which I should have to subject it. I shall submit to you the reports of the heads of the several departments, in which these subjects are set forth in careful detail, and beg that they may receive the thoughtful attention of your committees and of all Members of the Congress who may have the leisure to study them. Their obvious importance, as constituting the very substance of the business of the Government, makes comment and emphasis on my part unnecessary.[78]

With this statement, Wilson dispenses with discussing what had traditionally been one of the main aspects of past annual messages, the summaries of department reports. Indeed, the oral delivery of these items would have required much forbearance on the part of the listening audience, even if it was the president who was delivering them. The only foreign policy issue that Wilson addresses, traditionally another major aspect of past annual messages, is American relations with Mexico; compared to domestic concerns, the space devoted to foreign affairs is small. Wilson then proceeds to advocate multiple domestic legislative proposals, such as a banking and currency bill that was then before Congress, a system of farm credit, expansion of the Sherman Anti-trust Law, reforms for the way parties choose their presidential nominees, and several items relating to US territories. Because Wilson was delivering a speech, rather than sending a written message, it was also necessary for him to prioritize. He could not speak about all things, but could only include the ones that held the most importance. In this way, the oral SUAs are an excellent means of identifying what the most important issues were to the president at that point in time.

It should be noted that Wilson's final two annual messages were not speeches, but written messages. Wilson suffered a stroke in 1919, which prevented him from personally appearing before Congress. He states in his seventh message, "I sincerely regret that I cannot be present at the opening of this session of the Congress. I am thus prevented from presenting in as direct a way as I could wish the many questions that are pressing for solution at this time."[79] Wilson alludes to the reason why he reinstituted oral delivery of these messages; they provided the president with a very direct means of communication with Congress and, by extension, the people. In his final two messages, aside from the delivery, the nature remained much the same; they continued to ask Congress for legislative action, very often specific, on the issues the president deemed of paramount importance.

This spirited approach to presidential leadership of twentieth-century congresses, practiced by Teddy Roosevelt and Woodrow Wilson, was not seen again until Franklin D. Roosevelt became president. The three Republican presidents between Wilson and FDR (Warren Harding, Calvin Coolidge, and Herbert Hoover) followed the example of their predecessor Taft in their view of presidential leadership of Congress and eschewed the activist vision of Wilson. As an indication of this view, Harding, Wilson's immediate successor, addresses presidential powers in his first SUA.

> I am very sure we shall have no conflict of opinion about constitutional duties or authority. During the anxieties of war, when necessity seemed compelling there were excessive grants of authority and all extraordinary concentration of powers in the Chief Executive. The repeal of war-time legislation and the automatic expirations which attended the peace proclamations have put an end to these emergency excesses but I have the wish to go further than that. I want to join you in restoring, in the most cordial way, the spirit of coordination and cooperation, and that mutuality of confidence and respect which is necessary in representative popular government.[80]

Because he speaks of *restoring* coordination, cooperation, and confidence, Harding is taking issue with the leadership style of his predecessor Wilson. Presidents Harding, Coolidge, and Hoover would not be presidents who sought to exhibit strong leadership of Congress, either rhetorically through their annual messages, or in general.

In terms of the mode of delivery, there was some variation during the period between Wilson and FDR. Harding's two SUAs were delivered orally, and in 1923, Coolidge was the first president to have his SUA broadcast over the radio.[81] He was apparently not impressed either with the practice of oral delivery or the new technology's use in this regard; his subsequent messages would be written. None of Hoover's four annual messages was delivered before Congress as speeches. Ironically, even though technological advances in electronic media would give presidents the capability to reach more of the public with their SUA and have broader influence, these presidents chose not to capitalize on the new technology available for communication and, in addition, chose not to assert strong leadership of Congress.

Cementing the Role of Chief Legislator

When FDR became the thirty-second president of the United States, he ushered in a new era of the presidency. Modern presidents since Roosevelt's path-breaking tenure look to the precedents established during his time in office. Roosevelt fundamentally transformed the office on multiple levels of presidential power and communications.

FDR was sworn in on March 4, 1933, and the next day called the Seventy-third Congress into special session to begin work on the problems facing the country in the midst of the Great Depression. FDR would not give an SUA until January 3, 1934.[82] Roosevelt was, however, from the time of his swearing in to his first SUA, leading the Congress in the Wilsonian fashion, but to an even greater extent. Executive leadership of Congress was firmly established during the first 100 days of that special session, during which the first wave of New Deal legislation was passed. "Confronted by an undisciplined Congress and an inchoate public sentiment, the President nevertheless managed to control the situation."[83] FDR firmly established in the minds of the public and even Congress that the president was chief legislator. Wilfred Binkley observes of the twentieth-century environment after FDR, "In fact the citizen, as a voter, scarcely shows any consciousness whatever of the President's executive function, but instead manifests a quadrennial concern as to the legislation the presidential candidates if elected may promote or prevent."[84] All presidents in the modern era have actively assumed the role of chief legislator, and they have been aided by their use of SUAs.

Interestingly enough, Roosevelt's first SUA did not include recommendations, and he opens with a statement that tells why this is the case.

> I come before you at the opening of the Regular Session of the 73d Congress, not to make requests for special or detailed items of legislation; I come, rather, to counsel with you, who, like myself, have been selected to carry out a mandate of the whole people, in order that without partisanship you and I may cooperate to continue the restoration of our national wellbeing and, equally important, to build on the ruins of the past a new structure designed better to meet the present problems of modern civilization.[85]

During the special session that preceded his first SUA, Roosevelt had a very active legislative agenda, and his first SUA does include much discussion of what had transpired thus far in his term. He claims credit for various policies enacted to help bring the country out of depression. Like presidents before him, he talks of executive actions and foreign affairs. His main purpose, however, is to assure Congress and the nation that they are on the right track to recovery. In addition, he is consciously trying to foster good will between the two branches. FDR was certainly aware he was taking the presidency in new directions. As a recognition of this, he closes his first SUA with a thanks to Congress and a nod to the direction in which he is taking the institution of the presidency.

> I know that each of you will appreciate that I am speaking no mere politeness when I assure you how much I value the fine relationship that we have shared during these months of hard and incessant work. Out of these friendly contacts we are, fortunately, building a strong and permanent tie between the legislative and executive branches of the Government. The letter of the Constitution wisely declared a separation, but the impulse of common purpose declares a union. In this spirit we join once more in serving the American people.[86]

It was FDR's second SUA that really highlighted the role the president was forging. He states, "We have undertaken a new order of things; yet we progress to it under the framework and in the spirit and intent of the American Constitution. We have proceeded throughout the Nation a measurable distance on the road toward this new order."[87] Whereas in the first address he did not make recommendations, in the second, he includes many proposals for policies that would be known as the "Second New Deal." FDR first establishes a broad theme of policy that should be undertaken in the coming session: security. He provides three types of security that are paramount, the security of a livelihood by better utilizing resources, security against unforeseen events, and the security of adequate housing.[88] Having established the major thrust of his legislative program, he then gets to specifics. In outlining a public works plan, for example, FDR lists seven principles included in the plan he is sending to Congress.[89] Roosevelt, in Wilsonian fashion, relies on the pronoun *we* in the address. Where Wilson used *we* to include himself with the legislature, FDR's usage often specifically encompasses the American public as well.

> Thus, the American people do not stand alone in the world in their desire for change. We seek it through tested liberal traditions, through processes which retain all of the deep essentials of that republican form of representative government first given to a troubled world by the United States.[90]

Having incorporated the American public in language, FDR seeks to expand their ability to hear the speech also. Another significant event in the history of the SUA occurred in 1936 when FDR moved the time of his speech to nine o'clock in the evening, allowing him to have a wider national radio audience.[91] This move, no doubt, was influenced by two things. One, the state of international affairs in Europe was causing concern for the administration. Therefore, it is perhaps not surprising that the subject of this particular SUA is focused, unlike any of FDR's previous SUAs, on foreign affairs. America after World War I had returned to isolationism. FDR felt international events were portending a dangerous future; he used this particular SUA especially to elucidate and educate the public about international events. The first half of the speech is given over to a discussion of the state of international affairs. At the same time, FDR understood just how far he could go in the isolationist environment and also stressed US neutrality. After explaining the state of international affairs, FDR says,

> I realize that I have emphasized to you the gravity of the situation which confronts the people of the world. This emphasis is justified because of its importance to civilization and therefore to the United States. Peace is jeopardized by the few and not by the many. Peace is threatened by those who seek selfish power. The world has witnessed similar eras—as in the days when petty kings and feudal barons were changing the map of Europe every fortnight, or when great emperors and great kings were engaged in a mad scramble for colonial empire. We hope that we are not again at the threshold of such an era. But if face it we must, then the United States and the rest of the Americas can play but one role: through a well-ordered neutrality to do naught to encourage the contest, through adequate defense to save ourselves from embroilment and attack, and through example and all legitimate encouragement and assistance to persuade other Nations to return to the ways of peace and good-will.[92]

The second influence that likely prompted the move of the timing of the speech was that 1936 was an election year. Consequently, the second half of FDR's SUA specifically speaks to his unnamed critics at home.

> If these gentlemen believe, as they say they believe, that the measures adopted by this Congress and its predecessor, and carried out by this Administration, have hindered rather than promoted recovery, let them be consistent. Let them propose to this Congress the complete repeal of these measures. The way is open to such a proposal.
>   Let action be positive and not negative. The way is open in the Congress of the United States for an expression of opinion by yeas and nays. Shall we say that values are restored and that the Congress will, therefore, repeal the laws under which we have been bringing them back? Shall we say that because national income has grown with rising prosperity, we shall repeal existing taxes and thereby put off the day of approaching a balanced budget and of starting to reduce the national debt? Shall we abandon the reasonable support and regulation of banking? Shall we restore the dollar to its former gold content?[93]

By throwing down the gauntlet in this fashion at the beginning of an election year, FDR is setting the stage, not only for his own reelection, but also for the election of a supportive Congress as well. The public is presented with a choice by FDR: me, or my critics.

Roosevelt's eloquence and use of language to capture the hopes of the nation were very evident in his 1941 SUA. Here he first articulates the four freedoms: freedom of speech and expression, freedom of worship, freedom from want, and freedom from fear.[94] This particular speech is one of Roosevelt's most visionary and fully represents the extent of his rhetorical abilities and their use in a time of crisis. It is also an example of the importance and lasting impact SUAs can have. FDR's "four freedoms speech," as his eighth SUA is better known, is one of his most memorable, and would even be immortalized by Norman Rockwell in a series of paintings.

FDR's final two messages in 1944 and 1945 were sent to Congress in a written format. In both instances, FDR was ill. Shortly after the delivery of the documents to the Congress, FDR gave evening radio addresses in which he virtually repeated (1944) or summarized (1945) the document he had sent to Congress.[95] In this manner, FDR still accomplished what had come to be a major purpose of the SUA in his presidency, direct communication with the public.

The larger point to be made about FDR's SUAs is that he utilized them unlike others before him. Although previous SUAs have provided examples, often isolated, of eloquence, congressional leadership, policy leadership, and leadership of public opinion, FDR combined all of these elements. In addition, he attempted public opinion leadership on a larger scale than ever before by utilizing the radio and changing the time of the address, reaching a much wider public audience. He also included the public by using inclusive language and projecting the feeling that everyone (the president, the Congress, and the public) was in the same boat.

With the death of Franklin Roosevelt, the next president faced choices about the direction the institution would go. Would he continue with the new precedents set by FDR, or would he choose to return the presidency to the position it had occupied for most of its history? Harry S. Truman was not someone who had wanted to be president. When FDR died on April 12, 1945, Truman had been vice president for less than three months. He had been woefully unprepared by FDR for any succession to the presidency; Truman, famously, was not in the loop regarding US work on atomic weapons, for example.

Truman experimented with his first SUA. In it, he combined both the information on the state of the Union and the annual budget message into a written document he sent to the Congress. Truman justified the change at the beginning of the message.

It is clear that the budgetary program and the general program of the Government are actually inseparable. The president bears the responsibility for recommending to the Congress a comprehensive set of proposals on all Government activities and their financing. In formulating policies, as in preparing budgetary estimates, the Nation and the Congress have the right to expect the President to adjust and coordinate the views of the various departments and agencies to form a unified program. And that program requires consideration in connection with the Budget, which is the annual work program of the Government.[96]

While this justification was theoretically sound, in practice it made for a very long and detailed document. The experiment was not successful.[97] He would not again combine the two and in future years would revert to the practice of orally delivering the SUA.[98]

In 1947, Truman would once again like his predecessor FDR make the trip to Capitol Hill to talk about the state of the Union. With this speech, another significant event in the history of the SUA would occur. Given in the afternoon, it was the first televised SUA.[99]

Truman's SUAs did not match FDR's in terms of their eloquence. They are, however, reflective of Truman's style and character. He used short, staccato sentences, going right to the point. Referring to the Taft-Hartley Act, he bluntly states, "That act should be repealed!"[100] An example of Truman's plainspokenness occurs at the beginning of his fifth SUA. "A year ago I reported to this Congress that the state of the Union was good. I am happy to be able to report to you today that the state of the Union continues to be good."[101] He was similarly direct in his proposals for Congress.

To reach our long-range goal of adequate housing for all our people, comprehensive housing legislation is urgently required, similar to the nonpartisan bill passed by the Senate last year. At a minimum, such legislation should open the way for rebuilding the blighted areas of our cities and should establish positive incentives for the investment of billions of dollars of private capital in large-scale rental housing projects. It should provide for improvement of housing in rural areas and for the construction, over a 4-year period, of half a million units of public low-rental housing. It should authorize a single peacetime federal housing agency to assure efficient use of our resources on the vast housing front.[102]

At the beginning of the era of Dwight D. Eisenhower, Ike did not follow the lead of the previous two presidents and give Congress a specific legislative agenda. Shortly after taking office, Eisenhower did, however, deliver an SUA that was very lengthy and set the broad outlines of the direction the new administration would take. It was only after criticism from congressional Republicans that he would provide Congress a list of legislative priorities.[103] It would then be firmly entrenched in the modern presidency that not only did the president play a role at the end of the legislative process with his ability to accept or reject bills, but he also had a role to play at the beginning in initiating a policy agenda. No modern president since has failed to initiate policy, tout them, and highlight these policies in the SUA for the Congress and the public.

Embracing the Public

With the SUA firmly established as an oral address and Congress fully expecting the president to advance a legislative agenda, the next series of significant changes in the SUA relate to the further inclusion of the public audience. Lyndon B. Johnson (LBJ) was the next president to adapt, in two ways, the SUA to changing times. A subtle, but significant change occurred in 1964 with the delivery of LBJ's first SUA. Despite the recognition by previous presidents that the public was an audience, they had never been formally included in an SUA's salutation. Rather than recognizing solely the members of Congress as his predecessors had done in various formulations (Fellow-Citizens of the Senate and House of Representatives; Gentlemen of the Congress; Members of the Senate and the House of Representatives; Mr. Speaker, Mr. Vice President, Members of the Congress), Johnson became the first president to formally include the American public in his opening by beginning, "Mr. Speaker, Mr. President, Members of the House and Senate, my fellow Americans."[104] The typical salutation now includes some formulation of the American public. The second significant change that Johnson would make occurred in 1965. He moved the speech's delivery to the evening, enabling him to capture a prime-time viewing audience on television. All presidents since have followed this practice for most of their SUAs.[105]

Another significant practice was added to the delivery of the modern SUA by Ronald Reagan. He began introducing key guests in the gallery, and this practice has been followed by subsequent presidents. Typically, the guests are not famous people, but ordinary Americans. Presidents have used this practice to introduce people who exemplify values or characteristics they want to uphold or to link these guests to a policy initiative, goal, or successful program. For example, in Bill Clinton's 1994 address, he urged Congress to support his community policing program to put more policemen on the streets. After explaining why he believed in this initiative, he introduced a New York City policeman, Kevin Jett, who was seated in the gallery.[106]

A final significant event in the history of the SUA occurred in 1997 when, for the first time, the Internet became the newest communication medium to carry the speech live. Clinton even notes this significant event in his speech.

> To prepare America for the 21st century, we must harness the powerful forces of science and technology to benefit all Americans. This is the first State of the Union carried live in video over the Internet, but we've only begun to spread the benefits of a technology revolution that should become the modern birthright of every citizen.[107]

Clinton capitalizes on this "first" and goes on to discuss the promise of the Internet as an introduction to his technological and research goals.

Conclusion: From a Duty to a Power

Binkley notes, "Where can one find a finer example of the natural history of our political institutions than the way in which the dynamic forces of American society have transformed the Chief Executive of the written Constitution into the Chief Legislator of our unwritten constitution?"[108] However, it was more than just the "dynamic forces of American society," as Binkley put it, that transformed the SUA, a key component of the chief legislator's power.

The two constitutional provisions at the root of the SUA have always been there, but how they have been utilized by presidents has changed over time. The president has not always been the chief legislator, but presidents have always given annual messages or SUAs. The history of SUAs illustrates the extent to which key presidents were able to mold and shape it to fit their view of the presidency. In the nineteenth century, the annual message was viewed as a duty that presidents needed to fulfill; it was not seen as a power. In general, the written annual messages of this era gave Congress lots of information, but the recommendations tended simply to call the attention of Congress to a broad issue area rather than give any detailed policy guidance or leadership.

In the twentieth century, the SUA became a key power of the chief legislator. Activist presidents such as Teddy Roosevelt, Woodrow Wilson, and Franklin Roosevelt firmly believed in leading Congress and taking the initiative with a legislative agenda. They did not believe, as many of their predecessors did, that legislative leadership crossed a constitutional line. Chief legislators began utilizing the SUA as a way to exhibit leadership of Congress. Technological advances played a role in the ability of presidents to reach beyond just Congress. Presidents came to realize the SUA provided them with a forum not only to appeal to Congress, but also to appeal to the public. Modern presidents have fully exploited its communicative power.

Many have recognized that "the oldest and toughest problem of our governmental system is the relationship of the President and Congress."[109] This relationship is rarely static; there is an ebb and flow in the sharing of powers. A historical look at SUAs allows one to chart the evolution of presidential powers and the way presidents have utilized the document or speech, first as a means of fulfilling a duty, and later as a power that could fully exploit the president's position in the political system behind the bully pulpit.

Notes

1. US Constitution, Art. II, Sec. 3.

2. To avoid wordiness and confusion, when speaking of annual messages and State of the Union addresses as an aggregate unit, we will simply refer to them as *State of the Union addresses (SUAs)*. If we are referring to a particular message or speech, then we will generally refer to it with the term in use at the time. From 1790 to 1934, the document was referred to as an *annual message,* whether it was a written document or an oral speech. In 1934, the speech was officially titled the "Annual Message to Congress on the State of the Union." See Thomas H. Neale, "The President's State of the Union Message: Frequently Asked Questions" Report RS20021 (Washington, DC: Congressional Research Service, Library of Congress, 2003). Since the 1940s, the annual message has been referred to as the *State of the Union address.* Even though it is not until the 1940s that the terminology changes, we will, however, from Woodrow Wilson forward begin to uniformly refer to these documents (when delivered orally) as *State of the Union addresses.*

3. Alexander Hamilton, James Madison, and John Jay, *The Federalist Papers,* ed. Garry Wills (New York: Bantam, 1982), 349.

4. Ibid., 391.

5. *Annals of Congress,* 1st Cong., 1st sess., Senate, 1789, 28.

6. Ibid.

7. *Annals of Congress,* 1st Cong., 2nd sess., Senate, 1790, 970–971.

8. Hamilton, Madison, and Jay, *Federalist Papers,* 391.

9. Ibid., 349. But Hamilton does not mention the president giving information to Congress here, a further indication of the provisions' separate nature.

10. Ibid.

11. C. Ellis Stevens, *Sources of the Constitution of the United States* (New York: Macmillan and Co., 1894), 141.

12. Willi Paul Adams, *The First American Constitutions: Republican Ideology and the Making of the State Constitutions in the Revolutionary Era* (Chapel Hill: University of North Carolina Press, 1980), 272–273.

13. Constitution of New York 1777, art. XIX.

14. Herbert J. Storing, ed., *The Complete Anti-Federalist,* vol. 2 (Chicago: University of Chicago Press, 1981), 6.31: 115.

15. Hamilton, Madison, and Jay, *Federalist Papers,* 369.

16. The ambiguity evident in these provisions could also have been meant to serve the larger purpose of promoting competition between the executive and legislative branches as a means of keeping both in check. See Madison, *Federalist 51,* in Hamilton, Madison, and Jay, *Federalist Papers,* 261–265.

17. *Annals of Congress,* 1st Cong., 2nd sess., Senate, 1790, 968–969.

18. Constitution of New York 1777, sec. 19.

19. US Constitution, Art. II, Sec. 3.

20. *Annals of Congress,* 1st Cong., 1st sess., Senate, 1789, 28.

21. Seymour H. Fersh, *The View from the White House: A Study of the*

Presidential State of the Union Messages (Washington, DC: Public Affairs Press, 1961), 9.

22. *Annals of Congress,* 1st Cong., 3rd sess., Senate, 1790, 1772.

23. *Annals of Congress*, 4th Cong., 2nd sess., House, 1796, 1595.

24. Karlyn Kohrs Campbell and Kathleen Hall Jamieson, *Deeds Done in Words: Presidential Rhetoric and the Genres of Governance* (Chicago: University of Chicago Press, 1990), 74.

25. Stephen J. Wayne, *The Legislative Presidency* (New York: Harper & Row, 1978), 8.

26. Stephen Skowronek, *The Politics Presidents Make: Leadership from John Adams to Bill Clinton* (Cambridge: Harvard University Press, 1997), 73.

27. Stevens, *Sources of the Constitution,* 158.

28. Fersh, *View from the White House,* 16.

29. *Annals of Congress,* 7th Cong., 1st sess., Senate, 1801, 11.

30. *Annals of Congress*, 10th Cong., 2nd sess., Senate, 1808, 15.

31. This is evident, for example, in his feelings over the establishment of a national bank as well as the language he writes for a draft Constitutional amendment that pertained to the Louisiana Purchase. See Thomas Jefferson, "Opinion on the Constitutionality of a National Bank," 1791, Avalon Project at Yale University Law School; and Thomas Jefferson, "Draft on an Amendment to the Constitution," 1803, Avalon Project at Yale University Law School.

32. Skowronek, *The Politics Presidents Make,* 74.

33. *Annals of Congress,* 8th Cong., 1st sess., Senate, 1803, 12.

34. Fersh, *View from the White House,* 21.

35. Wilfred E. Binkley, "The President as Chief Legislator," *Annals of the American Academy of Political and Social Sciences*, 307 (1956):93.

36. *Annals of Congress,* 18th Cong., 1st sess., Senate, 1823, 19.

37. Ibid., 22–23.

38. Fersh, *View from the White House,* 28.

39. *Register of Debates in Congress*, 21st Cong., 1st sess., House, 1829, 472; 21st Cong., 1st sess., Senate, 1829, appendix, 1.

40. Darrell M. West, *The Rise and Fall of the Media Establishment* (Boston: Bedford/St. Martin's Press, 2001), 19.

41. Ibid.

42. Samuel Kernell, *Going Public: New Strategies of Presidential Leadership*, 3rd ed. (Washington, DC: CQ Press, 1997).

43. We refer to this as a variation of "going public" because the president is using the public, in a sense, to put pressure on Congress by referring to the public will or public opinion.

44. *Register of Debates in Congress*, 21st Cong., 1st sess., Senate, 1829, appendix, 6–7.

45. Fersh, *View from the White House,* 30.

46. Lyn Ragsdale, *Vital Statistics on the Presidency* (Washington, DC: CQ Press, 1996), 396.

47. *Register of Debates in Congress*, 21st Cong., 2nd sess., Senate, 1830, appendix, vi.

48. *Congressional Globe,* 37th Cong., 2nd sess., 1861, appendix, 1.

49. Ibid.

50. *Congressional Globe,* 37th Cong., 3rd sess., 1862, appendix, 3–4.

51. Fersh, *View from the White House,* 45.

52. *Congressional Globe,* 38th Cong., 2nd sess., 1864, appendix, 3.

53. *Congressional Globe*, 38th Cong., 1st sess., 1863, appendix, 3.

54. *Congressional Globe,* 37th Cong., 2nd sess., 1861, appendix, 4.

55. Ibid.

56. Andrew Johnson, "Annual Message to Congress, 1865," in Fred L. Israel, ed., *The State of the Union Messages of the Presidents, 1790–1966,* vol. 2 (New York: Chelsea House, 1966): 1112.

57. Johnson, "Annual Message to Congress, 1866," in Israel, *State of the Union Messages,* Volume 2: 1131–1133.

58. Wayne, *Legislative Presidency,* 12.

59. Fersh, *View from the White House,* 70.

60. Binkley, "The President as Chief Legislator," 93.

61. Theodore Roosevelt, "Annual Message to Congress, 1903," in Israel, *State of the Union Messages,* 2:2037.

62. Roosevelt, "Annual Message to Congress, 1904," in Israel, *State of the Union Messages,* 2:2134

63. Roosevelt, "Annual Message to Congress, 1901," in Israel, *State of the Union Messages,* 2:2018–2019.

64. Ibid., 2:2020.

65. Roosevelt, "Annual Message to Congress, 1908," in Israel, *State of the Union Messages,* 3:2308.

66. Emphasis added. Ibid.

67. William H. Taft, "Annual Message to Congress, 1911," in Israel, *The State of the Union Messages,* 3:2432.

68. Daniel D. Stid, *The President as Statesman: Woodrow Wilson and the Constitution* (Lawrence: University of Kansas Press, 1998).

69. Binkley, "The President as Chief Legislator," 95.

70. Jeffrey K. Tulis, "The Two Constitutional Presidencies," in *The Presidency and the Political System,* 7th ed., ed. Michael Nelson (Washington, DC: CQ Press, 2003), 79–110.

71. Emphasis added. Woodrow Wilson, "Annual Message to Congress, 1914," in Israel, *State of the Union Messages,* 3:2551.

72. Emphasis added. Wilson, "Annual Message to Congress, 1915," in Israel, *State of the Union Messages,* 3:2574.

73. Ryan Teten's analysis of SUAs calculated the average percentages of the use of *we* and *our* and noticed a large increase in usage in Wilson's addresses. Teten does not, however, distinguish between when use of *we* refers to Congress, the public, or both. Ryan L. Teten, "Evolution of the Modern Rhetorical Presidency: Presidential Presentation and Development of the State of the Union Address," *Presidential Studies Quarterly* 33 (June 2003):342.

74. Wilson, "Annual Message to Congress, 1914," in Israel, *State of the Union Messages,* 3:2552.

75. Tulis, "The Two Constitutional Presidencies," 99.

76. Wilson, "Annual Message to Congress, 1914," in Israel, *State of the Union Messages,* 3:2556.

77. Jeffrey Tulis, *The Rhetorical Presidency* (Princeton: Princeton University Press, 1987).

78. Wilson, "Annual Message to Congress, 1913," in Israel, *State of the Union Messages,* 3:2544.

79. Wilson, "Annual Message to Congress, 1919," in Israel, *State of the Union Messages,* 3:2598.

80. Warren G. Harding, "Annual Message to Congress, 1921," in Israel, *State of the Union Messages,* 3:2616.

81. Fersh, *View from the White House,* 93.

82. After the ratification of the Twentieth Amendment (1933), Congress would begin their new sessions in January, the president would be sworn-in in January, and SUAs would typically be given in that month.

83. Binkley, "The President as Chief Legislator," 97.

84. Ibid., 93.

85. Franklin D. Roosevelt, "Annual Message to Congress, 1934," in Israel, *State of the Union Messages,* 3:2806

86. Ibid., 3:2811.

87. Roosevelt, "Annual Message to Congress, 1935," in Israel, *State of the Union Messages,* 3:2811.

88. Ibid., 3:2813.

89. Ibid., 3:2816.

90. Ibid., 3:2812.

91. Fersh, *View from the White House,* 103. Delivery of the SUA, however, reverted back to the afternoon with Truman.

92. Roosevelt, "Annual Message to Congress, 1936," in Israel, *State of the Union Messages,* 3:2822.

93. Ibid., 3:2824.

94. Roosevelt, "Annual Message to Congress, 1941," in Israel, *State of the Union Messages,* 3:2860.

95. Fersh, *View from the White House,* 105.

96. Harry S. Truman, "Annual Message to the Congress on the State of the Union," *Public Papers of the Presidents of the United States: Harry S. Truman, 1946,* vol.1 (Washington, DC: GPO, 1962), 37.

97. Richard E. Neustadt, "Presidency and Legislation: Planning the President's Program," *American Political Science Review* 49 (December 1955):998.

98. Truman's final SUA in 1953 was another written message, but it was a lame-duck SUA. It was sent to Congress on January 7, 1953, and Eisenhower would take office in a matter of days.

99. Neale, "The President's State of the Union Message."

100. Truman, "Annual Message to the Congress on the State of the Union," *Public Papers, 1949,* 1:4.

101. Truman, "Annual Message to the Congress on the State of the Union," *Public Papers, 1950,* 1:2.

102. Truman, "Annual Message to the Congress on the State of the Union," *Public Papers, 1947,* 1:7.

103. Neustadt, "Presidency and Legislation," 1015; Lyn Ragsdale, *Vital Statistics on the Presidency,* rev. ed. (Washington, DC: CQ Press, 1998), 364.

104. Lyndon B. Johnson, "Annual Message to the Congress on the State of the Union," *Public Papers of the Presidents of the United States: Lyndon B. Johnson, 1964,* vol.1 (Washington, DC: GPO, 1965), 112.

105. Nixon's 1970 and 1972 SUAs as well as Ford's 1975 SUA were delivered in the afternoon.

106. William J. Clinton, "Annual Message to the Congress on the State of the Union," *Public Papers of the Presidents of the United States: William J. Clinton, 1994,* vol.1 (Washington, DC: GPO, 1995), 133.

107. Clinton, "Annual Message to the Congress on the State of the Union," *Public Papers, 1997,* 1:112.

108. Binkley, "The President as Chief Legislator," 92.

109. James MacGregor Burns, *The Power to Lead* (New York: Simon and Schuster, 1984), 182.

3

No Ordinary Speech

As the only nationally elected official, the president has many jobs to do. Clinton Rossiter identified five Constitutional tasks presidents fulfill: chief of state, chief executive, chief diplomat, commander-in-chief, and chief legislator. In addition, he counted another five extraconstitutional roles played by the president: party chief, voice of the people, protector of the peace, manager of prosperity, and leader of a coalition of free nations.[1] In one speech, the State of the Union address, we can see all of the various presidential roles on display. As it exists today, the SUA has extraordinary value as a speech, both for presidents as well as scholars. Through the ceremony involved in appearing in the House chamber with other governmental actors in attendance and the nation watching, presidents appear as the chief of state. In the capacity of chief executive, presidents report on the way certain policies are being carried out. They report on the state of foreign affairs, which involves both chief diplomat and commander-in-chief jobs. They will speak loftily of peace and freedom and the US role in maintaining and advancing these two values. As chief legislator, they discuss the legislation they do and do not support and explain their own proposals. As the only elected official with a national constituency, they use the opportunity to urge Congress to act on things they believe the public interest demands. Their role as party leader is often highlighted during an SUA when one side of the congressional audience stands and applauds, but the other side sits and remains silent. Most certainly, presidents report on the state of the economy, what the administration's role in it has been, and what they seek to do in regard to prosperity. The speech offers presidents the opportunity to appear very "presidential" and utilize their bully pulpit. For scholars, the SUA enables analysis of the way presidents communicate when at their most presidential. In short, the SUA encapsulates the various roles in the US presidency, as well as the symbolism and ceremony of the office.

Presidential roles, however, have not been static. While all of the various roles of the president are on display in the SUA, the one that is most prominent is that of chief legislator. As the president's role of chief legislator emerged, presidents became much more active in the realm of recommending policy than most nineteenth-century presidents, as they sought to more actively lead Congress, place their imprint upon policy, and secure their legacy, which became increasingly tied to legislative accomplishments. The president's legislative agenda-setting power, however, was not fully realized until the twentieth century. Although foreshadowed in the presidencies of Theodore Roosevelt and Woodrow Wilson, this power of the presidency was cemented when Franklin Roosevelt called the Seventy-third Congress into special session to enact his New Deal in 1933. In his first inaugural address, Roosevelt had stated, "I am prepared under my constitutional duty to recommend the measures that a stricken Nation in the midst of a stricken world may require."[2] He did, and Congress responded with a flurry of activity, enacting fifteen major public laws in the first 100 days of FDR's first term.[3] Since that time, Congress has come to expect that the president will send his legislative priorities, and presidents have been measured by their first 100 days in office. The SUA has become a major tool of the legislative president. Presidents can highlight to both Congress and the public the key items on which they want legislative action and use rhetoric in such a way that encourages action. They bring attention to issues of their choosing, which otherwise might not enter public debate. The SUA has become a power presidents can wield, not just a speech that fulfills the constitutional duties of reporting and recommending measures to Congress. The SUA is no longer just about presidents communicating with Congress, but involves presidents communicating with the public as well. The purpose of the speech remains, however, to rhetorically exert influence over Congress and get them to act on the president's recommendations. It is this communication in which we are especially interested, and we examine how the SUA functions as a means of presidential-congressional communication in a public setting.

Since the emergence of the president's role as chief legislator in the twentieth century, a president's legislative success has become intimately tied to our perception of leadership. The move from the written annual message to oral delivery of the SUA was a key component of how the president came to be viewed as the legislator-in-chief.[4] As this new presidential "hat" of chief legislator was being recognized, a related and fundamental change in the presidency had also taken place. Woodrow Wilson, who reinstituted the oral delivery of the SUA, was a key figure in the development of the rhetorical presidency in which the president is viewed as a popular leader.[5]

The president as popular leader and the president as chief legislator are connected roles. Legislators, as representatives, naturally appeal to their constituents for support; chiefs necessarily seek to lead. Rhetoric is one tool the chief legislator utilizes to accomplish both tasks. In the contemporary SUA, the chief legislators appeal to both their constituency and their legislature; as they report and recommend measures to Congress, the public is also listening and addressed. In this speech, the president seeks to exert leadership of both the public and Congress by setting the nation on a path, outlining an agenda, and using the art of rhetoric to further policy goals. Rooted in the Constitution, the SUA provides the president with an opportunity to say, in effect, "here is the situation, here is what has been done so far, and here is what I propose we do in the coming year." To bolster the case, the president uses images, examples, and symbols to appeal to the shared values and identities of constituents. While the policies mentioned in this speech do not encompass the whole of the president's agenda, the legislative requests indicate the items that the administration has chosen to highlight publicly before both Congress and the rest of the country.[6]

For our analysis of the nature of the communication that takes place in the SUA, we confine ourselves to the period of 1965–2002. We begin with 1965 because that is the year Lyndon Johnson established the practice of delivering the speech during prime-time television viewing hours, thus dramatically expanding the number of people he could potentially reach with the SUA. In the era that we study, the communications in the SUA are crafted both for congressional and public consumption. The president as chief legislator and the president as popular leader are roles that are firmly established during this time period. By beginning with 1965 for our content analysis, we can hold several factors constant as we examine how presidents as the chief legislator use the SUA. First, we examine only oral addresses delivered to joint sessions of Congress.[7] Reporting on the state of the Union in some way is a constitutional duty and, for modern presidents, has almost exclusively been in an oral format, the better to utilize this constitutional provision as a power. Second, evening delivery is the general rule.[8] Third, SUAs occur regularly and at the same point in the congressional calendar, near the beginning of a session. Fourth, the speeches occur in the same setting, the House chamber, and there is a constancy in the audiences. Both Congress and the public are addressed. Fifth, SUAs command widespread attention. The television networks carry the speech, the public is more likely to tune in to this speech than most others, the media report on it immediately afterward, and it becomes a reference point during the congressional session of the president's agenda. Finally, the address tells us what policy areas the president believes are important and has chosen to rhetorically highlight to the public and Congress. Paul Light notes the significance of what is contained in the SUA: "It is *the* statement of legislative priorities."[9] Furthermore, in a recent assessment of his time in office, President Clinton articulated the importance of the speech. "We used every State of the Union address to plan a specific detailed agenda for the coming year and then we just rammed it and worked at it."[10]

In the following chapter, we turn to an examination of the speech itself. We first examine the structure of the speech, which has remained a constant even as the format has changed. The policymaking rhetoric that presidents use both reports to Congress as well as recommends measures to Congress for consideration. In his policymaking rhetoric, the president seeks congressional influence by conveying substance about policy and using symbolism to convince his audiences to follow his leadership. The SUA is a unique tool of political communication for the chief legislator.

Reporting and Recommending: The Structure of the SUA

The SUA is rooted in two constitutional provisions that stipulate, "He shall from time to time give to the Congress Information of the State of the Union, and recommend to their Consideration such Measures as he shall judge necessary and expedient."[11] These constitutional provisions have never been amended. Therefore, the overall structure, or form, of the SUA has remained a constant.[12] The constitutional roots of the SUA provide for continuity in the form of the speech but are also vague enough to encompass different practices and views of the presidency. The Constitution does not dictate how, or even when, a president should report on the state of the Union, and it is silent on how the president should go about recommending "necessary and expedient" measures. Presidents have always reported to Congress and recommended measures to them. What has changed over time is the format, or the way presidential reporting and recommending has been done. SUAs have varied in arrangement, style, and substance as they carry out the two constitutional provisions at their root. Sometimes the format is written, and sometimes it is an oral address. Sometimes the recommendations simply seek to draw the attention of Congress to an issue area, leaving the details to them, and sometimes the recommendations are specific. Whatever its name—annual message or State of the Union address—and however presidents delivered it to Congress, presidents have always reported *to Congress* on the state of the nation, and recommended *to Congress* measures the president considered to be important. As the public became an audience and as *chief legislator* became a moniker applied to the president in the twentieth century, the SUA became a powerful tool for presidents to communicate with both Congress and the public.

The Policymaking Rhetoric of the SUA

Karlyn Kohrs Campbell and Kathleen Hall Jamieson, in their study of presidential rhetoric, examine the entire corpus of SUAs and emphasize the continuity in the form and function they found in the documents.[13] They specifically refer to the type of rhetoric in the SUA as "deliberative or policy related,"[14] characterized by the president detailing a problem and then providing a solution: "The overall structure of [State of the Union] addresses is problem-solution, the hallmark of deliberative, policy-making rhetoric."[15] Others have also used the term *deliberative rhetoric* when discussing presidential speeches more broadly. It has been used to describe presidential rhetoric aimed primarily at policymakers. Both Jeffrey Tulis and Michael Malbin distinguish what they call a president's *popular rhetoric* from his deliberative rhetoric—the former being aimed at the public (and indirectly at Congress), and the latter being aimed directly at Congress.[16] There are, however, difficulties with applying the *deliberative rhetoric* term to SUAs. The use of the term itself needs some qualification and clarification. A distinction should be made between the Aristotelian notion of the term and its application to presidential rhetoric in SUAs.

Deliberative rhetoric is one of the three types of rhetoric identified by Aristotle and can be viewed as "deliberation about the future action in the best interest of a state."[17] It is forward-looking and involves audiences of both "spectators" and "judges."[18] Judges in the sense of deliberative rhetoric would be the members of the policymaking assembly.[19] All three types of rhetoric (deliberative, judicial, and epideictic) are given in a setting in which "speakers seek to persuade or influence action or belief and thus to impose their own ideas or values on others."[20] In Aristotle's time, deliberative rhetoric would have involved multiple speakers all seeking to persuade their audiences as to their point of view about a particular policy or solution to a problem.

In modern parlance, however, the term *deliberative rhetoric* is often used in a different sense, especially when applied to presidential rhetoric. It has come to be used with rhetoric that is similar in some respects to Aristotle's original meaning of deliberative rhetoric; it is forward-looking and policy-oriented. The rhetoric of the SUA does seek to persuade "judges" and "spectators" regarding policy matters. There is an important distinction, however, to be made that relates to the actual notion of deliberation; the presentation of multiple viewpoints is absent in the forum in which the SUA is given. This is an important distinction that is typically not made when the term *deliberative rhetoric* is applied today. It is generally used to describe rhetoric that is meant to prompt deliberation about the path policy should take, as well as influence that path. The president's rhetoric in an SUA is one-sided; the rhetoric itself is not deliberative but is meant to promote deliberation. The actual act of deliberation takes place, if at all, in a separate forum. Deliberating about policy and attempting to spark deliberation about policy are different activities. Campbell and Jamieson neglect to make this distinction.

Deliberation is meant to be stimulated by the presidential rhetoric in the SUA, but it is not a given that deliberation will take place. It certainly will not be taking place during the event that is the SUA. Lack of deliberation is one of the concerns that Tulis has with the rise of the rhetorical presidency and the accompanying popular leadership the president seeks to exert through popular rhetoric. Tulis's case study of LBJ's War on Poverty initiatives is an example of presidential rhetoric where deliberation, in fact, did not take place, but the policies were nevertheless adopted.[21] It was policymaking rhetoric, but it did not spark much in the way of deliberation. As Tulis's case on LBJ points out, the president's overarching goal was to get his policies adopted; that deliberation was circumvented was of little concern to him. The rhetoric that was utilized, however, was an important factor in how deliberation was sidestepped. The rhetoric was policymaking in both its intent and effect, but it was not deliberative.

One additional difficulty with using the term *deliberative rhetoric* with SUAs relates to the audiences at which the rhetoric is directed. As noted above, Aristotle considered deliberative rhetoric to be aimed at both spectators and judges. Both Tulis and Malbin have used the term *deliberative rhetoric* to distinguish rhetoric aimed at policymakers (judges) from that aimed at the public (spectators). Each separates out the audiences of the public and the actual policymakers and notes the differences in the rhetoric presidents use in approaching these audiences, labeling one *deliberative rhetoric* and the other *popular rhetoric*.[22] While this distinction of audience may be useful if the president is addressing these two audiences separately, it is less so when one is discussing SUAs, where presidents are addressing both Congress and the public. It also is not consistent with the Aristotelian notion of deliberative rhetoric. In SUAs, presidents are simultaneously addressing both audiences with the same end in mind—persuading them that their policy proposals are good ones and should be supported and enacted.

Rather than rely on the term *deliberative rhetoric* to describe the rhetoric of the SUA, we will refer to the policymaking rhetoric of the SUA. In this sense, we alter slightly what Campbell and Jamieson see as the SUA's overarching form. Whereas they incorporate a notion of deliberative rhetoric, we feel the use of this term can be misleading and prefer to emphasize that the rhetoric of the SUA is policymaking, but not deliberative. This will hopefully avoid potential confusion that stems from the modern misuse of Aristotle's original labeling of a rhetorical genre. In addition, as the Tulis case on LBJ makes evident, a president's policymaking rhetoric may be successful in prompting policy, yet not spark deliberation. In addition,

Campbell and Jamieson note the SUA's rhetoric is intended to influence policy by identifying problems and offering solutions, but they put little emphasis on how this stems from the constitutional roots of the reporting and recommending provisions. The policymaking rhetoric that makes up the overall structure of the SUA is created by the constitutional basis of the address. Whether written annual messages or oral SUAs, this has always been the structure. The policymaking rhetoric of the SUA is one of the tools that presidents can utilize as they attempt to lead Congress and the public.

Although the emphasis on the components of reporting and recommending has varied, the end has always been congressional influence. Nineteenth-century annual messages typically put more emphasis on reporting than on recommending. In the twentieth century, as the president came to be regarded as both legislator-in-chief and popular leader, recommendations became much more specific. The overall structure of the SUA, therefore, is dictated by the president's twofold constitutional tasks of reporting and recommending to Congress. In this way, the SUA has always provided for presidential influence of Congress. The purpose of the SUA is for the president to report and recommend measures to influence the policy Congress will make; policymaking rhetoric is used in this regard. A case is presented regarding the policy ends the president is pursuing. In making this case, symbolism and information are used in an attempt to persuade the audiences that the policy recommendations are the correct course. This rhetoric, however, is one-sided and should not be considered deliberative. The constitutional roots of the SUA provide for continuity in its form and are reflected in the policymaking rhetoric presidents utilize to present the situation and offer their preferred actions.

Communicating with Congress and the Public in the SUA

Viewing the president as popular leader, according to Tulis, became "an unquestioned premise" in the twentieth century.[23] The use of rhetoric aimed at the public is the essence of this, giving us the "rhetorical presidency" where "presidents regularly 'go over the heads' of Congress to the people at large in support of legislation and other initiatives."[24] Since the emergence of the rhetorical presidency, the president's words in the SUA have been simultaneously aimed at both Congress and the public. Tulis traces the rhetorical presidency back to Wilson, who, not coincidentally, reestablished the oral delivery of the SUA in 1913. Shortly after this change in practice, the public audience began to be incorporated as a direct, rather than indirect, audience. The public first had the ability to hear the president's actual words in 1923, when the first radio broadcast of the president's speech occurred, and then had the opportunity to hear and see the president's speech when it was first televised in 1947. Not until 1965, however, would most Americans actually be able to see the SUA on television when Johnson moved its delivery to the evening to take advantage of a prime-time television viewing audience. This new tradition dramatically expanded the pool of potential viewers among the public, and the practice has become standard in SUAs since 1965.

In SUAs, presidents seek to convince two audiences to support their proposals by using policymaking rhetoric. They must convince a majority of members of both congressional chambers to act if they are to get anything accomplished legislatively. They may be aided in this task if they can convince the American public that their measures are necessary, putting pressure on Congress to act—this is the essence of "going public."[25] Members of Congress, as representatives of the people, are not immune to rhetorical devices designed to persuade, whether targeted at them directly or indirectly, as when rhetoric is aimed at the public. Thus, presidents seek to exhibit rhetorical leadership in an SUA through the use of policymaking rhetoric; exhortations for congressional action in the SUA are also understood as appeals for public support of the president's requests. The attempts at public persuasion in the SUA are part and parcel of how the president attempts congressional leadership. Presidents, therefore, simultaneously aim the policymaking rhetoric in the SUA at the public and Congress.

One excellent example of how the two audiences can become intertwined comes from Clinton's 1994 address.

> We must literally transform our outdated unemployment system into a new reemployment system. The old unemployment system just sort of kept you going while you waited for your old job to come back. We've got to have a new system to move people into new and better jobs, because most of those old jobs just don't come back. And we know that the only way to have real job security in the future, to get a good job with a growing income, is to have real skills and the ability to learn new ones. So we've got to streamline today's patchwork of training programs and make them a source of new skills for our people who lose their jobs. Reemployment, not unemployment, must become the centerpiece of our economic renewal. I urge you to pass it in this session of Congress.[26]

In framing the problem, Clinton addresses the American public: when *you* lose your job, here is what happens under the current system. His primary audience initially is not Congress; members rarely lose their jobs. In beginning this way, Clinton indicates to the American public that he understands the situation in which many individuals find themselves. Congress, however, is witness to the president's inclusion of the public audience. He then proposes his solution to the problem, which is reemployment, not unemployment, and urges Congress to pass his proposal. By the end of the statement, the target audience has shifted to Congress, but the public whom he had just involved in the framing of the issue is now a witness. In this example, the two audiences are simultaneously addressed.

How the State of the Union Address Functions as Presidential Communication

To understand the state of the Union, we must look not only at where we are and where we're going but where we've been.
—*Ronald Reagan,*
1982 SUA

While the overall form or pattern of the SUA is found in the reporting and recommending that takes place in the SUA, there are several functions the president's policymaking rhetoric fulfills. When presidents report to Congress, they say in effect not only, "here is the situation," but also, "here is what has been done so far" about this situation. In reporting, the president informs, frames the issue, and advertises actions already undertaken. The recommending provisions of the Constitution enable presidents to say, "here is what I propose for the future." The SUA is a vehicle in which presidents can convey substance about policy (background, past actions, proposals). In addition, they want to persuade their audiences that their reporting of the situation and recommendations about the situation are valid. They will incorporate symbolism and language that are significant to US citizens to further their leadership of Congress and the public. In this way they hope to make their policy recommendations meaningful and tangible.

Presidents will use the policymaking rhetoric of the SUA to build a case for their policy recommendations; the desired end is to get Congress to fulfill the legislative requests they highlight. As they report and recommend, they convey policy substance and use symbolism in their attempts to lead the Congress and the public. Campbell and Jamieson identify three processes or functions that characterize the genre of SUAs: meditations, assessments, and recommendations.[27] We characterize SUA functions in a slightly different, although related, way, because of our focus on the president's use of the speech as chief legislator. The functions we identify, conveying policy substance and persuading through symbolism, also are linked to the constitutional provisions that are the roots of the policymaking rhetoric in the SUA. Presidents report and recommend to Congress, and in doing so, convey policy substance; to help convince their audiences to follow their recommendations, they use symbols in the form of images and examples, as well as language that holds symbolic import.[28] The symbolism presidents employ partially corresponds to the function Campbell and Jamieson identify as "public meditations on values."[29] The policy substance of the SUA relates both to what Campbell and Jamieson call "the assessments of information and issues" and the "policy recommendations" that presidents make.[30] One aspect of SUAs that Campbell and Jamieson do not identify is the proclivity of presidents to claim credit for past successes as they build up to their policy recommendations. David Mayhew found that credit claiming was a key aspect of legislative behavior.[31] In addition, Pomper's evaluation of party platforms, documents similar in some respects to the SUA, identified evaluations of past performance as a key component of those political documents.[32] Thus, we see two key aspects in the policy substance of SUAs, credit claiming and recommending policy. Reporting to Congress, presidents detail the current state of affairs and take credit for what has been done about the situation thus far. They recommend measures judged "necessary and expedient" and detail the direction they want policy to take. Presidents convey policy substance by touting past actions and requesting future policy actions. Symbolism is incorporated throughout the SUA. To be persuasive and make their case, presidents will employ images and examples to inspire the audiences, appeal to shared values, harken back idealistically to an earlier age, and encourage thinking about shared identities, all in hopes that these will help audiences accept their recommendations as good ones.

Some examples from SUAs can aid in illustrating the substantive and symbolic functions of the SUA. Consider this example from Clinton's 1999 SUA where he reports on the state of the federal budget and recommends using the surplus for shoring up Social Security. He first frames the issue and gives an assessment of the situation.

How we fare as a nation far into the 21st century depends upon what we do as a nation today. So with our budget surplus growing, our economy expanding, our confidence rising, now is the moment for this generation to meet our historic responsibility to the 21st century.

Our fiscal discipline gives us an unsurpassed opportunity to address a remarkable new challenge, the aging of America. With the number of elderly Americans set to double by 2030, the baby boom will become a senior boom. So first, and above all, we must save Social Security for the 21st century.

Early in this century, being old meant being poor. When President Roosevelt created Social Security, thousands wrote to thank him for eliminating what one woman called "the stark terror of penniless, helpless old age." Even today, without Social Security, half our Nation's elderly would be forced into poverty.

Today, Social Security is strong. But by 2013, payroll taxes will no longer be sufficient to cover monthly payments. By 2032 the Trust Fund will be exhausted and Social Security will be unable to pay the full benefits older Americans have been promised.[33]

Woven into his assessment of the problem is the imagery of what retirement used to hold, and would still for many if not for Roosevelt's Social Security program. Clinton conjures the classic "heroic presidency" example of Roosevelt and one of his signature policy achievements, Social Security. Having given background and stated the problem, he then presents his solution to the problem.

> The best way to keep Social Security a rock-solid guarantee is not to make drastic cuts in benefits, not to raise payroll tax rates, not to drain resources from Social Security in the name of saving it. Instead, I propose that we make the historic decision to invest the surplus to save Social Security.[34]

And, he gives details regarding his solution.

> Specifically, I propose that we commit 60 percent of the budget surplus for the next 15 years to Social Security, investing a small portion in the private sector, just as any private or State Government pension would do. This will earn a higher return and keep Social Security sound for 55 years.[35]

Clinton also takes credit for actions already undertaken. In the first quotation, he stresses "our fiscal discipline." He again claims credit before reiterating his course of action. "Now, last year we wisely reserved all of the surplus until we knew what it would take to save Social Security. Again, I say, we shouldn't spend any of it, not any of it, until after Social Security is truly saved. First things first."[36]

Or, take the following example from Reagan's 1984 SUA and his discussion of an education policy proposal. He first sets the issue up by summoning a list of American values. Reagan uses these concepts that hold symbolic importance for Americans as a foundation from which he can encourage the impression that these values are represented by his policy request.

> But our most precious resources, our greatest hope for the future, are the minds and hearts of our people, especially our children. We can help them build tomorrow by strengthening our community of shared values. This must be our third great goal. For us, faith, work, family, neighborhood, freedom, and peace are not just words; they're expressions of what America means, definitions of what makes us a good and loving people.[37]

Reagan then begins to report his view of the situation.

> Families stand at the center of our society. And every family has a personal stake in promoting excellence in education. Excellence does not begin in Washington. A 600-percent increase in Federal spending on education between 1960 and 1980 was accompanied by a steady decline in

> Scholastic Aptitude Test scores. Excellence must begin in our homes and neighborhood schools, where it's the responsibility of every parent and teacher and the right of every child.[38]

Next, he reports on the actions that he has taken regarding this situation.

> Our children come first, and that's why I established a bipartisan National Commission on Excellence in Education, to help us chart a commonsense course for better education. And already, communities are implementing the Commission's recommendations. Schools are reporting progress in math and reading skills.[39]

He then arrives at his specific legislative request.

> I will continue to press for tuition tax credits to expand opportunities for families and to soften the double payment for those paying public school taxes and private school tuition. Our proposal would target assistance to low- and middle-income families. Just as more incentives are needed within our schools, greater competition is needed among our schools. Without standards and competition, there can be no champions, no records broken, no excellence in education or any other walk of life.[40]

Reagan wants his audiences to see a tuition tax credit as an embodiment of the key American values with which he framed the issue.

In these examples, we see all of the things presidents seek to do with their SUAs; they present the situation, tout the success of actions already undertaken, give their solution to the problem, and employ symbolism to help them make their case, all in hopes that they can affect Congress and get their legislative requests enacted. In this sense, the SUA is a document that accumulates evidence in order to persuade Congress (either directly, or indirectly through public pressure) to follow the president's legislative lead. Both policy substance and symbolism are part of the policymaking rhetoric of the SUA.

What substantive policy areas do presidents highlight in the SUA, and how do they attempt to get their audiences to accept their recommendations? We turn our attention first to examining the areas of policy to which presidents give attention in the SUA. Because the speech is about conveying policy substance, we examine the policy areas in which presidents are actively advocating recommendations. We then turn our attention to the symbolism of the policymaking rhetoric, or how presidents seek to convey substance in a convincing way.

Areas of Substance in the Policymaking Rhetoric of the SUA

Presidents recommend policies. Public policy can be made through a variety of processes, such as executive orders, bureaucratic rules and regulations, judicial decisions, as well as legislation. Policies come in different "taxonomies"[41] and in addition encompass a broad array of policy areas. In SUAs, presidents' recommendations are not limited to just legislative ones. Presidents can pledge action that they will take through an executive order, or they may recommend policy actions that they would like states to adopt, even though they have no formal role in the states' processes. We confine ourselves, however, to examining the direct communications of presidential recommendations to Congress that can be found in SUAs. Specifically, what are the areas of policy in which presidents request legislative action from Congress in their SUAs, and what can this tell us about the speech itself?

As part of our study of the SUA, we determine the policy areas in which presidents seek to actively and publicly insert themselves in the legislative process. To gauge the areas of policy substance presidents include, we coded all instances of requests for congressional action in SUAs from 1965–2002 using content analysis.[42] Requests had to be substantive legislative requests, not vague rhetoric about a policy area.[43] We then classify the requests according to nine policy areas. In studying political party platforms, Pomper analyzed statements of future policies to which the parties pledged themselves.[44] He classified these statements according to nine different policy areas. Legislative requests in SUAs can be treated in a similar fashion, and we adopt Pomper's policy categories, with some minor modifications.[45]

We seek to answer two questions about what presidents say in their SUAs that can shed some light on the nature of the SUA and its rhetoric. First, is the SUA a carefully targeted policy document in which presidents confine their legislative requests to a few key areas, or is it a speech in which presidents span a broad array of policy areas? Second, are the policy areas from which presidents make legislative requests static over time, or dynamic?

In assessing whether the speech is broad or targeted in terms of policy, we can assess what we know about presidential agendas in general. Modern chief legislators cannot attempt legislative leadership on everything; they must prioritize.[46] In the contemporary SUA, especially, we might expect presidents to target requests for two reasons. First, speeches have finite space. There is a limit to how long presidents can address their audiences and how many legislative requests they can make in a speech. In the era of the written annual message, there was less of a need for presidents to prioritize because they were not limited by the space constraints of a speech. Second, in the era before the president was considered the chief legislator, Congress did not expect legislative priorities of presidents as they now do.[47] The SUA has been represented as an indication of what those priorities are.[48] At the same time, the SUA has also been characterized as containing "laundry lists" of requests[49] and as a "garbage can" in which a whole host of things are thrown.[50] We expect, therefore, that there will be some breadth of policy areas, but that because of a need to indicate priorities, a few key areas will garner more requests than others as presidents highlight the key policy areas on which they want to work with Congress.

The SUAs' legislative requests give an indication of where the attention of presidents is focused at one point in time on issues they want to advertise to the public and Congress. Looking at these requests can offer insight into the nature of the speech. First, we examine the legislative requests of presidents as a whole from 1965 to 2002. As shown in Table 3.1, presidents tend to concentrate their requests for legislative action primarily in three policy areas: social welfare, economic policy, and governmental affairs. Legislative requests are generally concentrated in these three areas, and they make up the bulk of the typical speech's requests. Generally, more than one-third of the legislative requests of presidents will be in the area of social welfare policy.[51] Presidents tend to request almost nothing in the way of labor or agricultural policy and generally have relatively few requests in the areas of defense, resources, civil rights and liberties, and foreign policy. Whereas presidents may spend considerable space in the SUA discussing foreign and defense policy, they make fewer legislative requests in this area, largely due to their ability to undertake more unilateral action in these policy areas by virtue of being chief diplomat and commander-in-chief.

Broadly speaking, legislative requests tend to fall into three categories during the era of SUAs we study. One category is made up of what could be called high-tier policy areas composed of social welfare policy, economic policy, and governmental affairs. Another category comprises lower-tier policy areas; presidents include a much smaller relative percentage of requests in the areas of defense, resources, civil rights and liberties, and foreign policy. Presidents generally do not ignore these lower-tier policy areas, they just have few legislative requests from these areas. Finally, there are two policy areas that do not register much attention from presidents overall:

Table 3.1 Summary of Legislative Requests, by Policy Area, in State of the Union Addresses, 1965–2002

Policy Area	Median Percentage of Requests per SUA
Social welfare	34.1
Economic	19.2
Government affairs	19.0
Defense	7.0
Resources	5.3
Civil rights/civil liberties	4.5
Foreign policy	3.2
Labor	0.0
Agriculture	0.0

labor and agriculture. Thus, there is a hierarchy of policy areas from which legislative requests come in the SUA.

Aggregate figures of the median percentage of legislative requests in SUAs, however, may mask important patterns that would be evident from a more detailed examination of the policy areas from which a president's legislative requests are drawn. Therefore, we next turn to the legislative requests of individual presidents. We expect that presidents will differ in the policy areas from which their requests come because the nature of what they want to accomplish legislatively will differ both individually and on the basis of partisanship. We expect Democratic presidents to have more requests in social welfare policy and Republican presidents to have more requests in terms of economic policy. We expect Democrats to be more active in requesting policies in the area of civil rights and liberties as well as labor policy, and Republicans to be more involved in requesting measures related to defense policy. Table 3.2 contains the median percentage of legislative requests by president and also by partisanship.

Within the policy areas, we do find some differences in the concentration of legislative requests of presidents. Differences between presidents are statistically significant in the areas of social welfare, labor, and civil rights and liberties.[52] Furthermore, one can see that, more than any other president, Carter tended to spread his requests out more evenly among the policy areas. This is in keeping with Light's finding on the overall agenda of Carter, that he was unwilling to signal specific areas of priority.[53] Five of the eight presidents have the high-tier categories of social welfare, economic policy, and governmental affairs as the three most numerous categories for requests. The three who do not conform are Richard Nixon, Gerald Ford, and George W. Bush, and in each of these cases, changes in the political environment affected the nature of their requests. Both Nixon and Ford have a large median number of requests in resources policy. As awareness of and demand for environmental policies increased and an energy crisis ensued in the late 1960s and the 1970s, Nixon and Ford responded with a concentration of legislative requests from the resources category. G. W. Bush, in his two SUAs included in our analysis, also devotes more requests to defense policy rather than government affairs as most of his predecessors did, largely due to the influence of his post–September 11 SUA. Thus, where there is deviation from the overall pattern of higher and lower tier categories established above, it can largely be attributed to presidents responding in their SUAs to a particular environmental stimulus over the course of their presidency.

There are partisan differences in the median percentage of legislative requests, but most of them do not meet our expectations. First, Democratic presidents devote about ten percentage points more of their requests to social welfare policy than Republican presidents, but this difference is not

Table 3.2 Presidential Requests for Congressional Action, by Policy Area, in State of the Union Addresses, 1965–2002

President	Foreign Policy	Defense	Economic	Labor	Agriculture	Resources	Social Welfare	Government Affairs	Civil Rights/ Civil Liberties
Johnson	6.4	1.4	11.7	5.3	0.0	5.6	40.9	18.1	8.6
Nixon	0.0	2.7	5.6	0.0	0.0	20.4	40.3	22.5	6.5
Ford	0.0	1.2	31.7	1.5	0.0	29.8	13.5	20.4	1.7
Carter	5.6	10.0	25.0	11.1	0.0	10.0	15.0	11.1	0.0
Reagan	4.9	9.9	20.8	0.0	0.0	3.5	23.2	16.6	7.7
Bush, G. H. W.	1.3	5.9	28.7	0.0	0.0	9.3	27.0	16.1	0.0
Clinton	4.7	7.8	16.0	2.4	0.0	4.5	37.2	23.1	1.0
Bush, G. W.	4.9	14.6	20.5	0.0	1.7	6.2	45.9	6.4	0.0
All Democrats	5.6	6.9	16.7	4.5	0.0	5.2	36.2	22.2	1.9
All Republicans	2.8	7.4	22.5	0.0	0.0	5.5	26.8	17.2	4.7

Note: Numbers are the median percentage of requests per speech.

statistically significant.[54] Even for Republican presidents, social welfare policy requests are a plurality of all requests they make of Congress in the SUA. Republican presidents do tend to ask Congress for economic policy action more than Democratic presidents, but the difference of medians is not statistically significant.[55] Democratic presidents are more likely to devote a small percentage of their requests to labor policy, whereas Republican presidents have virtually no requests from that area, and this difference is statistically significant and thus meets our expectation that Democratic presidents would be more active in this policy area.[56] Republican and Democratic presidents do not differ much in the median number of requests they make relating to defense policy; both devote relatively little space to requests from this area. Interestingly enough, Republican presidents have a higher median number of requests relating to civil rights and liberties, but the difference with Democratic presidents is not statistically significant.[57] The difference is driven by the activity of both Nixon and Reagan. Nixon's requests related mostly to civil rights, whereas Reagan was particularly active in the area of civil liberties, especially relating to socially conservative requests for things such as constitutional amendments allowing for school prayer and to protect human life.

Thus, we find that individual presidents have largely drawn their legislative requests from the areas of social welfare, economic, and governmental affairs policy, but there is some variation from president to president. In the area of social welfare policy, significant differences exist in the number of median requests of presidents. There is a range of median requests, from 46 percent for G. W. Bush to about 14 percent for Ford. There are significant differences in the way presidents distribute their requests in labor and civil rights/civil liberties policy, as well. The policy areas from which presidents draw their legislative requests throughout their presidency exhibit some fluidity from president to president that was masked by the aggregate figures, but most of the policy areas did not register significant differences. In addition, of the expected partisan differences, only differences in labor policy were statistically significant.

Do the policy areas from which presidents draw their legislative requests change within a presidency? As presidents grapple with problems and offer solutions in their SUAs, we expect the speeches will be reflective of the environment in which they are given.[58] Presidents adapt their agendas to crises,[59] so we would expect that the highlights of their legislative agenda as presented in the SUA would be similarly affected by events that happened in close proximity to, or were ongoing at the time of, the speech. We posit that the SUA is primarily a reactive document; the legislative requests presidents highlight from year to year will be fluid as they adapt policy requests to position themselves according to changes in political circumstances. Examining the legislative requests presidents highlight from year to year for stability or fluidity as to policy area will show whether this expectation is true. The legislative requests of SUAs are expected to reflect the reactions of presidents to particular situations. These may be crises, but they may also be a change in partisan control of Congress or economic situations. Just as we found that the policy areas of legislative requests exhibited differences from president to president, we also expect legislative requests to be fluid within presidencies as well.

Table 3.3 presents the percentage of legislative requests from each SUA by policy area. From year to year within a presidency, there is often substantial variation in the policy areas from which legislative requests come. The differences within an administration tend to be greater than those between administrations. Reagan, for example, draws 56 percent of his requests from social welfare policy in his 1981 speech, but in 1986, just 5 percent of his requests come from that area. Nixon devotes more than half of his 1970 SUA to requests in the area of governmental affairs, but by 1974, he has no requests from that area. All presidents' SUAs show variation within their presidencies, sometimes even dramatic changes in focus from year to year. Nearly 25 percent of Clinton's requests are from the area of economic policy in 1993, a year in which the economy was recovering from a recession, but only 2.1 percent of his requests the next year are from that area. In 1975, less than 5 percent of Ford's requests are in social welfare policy as he requested legislative action in economic and resources policy. The next year, nearly a quarter of his requests are from the social welfare area.

In the presidencies of Reagan and Clinton, the only two-term presidents we study, we see an interesting shift in their second terms. If one combines the foreign policy and defense policy areas, one sees that both Reagan and Clinton incorporate more requests in these areas in their second term than in their first. Reagan's shift is especially pronounced in his final three SUAs. As second-term presidents tend to have less influence with domestic items,[60] they may choose to highlight more foreign and defense policy requests in their SUAs than they did in their first term, giving more attention to these areas to highlight the enhanced role they play in foreign and defense policy formulation.[61] In their study using presidential foreign policy speeches, Lydia Andrade and Garry Young conclude, "New emphasis on foreign policy may not reflect any particular increase in foreign policy problems, or any particular configuration of international interests, but simply an opportunity for a president to cultivate [an] image of power and influence in the wake of a declining ability to affect domestic policy."[62] In SUAs, presidents can change the emphasis of their legislative requests to suit the image they want to project. As second-term presidents, both Reagan and Clinton increased their requests in foreign and defense policy relative to their first-term SUAs. The fact that Reagan's and Clinton's SUAs included

Table 3.3 Yearly Presidential Requests for Congressional Action, by Policy Area, in State of the Union Addresses, 1965–2002 (percentage)

	Foreign Policy	Defense	Economic	Labor	Agriculture	Resources	Social Welfare	Government Affairs	Civil Rights/ Civil Liberties
Johnson									
1965	2.8	0.0	16.7	8.3	0.0	5.6	47.2	13.9	5.6
1966	8.3	2.8	19.4	11.1	0.0	2.8	36.1	11.1	8.3
1967	8.3	2.8	5.6	0.0	0.0	5.6	41.7	25.0	11.1
1968	4.4	0.0	6.7	2.2	6.7	8.9	40.0	22.2	8.9
Nixon									
1970	0.0	0.0	5.9	0.0	0.0	17.6	11.8	52.9	11.8
1971	0.0	0.0	4.8	0.0	0.0	23.8	47.6	23.8	0.0
1972	0.0	5.3	5.3	10.5	5.3	5.3	42.1	21.1	5.3
1974	0.0	7.7	23.1	0.0	0.0	23.1	38.5	0.0	7.7
Ford									
1975	0.0	0.0	31.0	0.0	0.0	44.8	3.4	17.2	3.4
1976	0.0	2.4	32.5	2.9	0.0	14.7	23.5	23.5	0.0
Carter									
1978	5.6	0.0	27.8	27.8	0.0	0.0	27.8	11.1	0.0
1979	5.0	10.0	25.0	10.0	0.0	10.0	15.0	25.0	0.0
1980	11.1	33.3	0.0	11.1	0.0	44.4	0.0	0.0	0.0
Reagan									
1981	0.0	3.7	22.2	0.0	0.0	3.7	55.6	14.8	0.0
1982	4.5	4.5	22.7	0.0	0.0	4.5	27.3	31.8	4.5
1983	3.2	9.7	19.4	0.0	0.0	3.2	38.7	16.1	9.7
1984	5.3	10.5	15.8	0.0	0.0	26.3	10.5	15.8	15.8
1985	2.9	8.6	37.1	0.0	2.9	5.7	20.0	17.1	5.7
1986	20.0	10.0	35.0	0.0	0.0	0.0	5.0	20.0	10.0
1987	15.8	10.5	15.8	5.3	5.3	0.0	26.3	15.8	5.3
1988	11.1	16.7	0.0	0.0	0.0	0.0	11.1	50.0	11.1

(continues)

Table 3.3 continued

	Foreign Policy	Defense	Economic	Labor	Agriculture	Resources	Social Welfare	Government Affairs	Civil Rights/ Civil Liberties
Bush, G. H. W.									
1989	0.0	7.0	18.6	0.0	0.0	18.6	30.2	25.6	0.0
1990	0.0	3.4	24.1	0.0	3.4	13.8	44.8	10.3	0.0
1991	9.5	4.8	33.3	0.0	0.0	4.8	23.8	19.0	4.8
1992	2.6	18.4	39.5	0.0	0.0	2.6	23.7	13.2	0.0
Clinton									
1993	2.0	2.0	24.5	2.0	2.0	4.1	40.8	22.4	0.0
1994	2.1	8.5	2.1	2.1	0.0	8.5	36.2	40.4	0.0
1995	2.3	9.1	9.1	4.5	0.0	0.0	34.1	36.4	4.5
1996	0.0	9.5	19.0	4.8	0.0	4.8	38.1	23.8	0.0
1997	7.0	5.3	8.8	1.8	0.0	3.5	54.4	19.3	0.0
1998	9.6	7.7	19.2	5.8	0.0	1.9	26.9	26.9	1.9
1999	7.8	7.8	13.0	2.6	2.6	5.2	42.9	11.7	6.5
2000	9.2	6.9	24.1	1.1	1.1	5.7	27.6	17.2	6.9
Bush, G. W.									
2001	3.0	9.1	24.2	0.0	0.0	9.1	48.5	6.1	0.0
2002	6.7	20.0	16.7	0.0	3.3	3.3	43.3	6.7	0.0

Note: Rows may not add to 100 percent due to rounding.

more attention to requests from these policy areas is consistent with the notion of the "cycle of decreasing influence" presidents confront over time, which affects presidential domestic agendas.[63]

In every speech that we examine from 1965 to 2002, there are only two speeches where the president did not have a majority of his legislative requests fall in the high-tier policy areas of social welfare policy, economic policy, and governmental affairs. Excepting these two speeches, the low ranges from 51.6 percent of requests in these areas for Ford's 1975 speech to a high of 92.6 percent for Reagan's 1981 speech. The two speeches that are anomalies are Carter's 1980 speech and Reagan's 1984 speech, both given in the year the president was pursuing reelection. In his 1980 SUA, Carter addresses the twin crises of the Soviet invasion of Afghanistan and the taking of US hostages in Iran. Not coincidentally, more than three-fourths of his legislative requests that year come from the area of resources and defense policy. Reagan's 1984 SUA was focused on reelection, unlike Carter's 1980 SUA, which was focused on crises even though it also took place in an election year. Reagan spread his requests out more evenly in 1984 than in any of his other SUAs and gave attention to a policy area he had few requests from previously, resources policy. A quarter of his requests in 1984 are in the area of resources. After his reelection was secured, his pattern of distribution returned to what it was previously, and legislative requests in resources policy were virtually nonexistent.

What do these data tell us about the nature of the policy substance of the SUA? SUAs are unique speeches in which presidents request legislative action on a broad array of issues. There are, however, a cadre of policy areas from which contemporary presidents draw most of their legislative requests: social welfare, economic policy, and governmental affairs. The requests emphasized will reflect the political environment and the needs of the president, but few policy areas are ignored. SUAs are individualized and the attention to policy areas varies both across presidents and within presidencies. SUAs are tactical speeches. Choices must be made about the areas presidents will target and highlight for congressional action. Above all, each SUA is a unique speech that offers a window on the way each president views his job as chief legislator at multiple and regular intervals throughout his presidency. The fluidity of policy areas from which individual presidents draw their legislative requests from year to year suggests a speech that serves different purposes for presidents at different times in their presidencies. Individual presidents will adapt the SUA to their own purpose and the political circumstances in which they find themselves. The SUA is less idiosyncratic, however, than it is reactive. It is a multifaceted speech that allows presidents to establish direction and offer a game plan in its first instance, react to political circumstances and portray themselves as responsive in subsequent years, lay the foundation for a reelection campaign in the fourth year, and if successful at reelection, perhaps address policy issues that hold long-term significance for them as they increasingly consider their own legacy after they leave office.

Symbolism in the Policymaking Rhetoric of the SUA

Another important aspect of the policymaking rhetoric of the SUA is the president's use of symbolism. Presidents seek to convince their audiences to follow their policy leadership. They use rhetoric in such a way that will encourage acceptance of their policy solutions. While symbolism abounds in the SUA and can be used by presidents for different purposes, we focus on the symbolism that aids presidents in making their case that their policy solutions ought to be preferred.[64] First, the SUA itself is an event that is symbolic and so is the person delivering it. The president appears in the setting of the US Capitol, addressing Congress and representatives of the executive branch, the judicial branch, the military, as well as the public. Second, presidents use symbolic language and images to remind Americans of commonalities and then portray their recommendations as being consistent with these things Americans share. In addition, all presidents incorporate religious language in their SUAs. Finally, we examine the way presidents since Reagan have incorporated symbolically important individuals in their SUAs, each for slightly different purposes.

The SUA as an event. When Wilson journeyed to Capitol Hill in 1913 and reestablished the practice of addressing a joint session of Congress for the purpose of reporting on the state of the Union, he recognized a fundamental factor about communication; it is best when one can communicate in person, engaging both the auditory and the visual senses. By appearing before Congress, Wilson could more effectively use the annual message to communicate with Congress. Once presidents had to prioritize to fit their message into the confines of a speech, the SUA became a primary means of communicating the highlights of what the president wanted to accomplish in the coming year. By formally addressing Congress in person, the SUA became an event, and one at which the president took center stage. Members of Congress in the nineteenth century could relatively easily ignore the written annual message if they chose; the length and detail of some of the annual messages probably encouraged this behavior. When the president came to Congress, however, and addressed them collectively, the communicative powers of the SUA increased. The speech now incorporates and illustrates the symbolic power of the presidency itself and also draws upon the symbolism of the setting in which the speech takes place.

A modern SUA is a unique political event. There is as much ceremony and pomp at this event as one will find anywhere in US politics. Initially, representatives mill about the House chamber as they await the coming speech. Some members will have earlier staked out the prime aisle seats, giving them maximum visibility. The Senate will be announced and enter the chamber, which takes some time as they make their way through the throng of the already assembled House members. The Speaker of the House will begin by announcing the House members of the escort committee, the members of Congress who will escort the president into the chamber. The Speaker is followed by the vice president, who, as president of the Senate, announces the senators to be included in escorting the president. These members exit to assemble with the president in preparation for his entrance in the chamber. In the meantime, the first lady will be seated in the gallery along with any special guests of the president who are to be recognized in the speech, a practice started by Reagan. Key government officials will be announced before they enter the chamber. First to enter will be the dean of the diplomatic corps, followed by the justices of the Supreme Court (although their attendance at recent SUAs has been spotty and was even nonexistent in 2000), and the Cabinet (except for the one designated missing department secretary to provide for the presidential line of succession). Also present in the chamber will be the Joint Chiefs of Staff. The president is subsequently announced by the Sergeant at Arms with a "Mr. Speaker, the President of the United States" and ushered into the chamber by the congressional escort.[65] He proceeds down the aisle, a gauntlet of congress-people, and typically takes several minutes shaking hands as he makes his way to the podium where the Speaker of the House and the vice president, in the capacity as president of the Senate, will be seated behind him. The Speaker gavels the chamber to order and introduces the president, who then begins his remarks.

The SUA is the only regular political event that brings all of these various actors together. They are all assembled to hear the president's pronouncement on the state of the Union and his policy recommendations for the coming year. The president is a symbol of the nation and appears before the assembled representatives of the government in a symbolic setting. In his 1970 SUA, Nixon refers to the symbolic nature of the Capitol from which he was speaking and uses it to remind his audiences of the things Americans share.

> In the majesty of this great Chamber we hear the echoes of America's history, of debates that rocked the Union and those that repaired it, of the summons to war and the search for peace, of the uniting of the people, the building of a nation. Those echoes of history remind us of our roots and our strengths. They remind us also of that special genius of American democracy, which at one critical turning point after another has led us to spot the new road to the future and given us the wisdom and the courage to take it.[66]

Murray Edelman discusses the symbolic importance of settings. Political settings, especially, are noted for their "contrived character," which

> make[s] for heightened sensitivity and easier conviction in onlookers, for the framed actions are taken on their own terms. They are not qualified by inconsistent facts in the environment. The creation of an artificial space or semblance thus sets the stage for a concentration of suggestions: of connotations, or emotions, and of authority.[67]

The president has a unique advantage over other political actors because of the setting in which the SUA takes place and his perceived position in the political system. Thus, the SUA has come to epitomize the way most Americans think of the president, as the powerful center of the government. Both the president giving the SUA, viewed as the symbol of government, and the setting in which the SUA takes place encourage and reinforce this view.

Symbolic language. The actor giving the SUA and the stage from which it is given are symbolically important, but so is the language that the president uses. Another way symbolism is employed in this regard is when presidents utilize language and images of symbolic value to Americans. In their SUAs, presidents all use symbolic language, and they consistently use it as a means to help them convince Congress and the public to support their policies. Presidents want to highlight commonalities and shared attributes that all Americans hold. To do this, they rely on articulating Enlightenment ideals stressed in the Declaration of Independence, such as popular sovereignty, political equality, and liberty. They refer to formulations of the American dream and American values and stress unity and shared history. They present their legislative requests as being consistent with the key concepts and images they have utilized. Presidents will employ this symbolic language and images in two ways in the SUA. They use it in a general sense by incorporating it into their introduction with uses that are meant to bring their audiences together, thereby setting the stage for the reporting and recommending that will commence. Presidents also employ symbolism in more specific ways by incorporating meaningful images and language as they frame specific policy recommendations.

In both good times and bad, presidents generally begin their speech by seeking to find ways of making their audiences identify with each other. Presidents will rely on key concepts, which hold such meaning for most Americans that the concepts themselves have become emblematic of what it means to be an American. For example, Clinton's 1993 speech begins with a call for a change in direction, but one that would be rooted in certain historically important American values. "I believe we will find our new direction in the basic old values that brought us here over the last two centuries: a commitment to opportunity, to individual responsibility, to community, to work, to family, and to faith."[68] Reagan used a similar formulation in his 1984 speech. "We're seeing rededication to bedrock values of faith, family, work, neighborhood, peace, and freedom—values that help bring us together as one people, from the youngest child to the most senior citizen."[69] Reagan and Clinton use almost identical values as they seek to bring their audiences together. Previous research noted that the way in which presidents discuss values in their SUAs does not materially differ for presidents of different parties.[70] In the SUA, the president wants to present himself as president of all the people and uses rhetoric that holds important symbolic meaning for most Americans. The SUA is not an occasion in which a president wants to highlight the differences of US citizens, but to find common ground from which to persuasively present policy recommendations.

Presidents utilize historical images as they begin their SUAs, not only to remind audiences of the shared nature of the US historical experience, but also to exemplify American fortitude. In his 1965 speech, Johnson asserts,

> Two hundred years ago, in 1765, nine assembled colonies first joined together to demand freedom from arbitrary power. For the first century we struggled to hold together the first continental union of democracy in the history of man. One hundred years ago, in 1865, following a terrible test of blood and fire, the compact of union was finally sealed. For a second century we labored to establish a unity of purpose and interest among the many groups which make up the American community. That struggle has often brought pain and violence. It is not yet over. But we have achieved a unity of interest among our people that is unmatched in the history of freedom. And so tonight, now, in 1965, we begin a new quest for union. We seek the unity of man with the world that he has built—with the knowledge that can save or destroy him—with the cities which can stimulate or stifle him—with the wealth and the machines which can enrich or menace his spirit.[71]

Ford's 1975 SUA is unique in that he is the only president in the contemporary period we study to portray the condition of the nation in a pessimistic light by bluntly stating, "the state of the Union is not good."[72] Even this SUA, while chronicling the unemployment, deficit, debt, energy crisis, and other "bad news," offered the president's recommendations and in urging their acceptance sought to awaken in the American ethos a display of historic American grit.

> At the end of World War II, we turned a similar challenge into an historic opportunity and, I might add, an historic achievement. An old order was in disarray; political and economic institutions were shattered. In that period, this Nation and its partners built new institutions, new mechanisms of

mutual support and cooperation. Today, as then, we face an historic opportunity. If we act imaginatively and boldly, as we acted then, this period will in retrospect be seen as one of the great creative moments of our Nation's history. The whole world is watching to see how we respond.[73]

By using language and images that make their audiences think of commonalities, presidents seek to set the stage for the acceptance of their policy recommendations.

Whereas presidents will rely on language and images in a generic fashion to set the stage for their policy recommendations, presidents will also couch their specific legislative requests in symbolically important language and images. Lyndon Johnson, in advocating for his Highway Safety Act in 1966, began by justifying attention to the area as a matter of securing life and property, saying, "we [cannot] fail to arrest the destruction of life and property on our highways."[74] In making a case for the creation of the Department of Transportation, he couches the need for change by saying, "It is the genius of our Constitution that under its shelter of enduring institutions and rooted principles there is ample room for the rich fertility of American political invention."[75] Before detailing his economic plan in 1992, George H. W. Bush begins, "The power of America rests in a stirring but simple idea, that people will do great things if only you set them free. Well, we're going to set the economy free."[76] Presidents, as a means of persuasion, will seek to cast their specific policies as being the epitome of the common concepts, values, and images that they employ. In this way, a tax cut can become the embodiment of freedom, or a civil rights bill can offer the fulfillment of the American dream.

Religious language.   Another way presidents employ symbolically important language is through their religious references. All presidents we studied incorporate religious language in their SUAs, but to varying degrees and for different reasons. In his historical study of SUAs, Fersh noted a trend that minimized religious language, which started after the Civil War and continued until his study ended with Eisenhower's 1959 SUA.[77]

We quantify both the mentions of the Deity and the specific religious references in the SUAs.[78] From Table 3.4, one can see the trend Fersh noted continued until Ronald Reagan, when there is a striking increase in the incorporation of religious language. From 1965 to 1980, presidents used religious language sparingly and for general purposes. From Reagan to G. W. Bush, presidents have utilized religious language much more, and some have specifically linked it to the policy substance of their SUA.

Before Reagan, mentions of God were relatively few in number. When there was a mention of God in these SUAs, it was used in a generic sense; it was in the introduction or, more typically, in the final paragraph where there

Table 3.4   Religious Content of State of the Union Addresses, 1965–2002

	Number of Addresses	Mentions of Deity (total)	Religious References (total)	Average Religious Content (per SUA)	Policy with Religious Context (total)
Johnson	5[a]	4	13	3.4	0
Nixon	4	2	4	1.5	0
Ford	3[a]	4	12	5.3	0
Carter	3	0	4	1.3	0
Reagan	8	36	62	12.3	14
Bush, G. H. W.	4	13	11	6.0	0
Clinton	8	20	42	7.8	0
Bush, G. W.	2	3	13	8.0	3

Note: a. Includes lame-duck SUA.

was a fairly standard inclusion of some form of "God bless America." In addition, all four of the presidents preceding Reagan had at least one SUA in which they did not invoke some formulation of the Deity at all. Mentions per address range from zero for Carter to 1.3 for Ford. Once Reagan took office, there was only one speech in which God was not mentioned by a president, and this was Reagan's 1981 address to a joint session of Congress. Since 1982, every SUA has mentioned God at least once. Mentions of the Deity per speech since 1982 range from 1.5 for the two speeches of G. W. Bush to 4.5 per speech from Reagan. Religious references were also incorporated by presidents, and these were generally less numerous from Johnson to Carter than in the period after Carter. Total religious content, which is the combination of religious references and mentions of God, is calculated per SUA in Table 3.4. Of the pre-Reagan presidents, Ford has the highest incidence of religious language. We should note, however, that Ford's 1977 lame-duck SUA, given after his defeat at the hands of Jimmy Carter, contains almost two-thirds of the total religious content of his SUAs. If this SUA were excluded, rather than having 5.3 uses of religious language per SUA, Ford would register only three per SUA.

Reagan well surpassed all of his predecessors, in addition to the presidents who followed him, in the incorporation of religious language. Not only did Reagan include an average of 4.5 mentions of God per address, but also these mentions were not confined to introductory or closing remarks, as was the case with previous presidents' addresses. He sprinkled his speeches with religious references, an average of almost eight per SUA. While Reagan uses more religious language than the presidents who came before him, presidents who followed him did not return to the pre-Reagan practice of minimizing religious mentions. G. H. W. Bush includes half as many mentions of God and religious references in his SUAs as did his predecessor, but his addresses do include more total religious content than the presidents before Reagan at six per message. Clinton and G. W. Bush, on the other hand, have virtually the same number of combined usages of religious language per SUA, about eight.

Reagan and G. W. Bush are unique among the presidents that we study, because some of the policy substance of their SUAs is itself religious in nature. This is a departure from all other presidents in our time period. The pre-Reagan presidents' SUAs contained little religious language, and when it was included, it was not tied to policy substance but generally was introductory or concluding material. After Reagan, SUAs do incorporate much more in the way of religious language, but neither G. H. W. Bush nor Clinton link their religious language specifically to the policy substance of their SUAs. They continue to use it in the generic fashion of the pre-Reagan presidents, but they do so more frequently.

Reagan is the first president of those we examine to include policy substance that was religious in nature. Every SUA Reagan delivered from 1983 to 1988 contained a plea for a constitutional amendment to return prayer to schools. The following excerpts are indicative of Reagan's persuasive attempts to incorporate policy recommendations in his SUA that were religious and would register with the religiously conservative.

> Finally, let's stop suppressing the spiritual core of our national being. Our nation could not have been conceived without divine help. Why is it that we can build a nation with our prayers but we can't use a schoolroom for voluntary prayer? The 100th Congress of the United States should be remembered as the one that ended the expulsion of God from America's classrooms.[79]

And,

> The Congress opens its proceedings each day, as does the Supreme Court, with an acknowledgment of the Supreme Being—yet we are denied the right to set aside in our schools a moment each day for those who wish to pray. I believe Congress should pass our school prayer amendment.[80]

His addresses of 1984, 1985, 1986, and 1988 also include his desire to see a human life amendment to the Constitution that would ban abortion, and his appeal is couched in religious language. There were also three SUAs in which Reagan pushed for vouchers, or tuition tax credits, for those attending private schools. In addition, his 1985 address also contains a section in which he congratulated Congress on legislation they had recently passed to give religious school groups access to after-school meeting facilities.

Finally, Reagan links the concept of religion to foreign policy goals by telling the nation,

> Freedom is not the sole prerogative of a chosen few; it is the universal right of all God's children. Look to where peace and prosperity flourish today. It is in homes that freedom built. Victories against poverty are greatest and peace most secure where people live by laws that ensure free press, free speech, and freedom to worship, vote, and create wealth.[81]

G. W. Bush follows Reagan's practice of including some policy substance with a religious nature. In both the 2001 and 2002 SUAs, Bush touts his policy of faith-based initiatives. In 2001, Bush also proposed to give those who do not itemize their tax returns a deduction for charitable contributions, a proposal that was introduced in a religious context.

Thus, we see a marked difference in the religious rhetoric used by presidents in our data. Presidents from Johnson through Carter use religion generically and minimally in their SUAs, while G. H. W. Bush and Clinton used religious language generically, but more frequently. Reagan and G. W. Bush used religion more frequently and also specifically tied it to some of their policy substance. Before Reagan, there are few mentions of God or religious references in SUAs. Starting with Reagan, much more religious language is incorporated in the SUA. Why did the use of religious language dramatically change beginning with Reagan? Jimmy Carter is known as being a devout, born-again Christian, yet he never mentions any formulation of God in his SUAs and has few religious references. Reagan's first true SUA in 1982 mentions God three times and contains another six religious references. In 1984, Reagan had a total religious content of twenty-four citations. Reagan does not prove to be an anomaly in his increased usage of religious language; later presidents do not return to the precedent of the pre-Reagan era of minimizing religious language. Reagan makes increased levels of religious language acceptable in the SUA, which previously had been used sparingly. The power of religious conservatives grew during the Reagan era; not only did increased religious language become acceptable in an SUA, but it also seems that religious language has now become expected in post-Reagan SUAs, regardless of the president. Reagan's inclusion of policy substance of a religious nature and appeal was unique at the time, but was subsequently followed by G. W. Bush. The constituency of religious conservatives is primarily a Republican one, and these two Republican presidents sought to activate them by including policy substance of a religious nature. G. H. W. Bush and Clinton use religious language more frequently, that is, they "talk the talk," but unlike Reagan and G. W. Bush, they do not "walk the walk" by linking their religious language to specific policy.

Using individuals as symbols. In 1982, Ronald Reagan began the practice of incorporating key individuals into SUAs. Many of these individuals would be seated in the House gallery and introduced by the president in the course of the speech. Some individuals would be referred to in speeches but not physically present. All presidents since Reagan have followed this practice, and all have used guests or referred to individuals for symbolic purposes. Each president, however, has utilized these individuals in slightly different ways.

All of the guests Reagan introduced, or the people to whom he referred in his SUAs, were representations of what he called American heroes, unsung heroes, or everyday heroes.[82] He was particularly fond of using those with Horatio Alger–like life stories. In 1984, Reagan referred to Barbara Proctor, "who rose from a ghetto to build a multimillion-dollar advertising agency in Chicago," and to Carlos Perez, "a Cuban refugee, who turned $27 and a dream into a successful importing business."[83] Reagan used these people as symbols of key American values that the president wanted to emphasize, and he generally did not tie them to any specific policy recommendation.

G. H. W. Bush continued Reagan's practice of recognizing key people, but on a much smaller scale; he introduced few individuals in his SUAs. In contrast to his predecessor, all of the persons whom Bush introduced in his speeches were not ordinary citizens. In 1990, Bush introduced several governors (Clinton among them) because of their work with the administration on education policy, and in 1991, he introduced the wives of General Norman Schwarzkopf and Chairman of the Joint Chiefs Colin Powell, as representatives of the families of soldiers in Iraq.[84] The individuals Bush introduced had connections to the government and were recognized primarily for their contributions to Bush policies. In each of his SUAs, Bush also made a practice of referring to a letter or telegram he had received from a citizen who had recently encountered hardship or been touched by death. One was from a man who lost his son to drug use, one from a soldier later killed in Panama, one from a woman writing about the adverse economic conditions, and one from a woman whose husband was killed in Iraq.[85] By referring to communications Bush had received from individuals, Bush showed himself as aware of, touched by, and responsive to the concerns of citizens.

Clinton's SUAs were unique in the way they integrated the use of individuals who served as symbols that would further his substantive policy purposes. In addition, he referred to or introduced more individuals than both Reagan and Bush combined. Clinton used guests as symbols of the policy successes for which he claimed credit. He also used guests as symbols to aid his push for legislative requests. Sometimes he used the same guest for both purposes. He was particularly fond of introducing

AmeriCorps participants as a way of touting the program as a success, emphasizing them as the embodiment of certain American values, and also making the case that Congress should not cut the program. In his 1995 SUA, Clinton introduces Cindy Perry who

> teaches second graders to read in AmeriCorps in rural Kentucky. She gains when she gives. She's a mother of four. She says that her service inspired her to get her high school equivalency last year. She was married when she was a teenager—stand up, Cindy. She was married when she was a teenager. She had four children. But she had time to serve other people, to get her high school equivalency, and she's going to use her AmeriCorps money to go back to college.[86]

Earlier in the speech, Clinton had requested that Congress not cut funds for AmeriCorps, his signature service program. Similarly, he also recognized guests involved in community policing in several speeches to both claim credit for that program and push for its continuance.

Clinton also utilized several people to push for specific legislative requests on which he especially wanted to pressure Congress and who served as particularly compelling examples of why his legislative requests were needed in the areas of crime/gun safety legislation, welfare reform, and his education initiatives. For example, Clinton introduced the parent of a child who was killed by school gun violence in Jonesboro, Arkansas, in his 1999 SUA, and another parent of a child killed at the Columbine high school shooting in Colorado in his 2000 address. In both instances, Clinton used them to advocate for tougher gun safety legislation.

In his SUAs, Clinton excelled at being able to put a human face on policies, not only to claim credit for his successes, but also to push for his legislative requests. His use of individuals in this fashion was also a way for the president to show himself as being connected to ordinary Americans.

G. W. Bush continued the practice of the introduction of key individuals. In his 2001 speech, he tied individuals introduced to two of his major policy recommendations, tax cuts and faith-based initiatives. He introduced a couple from Pennsylvania, billed as "representing many American families," and detailed how his tax cut recommendations would benefit them.[87] He also introduced the Democratic mayor of Philadelphia as someone who was making faith-based organizations work in his city. Bush used individuals differently in his 2002 SUA, the last we study. In this speech, given in the aftermath of September 11 and as military operations in Afghanistan were ongoing, Bush introduced both the interim leader of Afghanistan, Hamid Karzai, and the newly elected female minister of Women's Affairs, Sima Samar, to highlight the changes, especially for women, taking place in Afghanistan due to US involvement. He also introduced the widow of a CIA officer killed in Afghanistan and addressed her, stating

Shannon, I assure you and all who have lost a loved one that our cause is just, and our country will never forget the debt we owe Michael and all who gave their lives for freedom. Our cause is just, and it continues. Our discoveries in Afghanistan confirmed our worst fears, and showed us the true scope of the task ahead. We have seen the depth of our enemies' hatred in videos, where they laugh about the loss of innocent life. And the depth of their hatred is equaled by the madness of the destruction they design. We have found diagrams of American nuclear power plants and public water facilities, detailed instructions for making chemical weapons, surveillance maps of American cities, and thorough descriptions of landmarks in America and throughout the world.[88]

In the 2002 SUA, Bush advertises actions already undertaken by the administration to combat terrorism. As the political environment had dramatically changed since the previous year's speech, Bush used the SUA to emphasize his responsiveness to the new environment. This is evident not just in terms of policy substance, but also in the use of individuals as symbols. In Reagan-like fashion, Bush also introduced two flight attendants who had thwarted an attempted terrorist on an airplane to highlight individual heroic actions in the war on terror.

It is now standard practice for presidents to introduce and refer to key individuals in their SUAs. We find all presidents used these individuals for symbolic impact; presidents sought to put a human face or imprint on politics. Presidents, however, have utilized these symbolic individuals for different substantive purposes. Reagan typically did not tie them to particular substantive policy, but simply used them as exemplary US heroes, representations of all that he saw as good about Americans. G. H. W. Bush did not introduce "ordinary" Americans as Reagan did but preferred to introduce people connected to government largely as a means of simple recognition and thanks. In each speech, however, he did include a reference to a communication he had received from an ordinary US citizen. This helped him to portray himself as listening and being connected with the concerns of the American public. Clinton introduced, or referred to, more symbolically important individuals than all other presidents combined, and he is also the president who consistently linked these individuals to his specific policies, either to tout successes, push for recommendations, or both, thus specifically tying them to the policy substance of his SUAs. Finally, G. W. Bush's use of individuals in his initial speech was Clintonian in a sense, tying the small number of people he introduced to two of his major policy initiatives. After September 11, 2001, however, three of Bush's 2002 guests were symbolically used as justifications for policy actions the president had undertaken, specifically military operations in Afghanistan. Two others were recognized for their individual heroic actions in the war on terror. So, while presidents since Reagan have all incorporated symbolically important individuals in their SUAs, each president has utilized them differently. Furthermore, as

seen with G. W. Bush, even within a presidency the purpose for using symbolically important individuals can change.

Conclusion

The goal of this chapter was to examine the nature of the communication
that takes place in the SUA. The speech is a valuable one because the communications that take place offer a view of the presidency in microcosm, as
the many different roles of a president are on display. In addition, the
speech encapsulates views that presidents have of the past, the present, and
the future as they attempt to persuade audiences with their policymaking
rhetoric to see things as they do.

The SUA is a special form of presidential communication for several
reasons. Its roots are constitutional; its structure is determined by the provisions that require reporting to Congress and that allow for recommendations
of "necessary and expedient measures." The policymaking rhetoric of the
SUA is rooted in these constitutional provisions. While the format of
the SUA has changed over time, this structure has not. The chief end of the
SUA is congressional influence. Although presidents address multiple audiences, they primarily seek to exert rhetorical leadership of Congress—to
influence Congress's actions either directly, or indirectly through the aid of
public pressure.

With their rhetoric, presidents convey substance about policy. They
advertise successes and recommend new courses of action. They request
legislative action from Congress, and by examining the areas of their legislative requests, we get a better picture of the nature of the speech. We see
a speech that gives presidents an opportunity to request action on a broad
array of issues. Even so, presidents tend to concentrate their requests in the
areas of social welfare policy, economic policy, and government affairs policy. There are, however, differences from president to president, as well as
within presidencies, in the policy areas from which their requests come. The
SUA is a speech that is both tactical and reactive. Presidents choose the
requests they will highlight. These requests are reflective of their political
needs. SUAs also are reflective of the political environment and so the communications of the SUA are also reactive. This suggests that the speech
serves different purposes for presidents at different times.

Presidents also employ symbolic images, examples, and language in
their policymaking rhetoric. In so doing, they hope to encourage audiences
to see things in the same way, and this can set the stage for acceptance of
the president's requests. Presidents address the public as the symbolic head
of government in a setting, the House chamber, that encourages the view of
a president-centered government. They use language meant to make audi-

ences think of the things they hold in common, not their differences; this symbolic language helps them frame specific recommendations. Within the time period we study, we do see a change that merits attention. Reagan ushered in a new era of symbolism in the SUA. First, he began the practice of introducing individuals in his SUAs who were symbolically important, a practice all subsequent presidents have followed. Second, Reagan increased the incorporation of religious language in his SUAs. Presidents before Reagan, when they used religious language, typically used it sparingly and in a generic sense. In his use of religious language, Reagan surpasses all of the presidents we study. Not only does he use more total religious content than others, but he also links religion to specific legislative proposals. Presidents after him do not return to the pre-Reagan pattern of minimal inclusion of religious content. The change that we see in religious language can be attributed to the fact that Reagan made religious language acceptable, and the power of religious conservatives grew during the Reagan years and has yet to subside.

The SUA is a regular event, but this regularity should not connote ordinariness; it is precisely the opposite. While all presidents use policymaking rhetoric to convey substance and use symbolism to persuade, each does so in their own unique way. Presidents, acting as chief legislator, adapt each SUA to fit the particular circumstances they confront in an attempt to maximize their leadership and the likelihood of getting the policies they promote enacted.

Notes

1. Clinton Rossiter, *The American Presidency* (New York: Harcourt, Brace and Co., 1956), 4–25.
2. B. O. Zevin, ed., *Nothing to Fear: The Selected Addresses of Franklin Delano Roosevelt* (New York: Houghton Mifflin, 1946), 17.
3. Arthur M. Schlesinger Jr., *The Coming of the New Deal* (New York: Houghton Mifflin, 1959), 21.
4. Wilfred E. Binkley, "The President as Chief Legislator," *Annals of the American Academy of Political and Social Science* 307 (1956):92–105.
5. Jeffrey K. Tulis, *The Rhetorical Presidency* (Princeton: Princeton University Press, 1987).
6. We do not contend that the legislative requests in the SUA are all of the president's agenda. Other items may be part of the agenda that are not highlighted in the SUA. See George C. Edwards III and B. Dan Wood, "Who Influences Whom? The President, Congress, and the Media," *American Political Science Review* 93 (1999):330. We do, however, believe that the legislative requests in the SUA are of high priority to the president and his administration at the time of the SUA. See Andrew Rudalevige, *Managing the President's Program: Presidential Leadership and Legislative Policy Formation* (Princeton: Princeton University Press, 2002), 65. In addition, the legislative requests in the SUAs are the ones that the president has

chosen to publicly highlight. These will include his own initiatives, congressional initiatives, as well as things already on the agenda that may benefit from a boost in the form of a presidential mention. The SUAs also occur at the same time, near the beginning of the congressional session, thus making them comparable.

7. We examined thirty-seven oral addresses delivered to joint sessions of Congress from 1965–2002. Two SUAs from this period are specifically excluded: 1973 and 1981, both of which were written SUAs. In 1973, Nixon did not give an oral address on the State of the Union, but opted to send a series of six written messages to the Congress. Carter sent a written SUA to Congress in 1981 as a lame duck, which we also do not analyze. The 1981 (Reagan), 1989 (G. H. W. Bush), 1993 (Clinton), and 2001 (G. W. Bush) speeches we analyze are not SUAs but are oral addresses to joint sessions of Congress setting out goals of the new administration for the upcoming congressional session. It should be noted that often in modern practice, the address a president may deliver shortly upon taking office is not billed as an SUA. These addresses, however, do lay out a legislative program for the coming year. In the case of Reagan, his initial speech was billed as an economic one but actually laid out administration goals beyond just the economy. Clinton and both Presidents Bush gave addresses on administration goals. We include these speeches in our data because each lays out a legislative agenda, addresses the same audience, has the same pomp and circumstance as an SUA, occurs at the same time an SUA would occur (near the beginning of a congressional session), and is treated by both the media and public as virtually indistinguishable from an SUA. There have been presidents who did call their first speech right after taking office an SUA, most notably, Eisenhower in 1953 and Kennedy in 1961. More recent practice, however, has witnessed a subtle change in the nomenclature. Some have simply chosen not to give a first-year, beginning-of-session speech. For the presidents in the 1965–2002 time period, Nixon and Carter did not give an SUA upon taking office. Nixon did give an address to Congress on his domestic goals only, but it was in April 1969. We do not include it in our analysis as a proxy of an SUA. Carter gave a speech to the nation on February 2, 1977, but it was given from the White House, not before a joint session of Congress, and we do not include it in our analysis, either. In the case of both Nixon and Carter, the outgoing president gave a lame-duck, orally delivered, farewell SUA in January shortly before leaving office (in the case of Eisenhower and Kennedy, mentioned above, the outgoing president had sent a written message on the state of the Union right before leaving). Johnson's lame-duck SUA of 1969 and Ford's of 1977 are included in our analysis, except where noted.

8. The 1970, 1972, and 1975 SUAs were delivered in the afternoon.

9. Emphasis original, Paul C. Light, *The President's Agenda: Domestic Policy Choice from Kennedy to Clinton*, 3rd ed. (Baltimore: Johns Hopkins University Press, 1999), 160.

10. William J. Clinton, *Clinton Presidential Legacy,* speech given November 10, 2005, at Hofstra University, Hempstead, New York, 11th Presidential Conference, "William Jefferson Clinton: The 'New' Democrat from Hope," C-SPAN National Cable Satellite Corporation, 2005, DVD.

11. US Constitution, Art. II, Sec. 3.

12. We should note that Mark Peterson maintains of SUAs "there is no consistency in their form." He is actually referring to the format of the speech, however, as his subsequent examples make clear. He does not study the speech itself, but the president's agenda writ large. Mark A. Peterson, *Legislating Together: The White House and Capitol Hill from Eisenhower to Reagan* (Cambridge: Harvard University Press, 1990), 164.

13. Karlyn Kohrs Campbell and Kathleen Hall Jamieson, *Deeds Done in Words: Presidential Rhetoric and the Genres of Governance* (Chicago: University of Chicago Press, 1990), 52–78.

14. Ibid., 6.

15. Ibid., 74.

16. Tulis, *The Rhetorical Presidency,* 201; Michael J. Malbin, "Rhetoric and Leadership: A Look Backward at the Carter National Energy Plan," in *Both Ends of the Avenue: The Presidency, the Executive Branch, and Congress in the 1980s,* ed. Anthony King (Washington, DC: American Enterprise Institute, 1983), 217.

17. George A. Kennedy, introduction to *On Rhetoric,* by Aristotle (New York: Oxford University Press, 1991), 7.

18. Aristotle, *On Rhetoric,* trans. George A. Kennedy (New York: Oxford University Press, 1991), 47.

19. Ibid., 32, n. 21.

20. Kennedy, *On Rhetoric,* 7.

21. Tulis, *The Rhetorical Presidency,* 161–172.

22. Ibid.; Malbin, "Rhetoric and Leadership."

23. Tulis, *The Rhetorical Presidency,* 4.

24. Ibid.

25. Samuel Kernell, *Going Public: New Strategies of Presidential Leadership,* 3rd ed. (Washington, DC: Congressional Quarterly Press, 1997).

26. William J. Clinton, "Address Before a Joint Session of the Congress on the State of the Union," *Public Papers of the Presidents of the United States: William J. Clinton, 1994,* vol.1 (Washington, DC: GPO, 1995), 129.

27. Campbell and Jamieson, *Deeds Done in Words,* 54.

28. Barbara Hinckley defines a *political* symbol as "the communication by political actors to others for a purpose, in which the specific object referred to conveys a larger range of meaning, typically with emotional, moral, or psychological impact. This larger meaning need not be independently or factually true, but will tap ideas people want to believe in as true." Barbara Hinckley, *The Symbolic Presidency* (New York: Routledge, 1990), 7.

29. Campbell and Jamieson, *Deeds Done in Words,* 54–55.

30. Ibid., 54.

31. David R. Mayhew, *Congress: The Electoral Connection* (New Haven: Yale University Press, 1974), 53.

32. Gerald M. Pomper with Susan S. Lederman, *Elections in America,* 2nd ed. (New York: Longman, 1980), 156–158.

33. Clinton, "Address Before a Joint Session of the Congress on the State of the Union," *Public Papers, 1999,* 1:62–63.

34. Ibid., 1:63.

35. Ibid.

36. Ibid.

37. Ronald W. Reagan, "Address Before a Joint Session of the Congress on the State of the Union," *Public Papers of the Presidents of the United States: Ronald W. Reagan, 1982,* vol.1 (Washington, DC: GPO, 1983), 91.

38. Ibid.

39. Ibid.

40. Ibid.

41. Theodore J. Lowi, "Four Systems of Policy, Politics, and Choice, *Public Administration Review* 32 (July/August 1972):299.

42. The 1969 and 1977 lame-duck SUAs of Johnson and Ford, respectively,

were not utilized in this portion of our analysis, giving us a total of 35 speeches. Each author independently coded each speech and identified specific legislative requests. Agreement on requests was achieved at 93 percent or higher, and discrepancies dealt with on a case by case basis.

43. We should note, however, that our calculation of the president's legislative requests in SUAs differs from presidential proposals identified and used by Light in his study of agendas. To be counted in Light's calculations, proposals mentioned in the SUA also had to be formally included in a specific legislative package and cleared as in accordance with the president's program by the Office of Management and Budget. See Light, *The President's Agenda,* 9. We, however, focus on the SUA itself and include all presidential requests for legislative action in the speech. These not only will include the president urging action on his own initiatives, but may also include him weighing in on congressional initiatives as well, which can include requesting both action or inaction from Congress.

44. Gerald M. Pomper, *Elections in America: Control and Influence in Democratic Politics* (New York: Dodd, Mead & Co, 1968), 156–158.

45. Criteria for the policy areas are listed in the Appendix.

46. Light, *The President's Agenda,* 154–168.

47. Richard E. Neustadt, "Presidency and Legislation: Planning the President's Program," *American Political Science Review* 49 (December 1955), 1015.

48. Light, *The President's Agenda;* Rudalevige, *Managing the President's Program;* Mathew C. Moen, "The Political Agenda of Ronald Reagan: A Content Analysis of the State of the Union Messages," *Presidential Studies Quarterly* 18 (1988):779; Jeffrey E. Cohen, "Presidential Rhetoric and the Public Agenda," *American Journal of Political Science* 39 (1995):87–107.

49. Light, *The President's Agenda,* 6.

50. John W. Kingdon, *Agendas, Alternatives, and Public Policies,* 2nd ed. (New York: Harper Collins, 1995), 188.

51. The category of social welfare is a broad one. Foreign policy is a broad category as well but does not register the attention to legislative requests that social welfare policy does, largely because of the more unilateral nature of presidential power in this area and the tendency of a president's constituency to care more about domestic, rather than foreign, policy. When the more specific categories of domestic policy (labor, agriculture, resources, and civil rights and liberties) are combined, however, they do not displace the top three categories.

52. We utilize nonparametric statistics due to the small number of observations and the presence of outliers in our data. A median test indicates the variation between presidents is statistically significant ($p \leq 0.05$) in the policy areas of labor, social welfare, and civil rights and liberties.

53. Light, *The President's Agenda,* 156–157.

54. For determining whether there was a statistically significant difference in the medians of Democratic and Republican presidents in policy areas, Mann-Whitney U tests were conducted. For social welfare, $z = -0.93$ ($p \geq 0.36$); thus the difference in medians is not statistically significant.

55. For economic policy, $z = -1.5$ ($p \geq 0.15$); thus the difference in medians is not statistically significant.

56. For labor policy, $z = -4.10$ ($p \leq 0.01$); thus the difference in medians is statistically significant.

57. For civil rights and civil liberties policy, $z = -0.56$ ($p \geq 0.61$); thus the difference in medians is not statistically significant.

58. Moen's analysis of the space devoted to certain policy areas in Reagan's

SUAs showed this to be true in Reagan's case. Moen, "The Political Agenda of Ronald Reagan," 779.

59. Light, *The President's Agenda,* 162–163.

60. Ibid., 36.

61. Paul E. Peterson, "The President's Dominance in Foreign Policy Making," *Political Science Quarterly* 109 (1994):215–234.

62. Lydia Andrade and Garry Young, "Presidential Agenda Setting: Influences on the Emphasis of Foreign Policy," *Political Research Quarterly* 49 (September 1996):603.

63. Light, *The President's Agenda,* 36.

64. See Hinckley for a view of the many symbolic aspects of presidential speech generally, including SUAs. See also, Vanessa B. Beasley, *You, the People: American National Identity in Presidential Rhetoric* (College Station: Texas A&M University Press, 2004) for a discussion of the way presidents have symbolically addressed differences in American identity in SUAs and inaugural addresses.

65. Previous to 1995, the announcement was the duty of the House Doorkeeper. That position was abolished by the House in 1995 as part of the rule changes made by the new Republican majority and the duties of the Doorkeeper were assumed by the Sergeant at Arms. See *Contract with America: A Bill of Accountability,* H. Res. 6, 104th Congress, 1st Session.

66. Richard M. Nixon, "Address Before a Joint Session of the Congress on the State of the Union," *Public Papers of the Presidents of the United States: Richard M. Nixon, 1970,* vol. 1 (Washington, DC: GPO, 1972), 14.

67. Murray Edelman, *The Symbolic Uses of Politics* (Urbana: University of Illinois Press, 1985), 96.

68. Clinton, "Address Before a Joint Session of Congress on Administration Goals," *Public Papers, 1993,* 1:114.

69. Reagan, "Address Before a Joint Session of Congress on the State of the Union," *Public Papers, 1984,* 1:88.

70. Craig Allen Smith and Kathy B. Smith, "Presidential Values and Public Priorities: Recurrent Patterns in Addresses to the Nation, 1963–1984," *Presidential Studies Quarterly* 15 (1985):743–753.

71. Lyndon B. Johnson, "Address Before a Joint Session of Congress on the State of the Union," *Public Papers of the Presidents of the United States: Lyndon B. Johnson, 1965,* vol. 1 (Washington, DC: GPO, 1966), 1.

72. Gerald R. Ford, "Address Before a Joint Session of Congress on the State of the Union," *Public Papers of the Presidents of the United States: Gerald R. Ford, 1975,* vol. 1 (Washington, DC: GPO, 1977), 44.

73. Ibid.

74. Johnson, "Address Before a Joint Session of Congress on the State of the Union," *Public Papers, 1966,* 1:6.

75. Ibid.

76. George H. W. Bush, "Address Before a Joint Session of Congress on the State of the Union," *Public Papers of the Presidents of the United States: George H. W. Bush, 1992,* vol. 1 (Washington, DC: GPO, 1993), 159.

77. Seymour H. Fersh, *The View from the White House: A Study of the Presidential State of the Union Messages* (Washington, DC: Public Affairs Press, 1961), 98.

78. Mentions of the Deity in SUAs in our time period are: *Almighty, Creator, God, He, Him, One, Supreme Being.* Religious references used are: *Amen, angels,* biblical mentions and verses, *blessings, Christmas, Christian, church(es), clergy,*

creation (in religious context), *day of reckoning, divine, doubting Thomases, faith* (in religious context), *gospel, Islam, Islamic, Jewish, Judeo-Christian, Moslem, miracle, pray, prayer(s), prophesy, Puritan, sacred, spiritual* (not *spirit*), *temples, worship*.

79. Reagan, "Address Before a Joint Session of Congress on the State of the Union," *Public Papers, 1987*, 1:59.

80. Reagan, "Address Before a Joint Session of Congress on the State of the Union," *Public Papers, 1988*, 1:88.

81. Reagan, "Address Before a Joint Session of Congress on the State of the Union," *Public Papers, 1985*, 1:134–135.

82. Reagan, "Address Before a Joint Session of the Congress on the State of the Union," *Public Papers, 1982*, 1:72–79; *Public Papers, 1984*, 1:87–94; *Public Papers, 1985*, 1:130–136; *Public Papers, 1986*, 1:125–130.

83. Reagan, "Address Before A Joint Session of the Congress on the State of the Union, *Public Papers, 1984*, 1:87–88.

84. George H. W. Bush, "Address Before a Joint Session of the Congress on the State of the Union," *Public Papers, 1990*, 1:131; *Public Papers, 1991*, 1:78–79.

85. George H. W. Bush, "Address on Administration Goals Before a Joint Session of the Congress," *Public Papers, 1989*, 1:74–81, "Address Before a Joint Session of the Congress on the State of the Union," *Public Papers, 1990*, 1:129–134; *Public Papers, 1991*, 1:74–79; *Public Papers, 1992*, 1:156–163.

86. Clinton, "Address Before a Joint Session of the Congress on the State of the Union," *Public Papers, 1995*, 1:85.

87. George W. Bush, "Address Before a Joint Session of the Congress on Administration Goals," *Public Papers of the Presidents of the United States: George W. Bush, 2001*, vol.1 (Washington, DC: GPO, 2002), 143–145.

88. George W. Bush, "Address Before a Joint Session of the Congress on the State of the Union," *Weekly Compilation of Presidential Documents* 38, no. 5 (4 February 2002):134.

4

The President as Chief Legislator in the State of the Union Address

Presidents utilize symbolism as they try to convince audiences to follow their leadership on the substantive policy they discuss in their SUAs. We turn now to the president's power as chief legislator—how that role has not always been part of the presidency, how the role became available to the president, and how the oral SUA played an important part in that process. As the chief legislator appears in the SUA, it is apparent that he is no ordinary legislator. The president in this role does, however, share some goals with ordinary legislators, and the SUA helps him further these goals. In the policymaking rhetoric of the SUA, presidents convey policy substance by touting their successes and revealing their policy priorities. These activities, for which the SUA is uniquely suited, aid the chief legislator in furthering goals shared with regular legislators. While all presidents engage in credit claiming and position taking in their SUAs, the levels at which they engage in these activities vary depending upon presidents and the political circumstances they are confronting. SUAs come in different types depending on these factors, but all SUAs are political communications in which chief legislators seek to exert leadership of Congress.

Expanding the President's Legislative Powers

The president has five constitutional powers that are legislative in nature. Only one, the veto, is found in Article I, the article devoted to the legislative branch.[1] The remainder are all found in Article II, Section 3. In the first of these provisions, the president is charged with giving information to Congress. He is also given the power to recommend measures to Congress. The final two powers relate to congressional sessions. He can call Congress

89

into special session and adjourn them if they disagree on a time. These Constitutional provisions have not been formally altered or amended throughout American history. Yet, in the nineteenth century, the president was not considered to be the chief legislator; it is a role that emerged in the twentieth century. What changed?

There are two powers that relate to congressional sessions among the president's legislative powers. It should first be noted that no president has ever exercised his power to set adjournment if the two houses disagree.[2] This is, therefore, not a factor in the evolution of the chief legislator. The other power relating to congressional sessions is a power that became largely unnecessary in the latter half of the twentieth century. The last time a president called a special session of Congress was when Truman famously called the Republican-controlled Eightieth Congress into special session in the late summer of 1948.[3] There are two reasons why special sessions have not been used for more than fifty years. First, after the ratification of the Twentieth Amendment in 1933, Congress was sworn in and began sessions in January; the gap that previously occurred between new presidents taking office in March and Congress convening a regular session, typically in December, disappeared. Previous to the Twentieth Amendment, this gap frequently presented the need for presidents to call a special session. In addition, Congress now tends to be in session most of the year, making special sessions unnecessary. The adjournment and special session provision, therefore, cannot have affected the emergence of the chief legislator moniker; one power has never been utilized, and the other became virtually unnecessary during much of the time period in which we have called the president the chief legislator.

Moving to the veto power, one finds there have been changes both to the view of this power as well as the exercise of it. Rather than only vetoing measures considered to be constitutionally dubious, as his predecessors did, Andrew Jackson began the precedent of wielding the power to strike down measures he simply objected to on policy grounds.[4] Jackson's view of the veto was extraordinarily controversial; a controversy that did not end until after the Civil War.[5] Grover Cleveland was especially aggressive in his use of the veto, which "reflected his philosophy that the veto was and should be an integral component of his involvement in the legislative process."[6] Thus, the way presidents viewed and used the veto power changed in the nineteenth century, before the president was considered to have the hat of chief legislator. There were changes in the veto power's usage in the twentieth century as well, which have contributed to the enhanced legislative role that presidents gained. Robert Spitzer details the evolution of the veto power in this regard.

> The veto served as an important opportunity for presidents to exert greater influence over the legislative process (in particular as it advanced the abil-

ity of the president to involve himself in the legislative process before a bill reached his desk), first through the veto itself, then the veto threat, then anticipation by Congress of a veto threat, and thus to greater across-the-board consideration of the president's legislative and policy preferences by Congress.[7]

The evolution Spitzer details expands the veto power's influence to more than just a negative at the end of the legislative process; it gives the president power in the middle of the legislative process as a bill is being shaped. Vetoes are rather blunt instruments, however, and as Light points out, "the veto also engenders congressional hostility; for that reason, it is not the most effective means to accomplish policy goals."[8] Nevertheless, the veto's very presence in the chief legislator's toolbox gets the attention of Congress.

The remaining two constitutional powers are also key in the chief legislator's development and give presidents significant powers they can use at the beginning of the legislative process. As discussed in Chapter 2, the powers of giving information and recommending measures to Congress have been linked together since Washington's first annual message. SUAs have always been about presidents giving information to Congress; the extent to which measures were recommended in the nineteenth century varied, but the recommendations presidents made tended to be designed to focus the attention of Congress on large issues and lacked specificity. Two key happenings occurred in the twentieth century that contributed to the development of the chief legislator. A combination of practice and law expanded the reporting and recommending powers of the presidents. First, presidents with different views of presidential power than nineteenth century presidents, such as Teddy Roosevelt, Woodrow Wilson, and Franklin Roosevelt, asserted strong leadership of Congress. Second, the information-giving and recommendation powers of the president expanded through statute, specifically the Budget and Accounting Act of 1921 and the Employment Act of 1946. Furthermore, FDR's creation of the Executive Office of the President in 1939 through an executive order gave the president key policy advisors, giving him ready access to a repository of expertise and information he did not previously have. What simply needs to be noted here is that twentieth-century presidents gained enhanced ability to use their congressional reporting and recommending powers, ones that are important at the beginning of the legislative process.

What has changed that is significant to the development of the president's chief legislator role is the extent to which presidents could be involved in the legislative process from beginning, middle, to end. This is what makes the president an extraordinary legislator. Presidents have always played a role at the *end* of the legislative process by having to accept or reject bills placed before them. Before the Civil War, there were serious debates over the propriety of the veto's use by presidents.[9] As the veto power changed through its application in the nineteenth and early twentieth century, the effect was to give presidents a role to play in the *middle* of the legislative process. While presidents of unusual strength had periodically been forceful with their recommending powers, as presidents were given more opportunities for reporting and recommending to Congress in the twentieth century, all presidents began to develop specific legislative programs; Congress would even come to demand it of them.[10] Presidents began to have an enhanced function at the *beginning* of the legislative process. Key in the development of the chief legislator role is presidential expansion into the middle and the beginning of the legislative process through his changed usage of three constitutional powers: the veto and the information-giving and recommending provisions. Primary, however, in the development of chief legislator are the changes that occurred in the way information was given and legislation recommended.

It is not our purpose to analyze how the president's role in the middle, or even the end, of the legislative process evolved due to the veto power; much of this happened in the nineteenth century before the chief legislator role developed. Also, while the evolution of the veto power did contribute to the development of the chief legislator role, it is not a power that can be used all the time. As Light points out, the more effective policy strategy for presidents is one of proposal, not opposition.[11] We seek to better understand how the chief legislator uses the SUA at the beginning and middle of the legislative process, both for the purpose of proposing, but also for taking positions on proposals that may already be in the legislative pipeline. The changes in the view and use of these powers are primary in the development of the chief legislator; further, these provisions are also at the root of the SUA. We do not claim that the reporting and recommending provisions are the only things that have contributed to the chief legislator's role, but we do maintain that the SUA, which is based on these constitutional provisions, is integral in the extension of the president's role to more than just the end of the legislative process. The modern SUA exemplifies why we call the president the chief legislator. Since we have already detailed how the SUA is no ordinary speech, we now turn to an examination of how the president's use of the SUA exemplifies that he is no ordinary legislator.

Becoming Chief Legislator in the Twentieth Century

What conditions made it possible for presidents to play an enhanced role in the legislative process at the beginning and middle, in effect, giving the president a new hat to wear? Stephen Wayne identifies four factors that were key in increasing the legislative activity of presidents: visibility of the presidency; activist view of the presidency; congressional parties more open to leadership; and an enhanced need for presidents, with their national constituency, to respond to new social and economic conditions that called for regulation.[12] Presidents became chief legislators primarily because of a convergence of factors in the early twentieth-century environment that enhanced their effectiveness, willingness, and ability to give information and recommend legislation to Congress. Presidents were able to use these two constitutional provisions, heretofore viewed as presidential duties, to expand their influence in Congress and with the public. These two constitutional duties became powers and are at the root of the development of the chief legislator; these two powers are also the basis of the SUA. The SUA became a key tool through which presidents could exercise power as chief legislator. The SUA is not the only tool chief legislators utilize, but it is a very important power. The SUA is part and parcel of the development of the chief legislator; it is both integral to and reflective of the chief legislator's role.

Taking each of the four factors Wayne identified, we can examine the role the SUA played in each, as the chief legislator role was being established. The first factor Wayne identified was more visibility for the presidency. From Jefferson until Wilson, annual messages were sent to Congress in written form, but when Wilson reinstituted Washington's and Adams's original practice of delivering the annual message as a speech, the SUA became an event that would focus attention on presidents and their information and recommendations. Rather than giving information in a passive form and considering it a duty, presidents began giving it in an active form to which the public had more access. Wilson made the president more visible with the Congress by changing the mode of delivery of the annual message. In doing so, he made the presidency more visible to the public as well, although indirectly. None of Wilson's oral addresses was broadcast over the radio (the first would be Coolidge's 1923 address), but a presidential speech would merit more coverage in the newspapers than a written message sent to the Congress. Wilson was also a president who consciously sought to mold public opinion. Before he was president, the political scientist Wilson wrote, "a President whom [the country] trusts can not only lead it, but form it to his own views."[13] Appeals to the public became the root of the rhetorical presidency Tulis sees originating with Wilson.[14] The SUAs served an important purpose in this regard. Presidents with enhanced visibility had an enlarged platform from which to lead both the Congress and the public; the SUA provided such a platform. As electronic media developed and SUAs were broadcast over the airwaves, the public audience grew, giving the president an enhanced opportunity to talk directly to the people.

The second factor Wayne identified was a change in the way presidents viewed the presidency; presidents became more activist. As shown in

Chapter 2, most nineteenth-century presidents believed their information-giving and recommending role was a duty, not an opportunity to wield legislative leadership. Further, they adhered to a stricter interpretation of separation of powers that did not allow for extensive executive involvement. Particularly important presidents regarding this changing view were Teddy Roosevelt and Woodrow Wilson. Both of these presidents used their SUAs to inform and recommend measures to Congress that were more specific than most of their predecessors. They also had different views about the role of public opinion and the president's ability to discern and lead it. Activist presidents have legislative agendas and are assertive about advertising them before Congress and the public. SUAs reflected the more assertive stance presidents took regarding legislative leadership and public leadership.

In accordance with Wayne's third factor, Congress became more open to leadership from the executive in the twentieth century. At the turn of the century, presidents began to actively involve themselves with the congressional leadership, aided by some strong personalities and coupled with a view of the presidency that was less constrained by separation of powers.[15] In this regard, the SUA provided one forum for the president to exercise leadership of Congress. A reading of Teddy Roosevelt's and Wilson's SUAs reflect the different attitudes they had about the office and congressional (as well as public) leadership. Furthermore, Congress eventually adjusted to increasingly activist presidents and made more specific the information-giving and recommendation requirements of the president through statute. Shortly after Wilson left office, Congress passed the Budget and Accounting Act of 1921, which requires the president to submit a budget to Congress. Along with the formal budget, presidents transmit a budget message to the Congress. Details about the budget, which had been standard fare in the written nineteenth-century annual messages, after 1921 would be expanded and covered in the written budget messages. The Employment Act of 1946 required the president to submit an economic report to Congress and established the Council of Economic Advisors to assist the president in preparing the report, among other things. By 1947, there were three "annual messages," the annual message on the State of the Union, the annual budget message, and the annual economic report.[16] When Congress began mandating the president give information and recommend measures on the budget and the economy, administrations had to develop more detailed information and recommendations than previously had been required of presidents in the nineteenth century. The various entities in the Executive Office of the President, created in 1939, housed key policy staff and gave presidents the information they needed to prepare the budget, economic report, and other policy areas in addition. Whereas Teddy Roosevelt, Wilson, and FDR were significant in the role of chief legislator developing in the presidency because of their own particular views about presidential power and executive-congressional relations, Congress also began to require more activity and leadership from the president. Future presidents would not be able to retreat from this course (even should they desire) as executive leadership of Congress became institutionalized.

As the chief legislator role developed in the twentieth century, presidents' legislative recommendations in SUAs became more specific. During the Truman and Eisenhower administrations, detailed and comprehensive legislative programs began to emanate from the executive branch, and Congress began to expect them from presidents.[17] SUAs began to reflect administrations' greater involvement in the legislative process, provided a way for presidents to highlight the most important aspects of their legislative program, and became what Neustadt called the "psychologically most important annual message."[18] With expanded opportunities to give information and recommend measures to Congress, presidents gained an enhanced role at the beginning of the legislative process. In addition, presidents could use the SUA to weigh in on congressional proposals already in the legislative process. The SUA was a way for the president to sum up for both Congress and the public, what road the country was headed down, how far the president had gone to get the country where it was, and where the president wanted to go in the next year.

Finally, the economic and social environment in the early twentieth century was such that national leadership was needed to address national problems. The problems of industrialization affected the nation, not just isolated pockets of it. The Great Depression was "great" because it was so deep and widespread. When the president appears before a joint session of Congress, addressing all of the elected officials in the federal government (and many of the nonelected ones as well), he is the only elected official in the room who represents the entire nation. Congress can lose sight of the national interest, especially if it does not have presidential leadership, because "legislators tend to view national policy proposals from a local perspective, asking before anything else, how the proposal will affect the various interests that they represent."[19] The SUA is an important speech with which a president can lead Congress and address his constituency, the nation. Both audiences want to be presented with a vision for the country, offered solutions, and reassured the president has a plan.

These four factors that converged in the early twentieth century enabled presidents to don the chief legislator's hat, and the oral delivery of the SUA played a role in each factor. SUAs now routinely provide a forum in which the president attains maximum visibility and can actively assert rhetorical leadership of both Congress and the public. An SUA is a key part of the chief legislator's power, which has become a key part of the presidency. We now turn to an examination of the chief legislator's uses for the SUA.

The SUA and the President as Chief Legislator

There are many things presidents do within the confines of the SUA; they wear many hats during its delivery and might even wear multiple ones at the same time. One sees the commander-in-chief reporting on the state of military affairs. Next, the chief executive may emerge to inform Congress of an executive order of particular importance. When discussing the state of foreign affairs, the chief diplomat hat is donned. The simple act of appearing to address a congressional joint session in a very ceremonial fashion means that the president's role as head of state is evident throughout the speech.[20] One major role on display in the SUA will be that of chief legislator. The SUA can afford the president, in his capacity as chief legislator, a forum to behave as a policy entrepreneur by promoting innovative new policies, to jump on the bandwagon of legislation that is already in the congressional pipeline, to urge Congress not to act on certain things, to threaten vetoes, and to advocate his budgetary priorities. The president specifically asks for Congress's action on numerous legislative items, explaining his position, clarifying why certain actions are necessary, and incorporating symbolic and emotional appeals in his policymaking rhetoric.

Since the development of the chief legislator power, it has become intimately tied to our perception of presidential leadership. A key determinant of whether presidents are judged successful or not is the influence presidents wield in the legislative process. Setting the nation on a path, outlining an agenda, and convincing Congress their policy solutions should be adopted are all at the heart of providing leadership. These are all things presidents seek to do with an SUA. The two constitutional provisions at the heart of the SUA were the same provisions whose evolution were key in the development of the president's role as chief legislator. The move from the written annual message to oral delivery of the SUA was a crucial component of how the president came to be viewed as legislator-in-chief.[21] As a tool of the chief legislator, the speech has become integral to the president's communication of his vision and policy priorities.

The policymaking rhetoric in the contemporary SUA is aimed simultaneously at two audiences, Congress and the public. For both, the way the policymaking rhetoric of the SUA frames the issue, advertises past successes, and recommends solutions is designed to facilitate presidential leadership. To begin with, the president is addressing a joint session of Congress, where attendance of members is virtually compulsory. This audience, what we might call the constitutional audience, is in attendance so the president can give information and recommend measures, thus fulfilling two constitutional duties. First and foremost, the SUA is a document of presidential leadership of Congress. Its constitutional roots dictate an accounting *to Congress* on the state of affairs and recommendations *to Congress* regarding necessary and expedient measures. Recall from our discussion in Chapter 2, however, that the constitutional provisions of reporting and recommending can be viewed as presidential powers, not just duties. In no small degree this is because a second audience, the public, is now included and plays an important role. While the president has always reported and recommended measures to Congress in some way, the extent to which the American public was included as an audience and had access to the president's words has evolved. In the age of the rhetorical presidency, a president seeks to convince the public to see things as he does in hopes they might put pressure on members of Congress, the essence of "going public."[22] The president's goal remains congressional action, but he hopes to use the public as an intermediary. The SUA is unique because it offers the president a regular, institutionalized opportunity to "go public" in the presence of Congress, in effect potentially providing for an end run around Congress under its very nose. Public appeals are part of a strategy the president utilizes for congressional leadership, made possible by the president's ability to appeal directly to the public. Our purpose is not, however, to examine public reaction to SUAs and the pressure citizens may or may not put on members of Congress.[23] Our purpose is to present an analysis of how the chief legislator uses the SUA. The attempts at public persuasion in the SUA are part of how presidents attempt congressional leadership; therefore, presidents simultaneously aim the policymaking rhetoric in the SUA at the public and Congress.

For the remainder of this chapter, we will be occupied with an analysis of how the chief legislator uses the substantive rhetoric of the SUA. We should note that we are not attempting to study agenda setting by the president; other things may be part of the president's agenda that he does not choose to emphasize in the State of the Union.[24] Ours is, however, an examination of the policy substance highlighted in the SUA, because we are interested in how the SUA functions as a communication tool of the chief legislator. We begin by looking at what we know about legislative goals and behavior in general and pose several questions. How do contemporary presidents utilize the SUA as chief legislator? What does this tell us about the SUA as a tool of political communication?

Furthering Legislative Goals with the Policy Substance of the SUA

As chief legislator, the president is not an ordinary legislator. To begin with, his position is external to the actual legislature. As the moniker itself implies, however, he does play an integral role in the legislative process. Constitutionally, he must accept or reject legislation before it can become law. Modern presidents play a role in the process, however, which begins long before the act of acceptance or rejection of a bill; chief legislators are involved in the beginning and middle of the legislative process, as well. Like every legislator, the chief legislator represents a constituency, but, unlike those in the Congress, his constituency is the whole nation. Furthermore, since FDR the public has increasingly turned its attention to the president as the one who formulates and implements policy, and the public and the president have forged a "personal connection."[25] Congress, in addition, expects the chief legislator to provide leadership. To examine how the president uses the SUA as chief legislator, it is constructive to consider what we know about legislative goals in general. In what ways might the *chief* legislator's goals be unique? In what ways might they be similar to regular legislators' goals?

Richard Fenno identifies three widely held goals of House and Senate members: reelection, chamber influence, and making public policy. Some will also have progressive ambitions.[26] Of the goals identified by Fenno, two are of little consideration for the chief legislator. Being external to the actual legislature, the president is not concerned about chamber influence in the same way as members. As president he has constitutionally built-in influence *with* Congress, but this is different from Fenno's notion of influence *within* the chamber, where members seek to amass power and prestige. In addition, the president has reached the pinnacle of political ambition; there is no higher elected office for which to aspire. The president as chief legislator is, however, concerned with two goals that regular legislators have: reelection (but only in his first term) and making pubic policy. How do these two aspects of legislative behavior manifest themselves in the chief legislator's SUA?

Mayhew begins with the premise that members of Congress are "single-minded re-election seekers."[27] The chief legislator, however, is term limited, unlike regular legislators. If he behaves as a legislator in this manner, it can only be applicable to his first term. There can be no doubt that reelection is a goal of all the constitutionally eligible presidents we study.[28] If a president is fortunate enough to be reelected, as was the case with four of the presidents studied in our time frame, his goal in this regard must shift in the second term.[29] Reelection can no longer be a consideration. A goal that is similar, and comes to the forefront in the second term pertains to the legacy a president will leave behind when his tenure is complete. Even in a first term, a president will have an eye toward history.[30] When the reelection goal is fulfilled, however, concerns about one's legacy increase and replace the concern and attention previously given to reelection considerations. Reelection goals are short-term ones for a president; after reelection is secured, the focus changes to long-term considerations of the president's legacy. Furthermore, these goals are connected; an ability, or inability, to secure reelection affects one's legacy. Both reelection and legacy goals have similar ends that are based on the public's view and assessment of the president. The end of reelection is to have popularity manifest itself in a successful vote. The goal of securing a favorable legacy entails being viewed as a popular and effective president after one has left office. Once a president is out of office, he awaits the judgment of history.

The major activities that Mayhew sees in legislative behavior given the reelection premise with which he begins are advertising, credit claiming, and position taking.[31] Since we assert that the most visible hat the president wears during an SUA is the legislative one, and he is concerned with both reelection and legacy goals, we can use the activities Mayhew finds in legislative behavior to give us further insight into the nature and purpose of the chief legislator's SUA.

Advertising

Mayhew defines advertising as "any effort to disseminate one's name among constituents in such a fashion as to create a favorable image but in messages having little or no issue content."[32] A president has much less of a need to engage in advertising activities in the same way a congressperson does; Mayhew likens a legislator's actions in advertising to furthering one's "brand name."[33] A president has already secured brand name recognition or he would not be the occupant of the White House. In this regard, the chief legislator is different from the legislator. When legislators are engaging in the activity of advertising, their primary audience is their constituents, who often simply need to be reminded who the legislators are; thus, issue content is secondary at best. When presidents are delivering SUAs, they are concerned primarily with the two audiences of their constituents and Congress, both of whom are already aware of who they are. The purpose of the SUA is not to boost name recognition for the president. In addition, there is policy substance in an SUA. As the chief legislator, the president is expected to include substance and does so through the inclusion of policy recommendations. Advertising, in the sense Mayhew applies it to legislators, is not an activity in which we find chief legislators using SUAs to engage.

Credit Claiming

Mayhew defines credit claiming as "acting so as to generate a belief in a relevant political actor (or actors) that one is personally responsible for causing the government, or some unit thereof, to do something the actor (or actors) consider desirable."[34] Chief legislators most certainly engage in credit claiming in an SUA. In this respect, the chief legislator's behavior is similar to a regular legislator pursuing reelection. Credit claiming is a key part of the policy substance presidents convey in the document. There are, however, very important qualitative differences due to the president's role as chief legislator. Unlike the regular legislator's credit claiming, which is particular in nature, the president can claim credit for broad accomplishments. In addition, the president's credit claiming is not confined to just legislative accomplishments. Finally, the credit claiming in which presidents engage helps them make their case for new requests; reference to past success can help set the stage for future success.

For a single legislator, convincingly claiming credit can be a difficult proposition given that he or she is one actor among 535. Consequently, members of Congress claim credit for particular items.[35] For example, rather than seeking credit for the excellent condition of the interstate highway system across the country, legislators will claim credit for the excellent state of highways in their own district or state, made possible by the federal highway dollars they were able to secure for their constituency. It is not usually believable for one member of Congress to take credit for policy results that are not particular in nature. The American public, however, does not have difficulty assigning responsibility for large policy outcomes, such as a tax cut or the War on Poverty, to a single president, because of their perception of his position at the center of the political system. The president, however, has attention disproportionately focused on him in a way very unlike a legislator. As chief legislators in the era of the rhetorical presidency, it is expected that presidents appeal to the public and advance policy goals. Part of appealing to the public for future support includes reminding them of past successes.

Presidents will typically include some reference to Congress in claiming credit for legislative accomplishments in an SUA. For example, Reagan stated in his 1982 SUA,

> Together, we not only cut the increase in government spending nearly in half, we brought about the largest tax reductions and the most sweeping changes in our tax structure since the beginning of this century. And because we indexed future taxes to the rate of inflation, we took away government's built-in profit on inflation and its hidden incentive to grow larger at the expense of American workers.[36]

Credit claiming for legislative accomplishments in an SUA is generally spoken of as a team effort, but the president, by virtue of his position as "coach," gets assigned the credit by the public. The accomplishment Reagan is taking credit for above is known as the Reagan Tax Cut; as chief legislator, he proposed it and Congress accepted it, although they altered its contours. The president did not get everything he wanted in that legislation, but that is of little consequence to the president, or the public, when he claims credit for accomplishments in an SUA.

In addition to claiming credit for their share of legislative accomplishments, presidents can claim credit for achievements in which Congress plays little to no role, such as international negotiations, executive actions, or actions the president can take as commander-in-chief. Often, these accomplishments are still touted as things that "we" have done, but not always.

For example, G. W. Bush reported in the 2002 SUA,

> While the most visible military action is in Afghanistan, America is acting elsewhere. We now have troops in the Philippines, helping to train that country's armed forces to go after terrorist cells that have executed an American, and still hold hostages. Our soldiers, working with the Bosnian government, seized terrorists who were plotting to bomb our embassy. Our Navy is patrolling the coast of Africa to block the shipment of weapons and the establishment of terrorist camps in Somalia.[37]

As another example, President Johnson proclaimed, "Wherever waste is found, I will eliminate it. Last year we saved almost $3,500 million by eliminating waste in the National Government. And I intend to do better this year."[38]

Presidents can claim credit for the general state of the economy in which their own role is circumscribed, but in which the public may assign reward or punishment. Clinton pointed out,

> Record numbers of Americans are succeeding in the new global economy. We are at peace, and we are a force for peace and freedom throughout the world. We have almost 6 million new jobs since I became President, and we have the lowest combined rate of unemployment and inflation in 25 years. Our businesses are more productive.[39]

Presidents not only claim credit to boost their reelection/legacy prospects, but they also inform and remind audiences what the administration has accomplished in hopes of building support for their policy recommendations. Consider this example from Clinton's 1996 SUA:

> At last we have begun to find a way to reduce crime, forming community partnerships with local police forces to catch criminals and prevent crime. This strategy, called community policing, is clearly working. Violent crime is coming down all across America. In New York City murders are down 25 percent; in St. Louis, 18 percent; in Seattle, 32 percent.[40]

While there are numerous reasons why crime rates were going down in the 1990s, Clinton links the decline in murder rates specifically to his community policing program. Note that Mayhew's definition of credit claiming involves legislators acting in such a way as to "generate a belief" they are responsible for some action. After the above, Clinton goes on to say, "But we still have a long way to go before our streets are safe and our people free from fear,"[41] and then moves into discussing his legislative requests related to crime for the coming year. Besides reminding the audiences of the president's accomplishments, claiming credit helps him frame the situation and set the stage for his new requests in such a way as to encourage audiences to follow his leadership.

When the chief legislator engages in credit claiming in the SUA, he can tout broad accomplishments; he is not limited to legislative ones. A regular legislator claims credit for particular legislative accomplishments and lacks the forum and attention the chief legislator has in the SUA. Credit claiming is an activity that serves more than just the reelection goal of the chief legislator. It aids him with the larger and related goal of securing a positive legacy. Even so, credit claiming in the SUA is not just utilized for reelection/legacy purposes. It is also connected to the second goal Fenno identified, legislators' desire to make public policy.

Position Taking

Mayhew defines a legislator's position taking "as the public enunciation of a judgmental statement on anything likely to be of interest to political actors. The statement may take the form of the roll call vote."[42] While a president does not get to cast roll call votes as chief legislator, he does get to accept or reject bills before they become law. Position taking for the chief legislator, however, begins much earlier than the president's final acceptance or rejection of a bill. As chief legislator, he can play a vital role at the beginning or middle of the legislative process by taking positions. Whereas a legislator may take a position on a policy initiative early, it is unlikely to be of widespread interest; the roll call vote, however, does give the legislator's constituents tangible evidence of his or her position. The chief legislator's position taking is done to shape and influence the congressional agenda and the formation of public policy. The SUA is especially suited for the chief legislator to engage in this activity. Chief legislators take positions with the legislative requests they make of Congress in the SUA. Whereas members of Congress primarily take positions to aid their reelection goals, presidents take positions not only to serve reelection/legacy goals, but also to lead Congress and the public toward accepting their policy solutions. Position taking, therefore, for the chief legislator is also linked to the second goal Fenno identifies legislators having, that of making public policy.

Presidents convey policy substance in the SUA through both their credit claiming and position taking. Engaging in these activities enables presidents to further the goal of reelection, which they share with regular legislators. Credit claiming and position taking also further the chief legislator's goal of securing a positive legacy after reelection is no longer a possibility. In addition, both of these activities, which regular legislators engage in primarily for reelection purposes, assist the chief legislator in achieving the goal of making public policy, another goal shared with legislators.

Using the Policy Substance of the SUA

Presidents' reelection goals are furthered if they have been active and identified with making public policy, providing them achievements for which they can claim credit and campaign. They can no longer make public policy if they are defeated, and legacies are tied both to ability to secure reelection and policy successes. The credit claiming and position taking of presidents, therefore, further the mutually reinforcing goals of reelection/ legacy and making public policy. To further these goals, do all presidents utilize the policy substance of SUAs in similar fashion, or do uses vary from president to president? Furthermore, do presidents utilize the policy substance differently depending upon when the SUA takes place within their term?

Amount of claiming credit.   To gauge the presidents' use of credit claiming in SUAs, we identified sentences in which they claimed credit for outcomes.[43] Credit claiming was not limited to legislative outcomes and included both specific and general claims of credit.[44] A specific claim would include the following from G. H. W. Bush's 1990 SUA.

> One year—one year ago, the people of Panama lived in fear, under the thumb of a dictator. Today democracy is restored; Panama is free. Operation Just Cause has achieved its objective. The number of military personnel in Panama is now very close to what it was before the operation began.[45]

A general claim would include something such as Nixon's statement in his 1971 SUA, where he said, "The tide of inflation has turned. The rise in the cost of living, which had been gathering dangerous momentum in the late sixties, was reduced last year."[46] While there is no specific policy linked to the credit Nixon is seeking, he is drawing attention to the fact that inflation declined during his watch. Once credit-claiming sentences were identified, we computed the percentage of sentences in the SUA devoted to this activity.

Given that credit claiming is part of fulfilling reelection goals, we would expect a president's credit-claiming activity in the SUA to increase over the course of his first term as he gets closer to the election year and has more accumulated actions for which he can claim credit. Accordingly, it ought to peak in the year that the president is seeking reelection. If a president wins a second term, we would expect credit claiming to be maintained at a level roughly on par with the activity of the first term as the president's concern shifts to related legacy goals. Only two presidents in our time period serve out a full two terms, Reagan and Clinton. Our expectation is that in the second term, as presidents turn their attention, not to reelection, since it is a constitutional impossibility, but to their legacy, credit claiming will undergo what might be termed *maintenance*. Given that the space in an oral SUA is limited, credit claiming cannot increase indefinitely or it would displace other things to which the president will still pay attention, such as policy requests. Thus, we would not expect to see credit claiming successively increase in the second term. Second terms tend to be less successful than first terms;[47] it is likely that there will be fewer things for which to claim credit. We do not expect credit claiming to decrease, however, and our measure takes into account space devoted to claiming credit, not the number of accomplishments for which the president is claiming credit. In the second term, presidents will still have an incentive to tout successes when they can and devote space to them. Thus, we would expect to see credit claiming be maintained at a level sufficient for keeping major successes in front of the public while still allowing space for the other functions of the president's policymaking rhetoric. Our final expectation concerns lame-duck speeches, of which we have only two examples, Johnson's 1969 and Ford's 1977 SUAs. We expect the credit claiming of presidents in lame-duck speeches to be very high. It is the last opportunity for presidents to address their legacy, and there is no need for them to address their agenda in the coming year—it is irrelevant. More space, therefore, can be devoted to claiming credit.

Figure 4.1 charts the trends in credit claiming for first terms. Our first expectation, that credit claiming would increase over the first term, holds for four of our seven presidents.[48] For LBJ, Nixon, Ford, and Clinton, credit claiming increases to peak in their reelection-year SUA. Although each successive year does not, as with Nixon and Clinton, register an increase, the overall trend is still an upward one. The credit claiming of Carter, Reagan, and G. H. W. Bush does not peak in their reelection year, defying our expectations in this regard, but their reelection-year SUA does obtain the second highest level of credit claiming in their first term. Carter, however, is a bit of an anomaly in that his reelection-year SUA is the second highest percentage but also the lowest amount of credit claiming of his presidency. This is misleading, however, because Carter sustains a relatively high level of credit claiming in all three of his SUAs, even though there is a slight decline in space devoted to credit claiming in his final SUA. Carter claims credit in 13.9 percent of the sentences in his election year SUA, precisely the median for all election-year SUAs we examined.

What do we conclude about first-term credit claiming? In general, credit claiming shows the overall trend of increasing over the course of the first term; for all presidents, the percentage of the SUA devoted to credit claim-

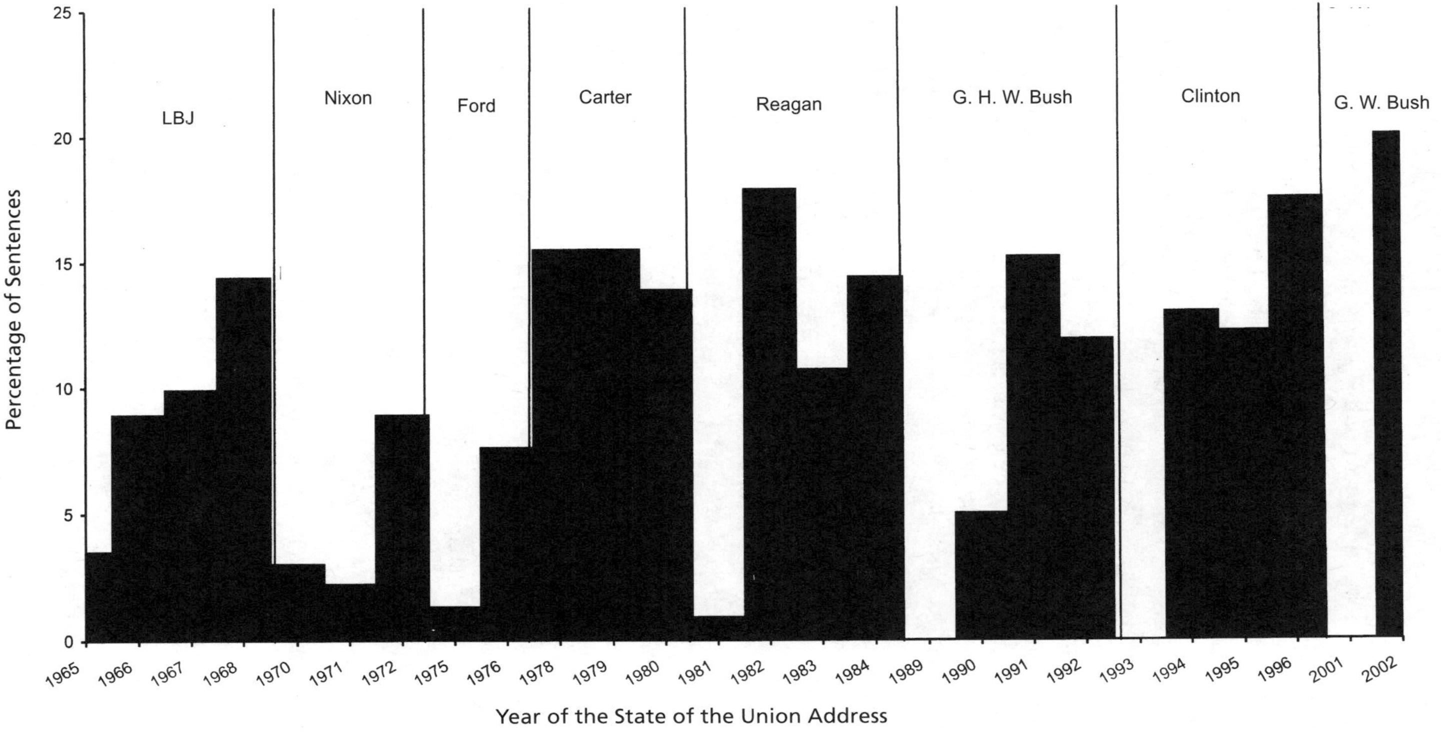

Figure 4.1   Credit Claiming in First-Term State of the Union Addresses

ing in the reelection year is either the highest or second highest of their first term. From these results, we observe that the credit claiming in contemporary SUAs generally moves in an upward pattern during the first term, but does not always peak in reelection years. There are explanations relating to specific circumstances for each of the three presidents whose first terms do not meet our expectations. Carter's 1980 SUA is unusual in that it is given on the heels of twin international crises—the taking of American hostages in Iran, and the Soviet's invasion of Afghanistan. G. H. W. Bush's 1991 SUA, in which credit claiming peaks, is given in the midst of a successful international event, the Gulf War. Reagan's peak credit-claiming SUA in 1982 follows his most successful year legislatively. Each of these events impacted the amount of credit claiming in the SUA. Credit claiming in SUAs serves different purposes for presidents depending on circumstances, a subject to which we will return when identifying the various types of SUAs. In addition, we note that presidents have different relative levels of credit claiming in their first terms as well. Both Nixon and Ford engage in credit claiming at much lower levels than Reagan and Clinton. We also see in the data that overall credit claiming in first terms, excluding inaugural years, has slightly increased over time. Of the three presidents before Carter, none had a median of more than 10 percent of their SUAs devoted to credit claiming; Nixon and Ford were substantially below that with 3 percent and 4 percent, respectively. From Carter to Clinton, each president devoted a median of 12 percent or more of their first-term SUAs to credit claiming. With only three presidents before Carter included in our data, it is impossible to state that this is a trend. This slight increase in overall first-term credit claiming, however, may be a manifestation of more-recent presidents who have increasingly linked governing with campaigning.[49]

While credit claiming in the first term can be utilized to set the stage for reelection, credit claiming in the second term can indicate the extent to which a president's attention has turned to legacy considerations. We have only two presidents in our time series who serve out two full terms, Reagan and Clinton. We include Nixon's 1974 SUA in Figure 4.2 as well, since he did win reelection, but did not serve out a full second term.[50] Our expectations were that, since reelection is no longer a concern, a president's reelection goals would be replaced by goals of securing his legacy in the second term. In this regard, credit claiming would not cease but continue to maintain some focus on accomplishments that would be on par with the credit claiming the president engaged in during his first term.

Both Reagan and Clinton continue to claim credit in their second terms, and there is not successively greater space devoted to credit claiming. However, Reagan's credit claiming in his second term is maintained at a much lower level than in his first; his noninaugural SUAs in the first term had a median 14.4 percent of space devoted to credit claiming. In his second

Figure 4.2　Credit Claiming in Second-Term State of the Union Addresses

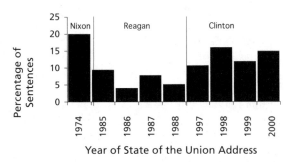

Year of State of the Union Address

term, the median space devoted to credit claiming was only 6.5 percent. Credit claiming was not an activity Reagan employed at the same level after his reelection. Clinton, on the other hand, does maintain a level of credit claiming on par with his first term. His noninaugural SUAs in the first term had a median 13 percent of space given over to claiming credit, and his second-term SUAs devote a median 13.4 percent to this practice. Finally, Nixon's 1974 SUA devotes a full one-fifth of the speech to credit claiming. Nixon confronted unusual circumstances in his 1974 SUA; the chorus of Watergate-related criticisms against his presidency was growing, eventually leading to his resignation in August of that year. As a result of the political environment, he devotes an extraordinary amount of space to reminding his audiences of his accomplishments, especially when one considers that he devoted only a median 3 percent of his first-term SUAs to credit claiming. Both Reagan and Clinton confronted similar crises in their second terms. Reagan's 1987 SUA addresses Iran-Contra allegations. Clinton's 1998 SUA came just days after reports of an affair with White House intern Monica Lewinsky surfaced, and his 1999 SUA was given after he had been impeached by the House, but before his acquittal in the Senate. We do see Clinton in 1998 devoting a higher level of his SUA to credit claiming, but 1999 witnesses less, not more, attention to credit claiming. We also do not encounter more relative credit claiming in Reagan's 1987 SUA. What our examination of second-term SUAs suggests, as did our analysis of first-term credit claiming, is that the activity of credit claiming is affected by the circumstances in which the SUA took place and not always in a way that is predictable. Credit-claiming activities can be highly individualized. Nixon, Reagan, and Clinton had different credit-claiming approaches in their second terms as they dealt with crises within their presidencies that would affect their legacies. Again, we will speak to these different circumstances and different purposes that SUAs hold for presidents below.

Our final expectation regarding credit claiming relates to lame-duck addresses given in the month that a president leaves office.[51] We expected credit claiming to be very high in these addresses given that the president is shortly leaving office and very attune to legacy concerns. In addition, specific policy requests of Congress for the coming year would not be relevant, and space typically devoted to these requests could be taken up by credit claiming. As represented in Figure 4.3, the two lame-duck addresses by Johnson in 1969 and Ford in 1977 both contain not only the highest percentage of credit-claiming sentences of their respective SUAs, but also the highest percentages of credit claiming of all our observations. Both are also leaving office under a cloud of unpopularity. Johnson withdraws from the race in 1968 because there was some danger he would not get the Democratic party's nomination. Ford, having replaced the disgraced Nixon, could not win the presidency in his own right in the 1976 election. These two presidents had a particular need to attend to concerns about their legacy in their final SUA. Therefore, they are particularly conscious of legacy considerations and accordingly devote more space to claiming credit for their accomplishments. In addition, they can devote more space to credit claiming because less space is taken up with policy proposals. It should be noted, however, that neither Johnson nor Ford totally ceased to make policy recommendations in their final SUAs, even though they would be leaving office in a matter of days. While the recommendations made are considerably fewer in number, they still urge a few legislative actions before they relinquish their chief legislator role.[52]

The SUA is a forum all presidents use to claim credit for outcomes. Of the policy substance presidents seek to convey, a portion of it will be devoted to credit claiming. They generally dedicate more space to claiming credit the closer they move to their reelection campaign, but circumstances such as crises can affect this activity. The only two presidents who served full

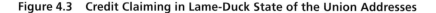

Figure 4.3   Credit Claiming in Lame-Duck State of the Union Addresses

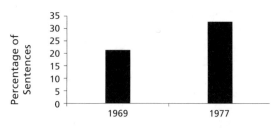

Year of State of the Union Address

second terms in our data treated credit claiming differently in their last term. We find the two highest levels of credit claiming were each obtained in lame-duck SUAs, when presidents were on their way out of office, were particularly concerned with the legacy they would leave behind, and took lengths to address it. Presidents, however, vary in their tendencies to engage in this SUA activity. As much as one-third of the SUA was devoted to this activity during the period we study, although the median percentage of space devoted to credit claiming, excluding first-year speeches, is 11.9 percent. Nixon and Ford devoted relatively little space in their SUAs to this practice, Carter's credit claiming was consistent, and Reagan's pattern varied from his first to second terms. Presidents use the SUA to claim credit differently, and this relates both to the presidents and the circumstances in which their SUA took place, a topic to which we will return.

Amount of position taking. While SUAs enable chief legislators to engage in credit claiming for reelection and legacy purposes, credit claiming can also be useful for setting the stage for their policy recommendations. When a president addresses where he wants to go in the coming year with his policy recommendations, he may incorporate an assessment of how far he has already taken the country in regard to a particular policy area. While a portion of the SUA's policy substance will be devoted to claiming credit, it generally does not make up a large percentage of the SUA. Position taking in the form of policy recommendations is another activity in which chief legislators will engage in the SUA. A far greater portion of the policy substance of the SUA is devoted to recommendations in which presidents outline where they want to go in the coming year.

An examination of the quantity of legislative requests details the extent to which presidents engage in position taking activity in the SUA. To gauge position taking, we coded all instances of presidential requests for congressional action in SUAs from 1965 to 2002.[53] Requests that were not legislative in nature, such as pledges of executive action or the president urging state actions, were not included. All legislative requests presidents made were counted, whether of a major or minor nature.[54] Requests had to be substantive legislative requests, not vague rhetoric about a policy area. For example, Clinton's 1993 address introduced broad goals of his economic recovery plan, saying it would shift "our emphasis in public and private spending from consumption to investment, initially by jumpstarting the economy in the short term and investing in our people, their jobs, and their incomes over the long run."[55] These remarks are introductory and too vague to count as any kind of congressional request for action. Later in his remarks, Clinton specifically states, "We propose a permanent investment tax credit for the smallest firms in the country, with revenues under $5 million."[56] This counts as a request for legislative action. Requests can be for positive action (do X) or for negative action (do not do X). For example, in 1996, Clinton made requests of Congress regarding both the Brady Act and the assault weapons ban, saying, "I challenge the Congress to keep those laws on the books,"[57] thus, requesting Congress not repeal them.

As Table 4.1 illustrates, presidents vary greatly in the number of requests they make in SUAs, from as few as nine in Carter's 1980 SUA, to as many as 87 in Clinton's final address. Johnson, Ford, and both presidents Bush all engage in position taking close to the median level. Four presidents, however, stand out in the way they utilized position taking. Nixon, Carter, and Reagan took positions the least, and Clinton took substantially more positions than any other president.

Nixon approached his SUAs in a manner unlike other presidents, and this contributed to the relative paucity of requests Nixon made in his speeches. In his first SUA in 1970, Nixon instructed his audience, somewhat cynically, on the purpose of the speech, "The State of the Union Address is traditionally an occasion for a lengthy and detailed account by the President of what he has accomplished in the past, what he wants the Congress to do in the future, and, in an election year, to lay the basis for the political issues which might be decisive in the fall."[58] He goes on to state that he will not follow this tradition. Rather than give details of his proposals, he will focus on what he calls "urgent priorities." In both 1970 and 1971, Nixon draws his requests from fewer policy areas than is typically the case; requests come from five and four areas, respectively (see Table 3.3). Nixon has fewer requests than are found in most SUAs and devotes more space to delving into reasons why the requests he does make are needed. Furthermore, in each of these speeches, he primarily addresses domestic policy, leaving most foreign policy issues for separate reports. His SUAs of 1972 and 1974 are unique in that he prepares a much longer "message" for the Congress on the State of the Union that he submits to them in addition to giving the oral address. The written messages, to which he refers in the SUAs, contain the details left out of the oral address, thereby streamlining it. Furthermore, Nixon's 1974 SUA has only thirteen legislative requests. As shown previously, as Nixon was embroiled in the Watergate crisis, he particularly ratcheted up his credit claiming in this SUA, devoting 20 percent of the SUA to this activity. The space and attention devoted to trying to mitigate the effects of Watergate through both claiming credit and directly addressing the situation, which he also does in this SUA, served to decrease the attention to legislative requests.

The overall level of Carter's position taking was affected by his 1980 speech; once again this particular speech turns out to be irregular. Carter makes only nine requests of Congress in that SUA, and they mostly come from the policy areas of resources and defense policy, two areas that figured heavily in the crises in Iran and Afghanistan that occurred shortly before the speech. In addition, this speech is the shortest of Carter's SUAs, containing

Table 4.1   Presidential Requests for Congressional Action, by Number, in State of the Union Addresses

	Number of Requests	Median Requests
Johnson		
1965	36	
1966	36	
1967	36	
1968	45	36.0
Nixon		
1970	17	
1971	21	
1972	19	
1974	13	18.0
Ford		
1975	29	
1976	34	31.5
Carter		
1978	18	
1979	20	
1980	9	18.0
Reagan		
1981	27	
1982	22	
1983	31	
1984	19	
1985	35	
1986	20	
1987	19	
1988	18	21.0
Bush, G. H. W.		
1989	43	
1990	29	
1991	21	
1992	38	33.5
Clinton		
1993	49	
1994	47	
1995	44	
1996	42	
1997	57	
1998	52	
1999	77	
2000	87	50.5
Bush, G. W.		
2001	33	
2002	30	31.5
Overall		31.0

only slightly more than 3,000 words. Much of the speech, however, is devoted to rhetoric meant to rally the American public during a time of international crises. Even without the influence of this speech, however, Carter had lower than normal levels of position taking in his first two

SUAs. In 1978, Carter followed the Nixon Administration's practice of sending a separate written message on the State of the Union to Congress, as well as delivering an oral address. Like Nixon, he leaves many of his legislative requests to that document rather than the oral address. In 1979, Carter discontinued the practice of issuing a companion written message, but he continued his pattern of including a low level of specific legislative requests.

Reagan also had a lower median number of legislative requests in his SUAs. As a whole, Reagan utilized much space in his SUAs explaining the current situation as he viewed it and justifying his legislative requests; this made for fewer overall legislative requests. As a conservative Republican, Reagan sought to bring a view to Washington that he felt had been long absent. As a result of this view, his SUA communications took on an educational quality as he explained and justified his policies. In 1982, Reagan spent a considerable amount of space rationalizing his program of economic recovery, which had been put in place in 1981. The country was in a recession, and Reagan explains,

> First, we must understand what's happening at the moment to the economy. Our current problems are not the product of the recovery program that's only just now getting underway, as some would have you believe; they are the inheritance of decades of tax and tax and spend and spend.
>
> Second, because our economic problems are deeply rooted and will not respond to quick political fixes, we must stick to our carefully integrated plan for recovery. That plan is based on four commonsense fundamentals: continued reduction of the growth in Federal spending; preserving the individual and business tax reductions that will stimulate saving and investment; removing unnecessary Federal regulations to spark productivity; and maintaining a healthy dollar and a stable monetary policy, the latter a responsibility of the Federal Reserve System.
>
> The only alternative being offered to this economic program is a return to the policies that gave us a trillion-dollar debt, runaway inflation, runaway interest rates and unemployment. The doubters would have us turn back the clock with tax increases that would offset the personal tax-rate reductions already passed by this Congress. Raise present taxes to cut future deficits, they tell us. Well, I don't believe we should buy that argument.[59]

Reagan's communication style was one that sought to present his alternatives as common-sense policies with which everyone ought to agree and he spent more space explaining his views than the other presidents we study. His penchant for anecdotes and the symbolic use of individuals to celebrate American heroism contributed to his rhetorical style. Finally, Reagan's last two SUAs, in which he has the two lowest levels of requests, were followed by Reagan sending more detailed written messages on specific aspects of his legislative requests to Congress. All of these factors contributed to Reagan having fewer legislative requests in his SUAs.

Unlike Nixon, Carter, and Reagan, Clinton had extraordinarily high numbers of legislative requests. Clinton's position taking is quite high throughout his two terms and increased over time. Throughout his presidency, Clinton sought to portray himself as an active chief legislator who had a grasp on a breadth of policy, seeking to lead Congress on many issues. Whereas Clinton's credit claiming was maintained in the second term rather than continuing to increase, this is not so with position taking. There is a marked difference from the first to second terms: the median number of requests for the first term is 45.5, but for the second, is 67. His number of first-term requests is still quite high, well above the median for all presidents, but it dramatically increases after the 1996 election. In Clinton's second term, considerations of legacy replaced reelection concerns as he had to continue dealing with an opposition Congress that became increasingly occupied with scandals in the White House. Clinton reacts by stressing his activity even more, using the SUA to advertise all of the things that he wanted to do. In this way, he could draw a contrast with what he wanted to accomplish and what Congress wanted to accomplish, which for a good portion of the second term revolved around investigating and impeaching the president. Clinton's position-taking strategy emphasized quantity in his final four years. He could position himself as an active chief legislator who was dealing with a recalcitrant Congress.

In examining the quantity of position taking in which presidents engage, we find that it can vary dramatically from president to president. This can partially be accounted for by differences in the way presidents approach their chief legislator role. Events, however, also impact the way chief legislators convey policy substance in their SUAs, and differences within a presidency can largely be attributed to the environment in which SUAs take place.

Our examination of the way chief legislators convey policy substance in the SUA reveals that while both credit claiming and position taking are activities of the chief legislator, all presidents do not utilize policy substance in the same fashion. Presidents approach their chief legislator roles differently. Some, such as Reagan, tend to engage in less credit claiming and position taking overall, while others, such as Clinton, engage in higher levels of each activity. Furthermore, the uses of these activities often vary depending upon the particular circumstances in which the SUA takes place. Circumstances such as an upcoming election, a crisis, or an opposition Congress may prompt a president to engage in more credit claiming than usual, or to increase the number of legislative requests made. Within the genre of SUAs, an analysis of credit claiming and position taking activities of chief legislators has revealed that there are different types of SUAs.

Types of State of the Union Addresses

All SUAs provide the president with a forum in which to act as chief legislator by reporting and recommending measures to Congress. Contemporary chief legislators use the SUA in the same fashion; they employ policymaking rhetoric to convey policy substance and use symbolism in their attempts to lead Congress. Each president puts his own stamp on the speech; each president's SUA has a character unique to that president. Within a presidency, however, we have also witnessed that the policy substance of SUAs can vary dramatically, and as we have periodically pointed out, these differences can often be attributed to the political context in which the speech is being given. Accordingly, we find that within the genre of SUAs, there are different types of speeches. The policy substance presidents convey in their SUAs is affected by the political environment in which the speech is given. SUAs are highly adaptable to serve the needs of the president and one must take into account the political context in which the speech occurs. We identify six different types of SUAs, types that are identifiable because of the political context in which they take place. Our six types, which are mutually exclusive, are inaugural, intermediate, election, lame-duck, legacy, and crisis SUAs.

Inaugural Joint Addresses to Congress

When a recently sworn in president addresses a joint session of Congress and puts forward his agenda highlights for the coming year, we have classified it as an inaugural SUA. Whereas in the past, some presidents, notably Eisenhower in 1953 and Kennedy in 1961, did call this speech an SUA, presidents in our time period did not.[60] Not all presidents choose to give a joint address shortly after being sworn into office. Neither Nixon nor Carter did, but they both followed presidents who gave lame-duck SUAs. Presidents from Reagan to G. W. Bush, however, all gave an initial speech of this type.

Inaugural SUAs are characterized by their desire to set the tone for the new administration. If the new president is of a different party than the previous one, he will emphasize how he will be different. Reagan characterized his economic recovery program as a "new beginning" and asked, "Are we simply going to go down the same path we've gone down before, carving out one special program here, another special program there?"[61] Clinton talked about embarking on a "great national journey" and stated, "Our nation needs a new direction."[62] G. W. Bush called for "a new approach for governing our great country."[63] G. H. W. Bush, however, whose administration followed into office an administration of which he had been a part, stated, "I don't propose to reverse direction. We're headed the right way, but we cannot rest."[64] These speeches are forward-looking, hopeful, and communicate the president's vision, and at the same time, they draw upon the past as they remind Americans of shared history, values, and experiences.

Since presidents giving this type of speech are new, there will be little to no claiming credit in the speech. Neither presidents Bush nor Clinton claimed credit for any actions, but Reagan did claim credit for an executive order he had recently signed regarding the regulatory process.[65] There will, however, be an ample amount of position taking as the president highlights agenda items his new administration wants to tackle. Of the presidents giving inaugural SUAs, three of the four have requests that number above their own median number of requests. Clinton, the exception, has 49 requests in his initial speech, slightly below his median 50.5, but well above the overall median of 31 requests for all SUAs. The first year is a critical juncture for presidents.[66] It is this period when they have the most leeway with Congress, and it is important they articulate the policy items on which they want to lead.

Intermediate SUAs

Twelve of the thirty-seven SUAs we study can be classified as intermediate SUAs, which are SUAs in the second and third years of a president's first term.[67] When presidents go before Congress to report on the state of the Union in the second and third year of their first term, they have been engaged in the business of governing and have accomplishments for which they can claim credit. Intermediate SUAs have moderate levels of credit claiming; a median 10.3 percent of the sentences are devoted to this activity.[68] During this point in their presidency, presidents are pursuing an active agenda with an eye toward both securing reelection and a positive legacy. The amount of position taking in these SUAs is typically moderate as well. There is a median of 30 legislative requests in this type of SUA, the median for all SUAs being 31.

Election-Year SUAs

Six of our SUAs are given in years in which the president is seeking reelection or election in his own right.[69] In these SUAs, presidents will generally make the case for their reelection or election, but not in an overt manner. They will do this by stressing their accomplishments while in office as well as using their legislative requests to signal themes for their reelection campaign. Credit claiming in election year SUAs is higher than the median of all SUAs (13.2 percent versus 10.7 percent), but it is somewhat restrained, as we do not encounter the highest levels of credit claiming in these SUAs. It is, however, slightly higher than SUAs as a whole. Presidents do not turn the SUA into a stump speech, but they certainly devote a bit more space to claiming credit for their accomplishments. Presidents in election-year SUAs also include a few more legislative requests than is typical, with a median of 36 requests per SUA.

Presidents may also refer to the upcoming election in these SUAs. If so, it is done in a way that exemplifies their role as the legislator with a national constituency and emphasizes a need to put partisanship aside. Johnson's 1968 SUA includes a mention of the upcoming election, and even though he governed during a period in which the Democrats controlled Congress, he stresses bipartisanship.

> Each of these questions I have discussed with you tonight is a question of policy for our people. Therefore, each of them should be—and doubtless will be—debated by candidates for public office this year.
>
> I hope those debates will be marked by new proposals and by a seriousness that matches the gravity of the questions themselves.
>
> These are not appropriate subjects for narrow partisan oratory. They go to the heart of what we Americans are all about—all of us, Democrats and Republicans.[70]

In 1972, Nixon especially stresses a need to focus on a national perspective, suitable for one representing a national constituency, before mentioning the upcoming election.

> However, there are great national problems that are so vital that they transcend partisanship. So let us have our debates. Let us have our honest differences. But let us join in keeping the national interest first. Let us join in making sure that legislation the Nation needs does not become hostage to the political interests of any party or any person.
>
> There is ample precedent, in this election year, for me to present you with a huge list of new proposals, knowing full well that there would not be any possibility of your passing them if you worked night and day. I shall not do that.[71]

He is true to his word and does not include an inordinate number of legislative requests. With just 19 requests for congressional action, he is well below the median for election-year SUAs. George H. W. Bush, however, is a bit more combative in urging Congress to work with him in a bipartisan fashion in the election year of 1992.

> Let's be frank. Let me level with you. I know and you know that my plan is unveiled in a political season. I know and you know that everything I propose will be viewed by some in merely partisan terms. But I ask you to know what is in my heart. And my aim is to increase our Nation's good. I'm doing what I think is right, and I am proposing what I know will help.
>
> I pride myself that I'm a prudent man, and I believe that patience is a

virtue. But I understand that politics is, for some, a game and that sometimes the game is to stop all progress and then decry the lack of improvement. But let me tell you: Far more important than my political future and
far more important than yours is the well-being of our country. Members
of this Chamber are practical people, and I know you won't resent some
practical advice. When people put their party's fortunes, whatever the
party, whatever side of this aisle, before the public good, they court defeat
not only for their country but for themselves. And they will certainly
deserve it.[72]

By increasing space devoted to claiming credit for accomplishments, incorporating slightly higher levels of legislative requests, and stressing bipartisan efforts in the context of the election, chief legislators use their election-
year SUAs to position themselves for a successful election without making
the SUA a blatant appeal for reelection. The functions of every SUA are
suited for fulfilling reelection/legacy goals. Presidents in an election year,
therefore, can stay within the normal framework of SUAs and simply
increase the attention to credit claiming and position taking that serves their
desire to be reelected.

Lame-Duck SUAs

Lame-duck SUAs are given by presidents who are leaving office within the
month. Only two presidents, Johnson and Ford, give oral SUAs as lame
ducks.[73] These SUAs prove to be very reflective and are given at a time
when the president is very conscious of legacy considerations; it is one of
his last opportunities to address the Congress and the public. In these SUAs,
the presidents stress their accomplishments in a way unlike what we found
in any other SUA. The highest levels of credit claiming occur in these
addresses. Johnson devotes slightly more than one-fifth of his speech to this
activity, while Ford devotes one-third of his final SUA to credit claiming.
While lame-duck SUAs afford presidents final opportunity to advertise their
accomplishments, these SUAs also allow them to acknowledge their disappointments. And, even though they will not be in office during the session
of Congress they are addressing, these lame-duck chief legislators still recommend legislative actions, generally ones tied to the disappointments they
have had. Johnson in particular discusses the aspects of his domestic policy
that were not completed or fully funded. Ford laments the lack of a comprehensive energy policy and the little that was accomplished in the way of
organizational reforms at the federal government level. Each gives specific
recommendations pertaining to these unfulfilled requests. Even outgoing
chief legislators did not give up the goal of making public policy.

Finally, Johnson's and Ford's lame-duck SUAs each closed on an especially sentimental and personal note. Both had served in Congress and been

in the congressional leadership before becoming president. Each mentioned by name members of Congress with whom they have been long acquainted and worked with both when in Congress and as president. In this sense, these SUAs function as both SUAs and farewell addresses. Not all final-year SUAs are lame-duck SUAs, we should note. While Presidents Reagan and Clinton gave SUAs in their last year in office, they did so at the beginning of their final year, not when they were leaving office in a matter of mere days. Those speeches do not obtain the qualities of a lame-duck address.

Legacy SUAs

We identified six SUAs in presidential second terms that we classify as legacy SUAs. In the fifth and following years of presidential terms, presidents increasingly have an eye fixed on the legacy they will leave behind once they leave office. Reagan's 1985, 1986, and 1988 SUAs as well as Clinton's 1997, 1999, and 2000 SUAs classify as this type of SUA.[74] Reagan and Clinton treat both the level of credit claiming and quantity of legislative requests differently in their legacy SUAs. Reagan engages in these activities at a considerably reduced rate than in his intermediate SUAs, whereas Clinton's credit claiming is roughly the same as in his intermediate SUAs, and the quantity of his legislative requests is much higher. Reagan's legacy SUAs contain fewer requests (median of 20) when compared both with his own intermediate SUAs (median 26.5) as well as intermediate SUAs in general (median 30). Reagan did not request much that was new in his second term. He repeatedly asked for things such as the line-item veto, constitutional amendments allowing for school prayer, the protection of the unborn, and a balanced budget, as well as various spending cuts. Clinton, on the other hand, had a different approach in legacy SUAs. In sheer quantity of legislative requests, Clinton's legacy SUAs outpace every other president with a median 77 requests. One of the things affecting the increased number of requests in the second term are events that happened in his first term. Beginning with his 1995 SUA, the nature of Clinton's legislative requests changed and carried over into his second term, which affected the number of requests he made. The 1994 election and the failure of his health-care reform humbled Clinton. Referring to the demise of that reform, he states, "we bit off more than we could chew. So I'm asking you that we work together. Let's do it step by step."[75] His legislative requests became more incremental and smaller in scope. After the defeat of large-scale health-care reform, Clinton advocates incremental health-care changes for the rest of his tenure, things such as insurance portability,[76] ending drive-through mastectomies,[77] letting 55- to 65-year-olds buy into Medicare,[78] and allowing the disabled to keep Medicare coverage if they return to work.[79] Incremental requests also carried over into policy areas beyond health care. The effect of this strategy was to increase the number of legislative requests Clinton made of Congress. In addition, this strategy could help Clinton portray himself as an active chief legislator, especially when dealing with an opposition Congress that wanted to stymie much of his agenda.

In one significant way, Reagan and Clinton used their legacy SUAs in a similar fashion. As noted in Chapter 3, Reagan and Clinton increased the percentage of their legislative requests coming from the defense and foreign policy areas in their second term. This is true of the second-term SUAs we classify as legacy SUAs. Reagan especially concentrates more of his legislative requests in the foreign and defense policy areas, drawing a median 27.8 percent of his requests from these areas in his legacy SUAs. Clinton also increases his requests from these areas, obtaining a median 15.6 percent. The median number of requests from foreign and defense policy areas in intermediate SUAs is just below 10 percent. As presidents' reelection goals are replaced by legacy goals in second terms, they can increase their focus on making foreign and defense policy requests, which they might have paid less attention to in intermediate SUAs, where reelection is a concern and the constituency on which reelection depends tends to care more about domestic policy.

Crisis SUAs

Crisis SUAs can occur at any time within a presidential term. The effect of a crisis on the SUA makes the speech unique even though under normal circumstances its time frame might dictate it be in another category. Crisis SUAs are outliers and tend to have unique characteristics and objectives. In addition, the crises that presidents deal with are of different natures. There are three types of crisis SUAs we identify; in all of them, presidents use their rhetoric to rally audiences. The nature of the crisis, however, is different, and each type of crisis SUA is differentiated by the object around which the president seeks to rally his audiences. One type pertains to an SUA being delivered in a time of international crisis, where the rhetoric of the SUA is utilized to rally the audiences around the flag.[80] Presidents employ emotional appeals that seek to capitalize on the public's patriotism as they lead the country through the crisis. Three SUAs are identified as this type: Carter's of 1980, G. H. W. Bush's of 1991, and G. W. Bush's of 2002. The second type of crisis SUA is one where the president seeks to rally audiences around the presidency itself. Ford's 1975 SUA is the only example we have of this type of SUA. The final type of crisis SUA we encounter is one where the president seeks to rally audiences to himself due to a crisis brought on by presidential actions. Nixon's 1974, Reagan's 1987, and Clinton's 1998 SUAs are all of this type.

Rally-round-the-flag SUAs. When SUAs closely follow an international crisis, there is a disproportionate amount of attention given to the crisis in the speech. When a rally-round-the-flag SUA is given, much of the text addresses the crisis, often in language that might be termed *rally rhetoric,* specifically encouraging the nation to rally round the flag, and this rhetoric may displace other functions. Presidents do not have unlimited time to address their audiences in the SUA. While some SUAs are longer than others, a president cannot continue on indefinitely. The presence of international crises affects the way presidents engage in credit claiming and position taking. As a whole, there are higher levels of credit claiming in these SUAs than in normal SUAs. Increases in rally rhetoric and credit claiming leave less space for other activities, and there is a corresponding decrease in the number of legislative requests presidents make of Congress in these types of SUAs. Requests, though fewer in number, are focused more on foreign and defense policy areas when compared with that president's previous SUA (see Table 3.3). Each president, however, addresses the crisis he faces a bit differently in his SUA, as the nature of each crisis is unique.

Carter's 1980 speech is a prime example of a rally-round-the-flag SUA. In November of 1979, American hostages were taken in Tehran, Iran, beginning a period of captivity that would extend 444 days. In late December 1979, Soviet forces invaded Afghanistan. Carter explains the challenges these two events presented the United States in his January 21, 1980, SUA.

> Three basic developments have helped to shape our challenges: the steady growth and increased projection of Soviet military power beyond its own borders; the overwhelming dependence of the Western democracies on oil supplies from the Middle East; and the press of social and religious and economic and political change in the many nations of the developing world, exemplified by the revolution in Iran.
>
> Each of these factors is important in its own right. Each interacts with the others. All must be faced together, squarely and courageously. We will face these challenges, and we will meet them with the best that is in us. And we will not fail.[81]

Carter's SUA takes on a very combative tone as he tries to deal with the effect of these two events and portray himself as a tough, resolute leader. With regard to the situation in Iran, he states that "our Nation has never been aroused and unified so greatly in peacetime. Our position is clear. The United States will not yield to blackmail."[82] In specifically addressing the challenge posed by the Soviet's movement toward the Middle East, Carter says,

> Meeting this challenge will take national will, diplomatic and political wisdom, economic sacrifice, and, of course, military capability. We must call on the best that is in us to preserve the security of this crucial region.

> Let our position be absolutely clear: An attempt by any outside force to gain control of the Persian Gulf region will be regarded as an assault on the vital interests of the United States of America, and such an assault will be repelled by any means necessary, including military force.[83]

He ends by exhorting, "Together as one people; let us work to build our strength at home, and together as one indivisible union, let us seek peace and security throughout the world. Together let us make of this time of challenge and danger a decade of national resolve and of brave achievement."[84] Carter's speech is primarily about rallying the nation and reflects the country's indignation at the occurrence of these international events.

The vast majority of Carter's 1980 SUA is devoted to discussing items stemming from these crises. Carter devotes only seven paragraphs of this SUA to a discussion of purely domestic policies unconnected to the crises. This SUA actually contains Carter's lowest percentage of credit claiming. Carter's three SUAs, however, all had relatively high levels of this activity. Of the 1980 SUA, he devoted 14 percent of the speech to credit claiming, about 3 percent more than the typical SUA. 1980 is also an election year, but Carter does not have increased levels of credit claiming. Nor does Carter devote lots of space to his legislative requests, as he has only nine of them, the least of any SUA we analyze. Carter's rallying rhetoric takes up space that might have been devoted to more credit claiming and policy recommendations in a normal election year SUA.

George H. W. Bush has a crisis SUA in 1991, which was given shortly after the first Gulf War began. The Iraqi invasion of Kuwait took place in August 1990.[85] Over the fall, the coalition of countries to dispel Saddam Hussein from Kuwait was put together. The air war portion of Operation Desert Storm began on January 16, 1991.[86] Bush gave his SUA on January 29, 1991. Unlike Carter's 1980 speech, however, the crisis effect does not depress credit claiming; this is the SUA in which Bush's credit claiming peaks. This differing effect can be attributed to the fact that the crises of 1980 and 1991 were different in character, and presidential actions were different as well. Carter was dealing with external events beyond his control whose proximity to the speech did not allow for much reaction time. By the time of Bush's 1991 speech, five months after Saddam Hussein invaded Kuwait, he does have things related to the crisis for which he can take credit.

> The world has said this aggression would not stand, and it will not stand. Together, we have resisted the trap of appeasement, cynicism, and isolation that gives temptation to tyrants. The world has answered Saddam's invasion with 12 United Nations resolutions, starting with a demand for Iraq's immediate and unconditional withdrawal, and backed up by forces from 28 countries of 6 continents. With few exceptions, the world now stands as one.[87]

Bush's 1991 SUA is shaped by the crisis at hand and includes a significant amount of rhetoric meant to rally the nation behind his actions related to Iraq. Bush opens his 1991 SUA by asserting why the United States is in the Persian Gulf.

> Halfway around the world, we are engaged in a great struggle in the skies and on the seas and sands. We know why we're there: We are Americans, part of something larger than ourselves. For two centuries, we've done the hard work of freedom. And tonight, we lead the world in facing down a threat to decency and humanity.
>
> What is at stake is more than one small country; it is a big idea: a new world order, where diverse nations are drawn together in common cause to achieve the universal aspirations of mankind—peace and security, freedom, and the rule of law. Such is a world worthy of our struggle and worthy of our children's future.[88]

He concludes his SUA by maintaining,

> We will succeed in the Gulf. And when we do, the world community will have sent an enduring warning to any dictator or despot, present or future, who contemplates outlaw aggression. The world can, therefore, seize this opportunity to fulfill the long-held promise of a new world order, where brutality will go unrewarded and aggression will meet collective resistance.
>
> Yes, the United States bears a major share of leadership in this effort. Among the nations of the world, only the United States of America has both the moral standing and the means to back it up. We're the only nation on this Earth that could assemble the forces of peace. This is the burden of leadership and the strength that has made America the beacon of freedom in a searching world.[89]

The crisis does provide the background for the SUA, but the crisis does not dominate to the exclusion of virtually everything else, as in Carter's 1980 SUA. There is plenty of rhetoric to rally the nation, and there is more credit claiming in this SUA (15.2 percent) than in both SUAs as a whole (10.7 percent) and in Bush's other SUAs. High levels of rally rhetoric and credit claiming make for less attention to legislative requests. Bush has the least number of requests of his presidency in this SUA, and of these requests, more are from the areas of defense and foreign policy than in Bush's previous SUAs (see Table 3.3).

The final rally-round-the-flag SUA is George W. Bush's 2002 speech given four months after the events of September 11, 2001. While Bush did not need to do much to rally the nation to the flag in January 2002, nevertheless, his rhetoric is stark in its attempt to do just that. "Our enemies believed America was weak and materialistic, that we would splinter in fear and selfishness. They were as wrong as they are evil."[90] Bush stresses the activities the administration has been engaged in during the war on terror and devotes one-fifth of the SUA to the activity of credit claiming.

> Our progress [in Afghanistan] is a tribute to the spirit of the Afghan peo-ple, to the resolve of our coalition, and to the might of the United States military. When I called our troops into action, I did so with complete con-fidence in their courage and skill. And tonight, thanks to them, we are win-ning the war on terror. The men and women of our Armed Forces have delivered a message now clear to every enemy of the United States: Even 7,000 miles away, across oceans and continents, on mountaintops and in caves—you will not escape the justice of this nation.[91]

He makes 30 specific legislative requests of Congress, slightly less than his inaugural SUA, and 26.7 percent of those requests are in the area of foreign and defense policy, almost double the percentage of requests from these areas in his previous SUA.

Rally-round-the-presidency SUA. Ford's 1975 SUA is a valiant attempt to rally the nation to the institution of the presidency itself. After having been sworn into office in August 1974 following Nixon's resignation from the presidency, Ford delivers his first SUA in January 1975. Ford's popular-ity had plummeted after his pardon of Nixon one month after taking office,[92] and Democrats strengthened their majorities in Congress in the November 1974 election.[93] The lingering effects of the Arab oil embargo of 1973–1974 still had the United States in the midst of an energy crisis, and this plays a role in Ford's SUA as well. Ford flatly declared in the 1975 SUA, "I must say to you that the State of the Union is not good."[94] He goes on to say, "Now, I want to speak very bluntly. I've got bad news, and I don't expect much, if any, applause. The American people want action, and it will take both the Congress and the President to give them what they want. Progress and solutions can be achieved, and they will be achieved."[95] As one might expect given this language and the fact Ford has only been in office a few months, he devotes very little space to claiming credit—about 1 percent. Even though it is his first SUA, Ford has fewer requests in this SUA than in his subsequent one. He follows Nixon's practice of sending some of his specific recommendations to Congress in separate written mes-sages.

The language and tone Ford incorporates in this SUA are colored by the state of the presidency. Confidence in the institution has been roiled by Watergate. He uses very assertive language in his legislative proposals and he emphasizes the actions he will undertake without Congress throughout his speech. First, he states, "I am using Presidential powers to raise the fee on all imported crude oil and petroleum products."[96] Later, he asserts, "I plan to take presidential initiative to decontrol the price of domestic crude oil on April 1."[97] Near the end of the SUA, Ford contends, "I am prepared to use presidential authority to limit imports, as necessary to guarantee success."[98] Ford also reminds his audiences of his veto power, saying "I vetoed the strip mining legislation passed by the last Congress,"[99] and "I will not hesitate to veto any new spending programs adopted by the Congress."[100] This would be a harbinger of things to come, as Ford would veto sixty-six items in the course of his short presidency.[101]

At the same time Ford is asserting presidential authority, he also makes many separate appeals for Congress and the president to work together. Consider the following examples:

> The moment has come to move in a new direction. We can do this by fashioning a new partnership between the Congress on the one hand, the White House on the other, and the people we both represent.[102]

And,

> But we have serious problems before us that require cooperation between the President and the Congress.[103]

However, given Ford's assertive language and emphasis on the unilateral actions he will take, his view of cooperation with Congress might be better captured when he states,

> If the Congress and the American people will work with me to attain these targets, they will be achieved and will be surpassed. From adversity, let us seize opportunity.[104]

He does not say he will work with Congress, but rather Congress needs to work with him.

Finally, as Ford closes out his SUA, he addresses the presidency and the situation in which the institution finds itself.

> In recent years, under the stress of the Vietnam war, legislative restrictions on the President's ability to execute foreign policy and military decisions have proliferated. As a Member of the Congress, I opposed some and I approved others. As President, I welcome the advice and cooperation of the House and the Senate.
>   But if our foreign policy is to be successful, we cannot rigidly restrict in legislation the ability of the President to act. . . .
>   For my part, I pledge this Administration will act in the closest consultation with the Congress as we face delicate situations and troubled times throughout the globe.
>   When I became President only 5 months ago, I promised the last Congress a policy of communication, conciliation, compromise, and cooperation. I renew that pledge to the new Members of this Congress.[105]

Ford's 1975 SUA makes a concerted effort to boost the institution of the presidency in the eyes of both the Congress and the public, while at the same time protecting the powers of the institution. Ford is concerned with the recently assertive Congress and the erosion of presidential power. He stresses cooperation with Congress, but cooperation in which the president leads. By using assertive language and emphasizing presidential prerogatives, he seeks to restore the executive's view of the proper balance between the legislative and executive branches.

Rally-round-the-president SUAs. The final type of crisis SUA we identify is one in which the president is embroiled in scandal and seeks to use the SUA to rally audiences around himself. Each president confronts a different type of crisis, each deals with it differently in their SUA, and each result is unique. All, however, seek to mitigate the fallout of the scandal with their SUAs.

Our first example of this type of crisis SUA is Nixon's 1974 speech, given on January 30. At the time of what would turn out to be Nixon's final SUA, criticism of the president was substantial. The "Saturday Night Massacre" occurred on October 20, 1973. Both the attorney general and deputy attorney general resigned rather than fire special prosecutor Archibald Cox (as Nixon had ordered), who was eventually fired by acting Attorney General Robert Bork.[106] It is this event that was instrumental in moving the discussion of impeachment forward in the halls of Congress. On January 4, 1974, a few weeks before the SUA, Nixon sent a letter to the Chair of the Senate Select Committee on Presidential Campaign Activities, involved in investigating Watergate, in which he responded to the committee's broad subpoenas of presidential tapes from the Oval Office. In this letter, Nixon asserts the tapes are privileged and will not be produced.[107] It is in this environment that the 1974 SUA would take place.

Nixon's 1974 SUA is especially unique because Nixon uses a substantial portion of the SUA to claim credit for various accomplishments in a way that he had not done previously. One-fifth of Nixon's SUA was devoted to the activity of credit claiming. This is almost double the amount of space the typical SUA devotes to this activity. Furthermore, Nixon claiming credit at this level was inconsistent with the pattern in his earlier SUAs; his 1972 election-year SUA devoted only 9 percent of the address to this activity. Furthermore, there are only 13 legislative requests in the 1974 SUA, the second smallest number of all the SUAs we analyze. Nixon's strategy for rallying the nation to the president was one of emphasizing his achievements. Rather than looking forward, Nixon chose to look backward to a large degree.

Nixon closes his 1974 SUA by directly addressing the "elephant in the room," Watergate. He begins by stating, "Mr. Speaker, and Mr. President, and my distinguished colleagues and our guests: I would like to add a personal word with regard to an issue that has been of great concern to all Americans over the past year. I refer, of course to the investigations of the so-called Watergate affair."[108] For the next six paragraphs, Nixon recognizes the "special responsibility" of the House Judiciary Committee, the committee in whose jurisdiction impeachment lies, and says he will cooperate so that the investigations may end. He adds,

> There is one limitation. I will follow the precedent that has been followed by and defended by every President from George Washington to Lyndon B. Johnson of never doing anything that weakens the Office of the President of the United States or impairs the ability of the Presidents of the future to make the great decisions that are so essential to this Nation and the world.[109]

Nixon refers here to the principle of executive privilege. He continues,

> Another point I should like to make very briefly: Like every Member of the House and Senate assembled here tonight, I was elected to the office that I hold. And like every Member of the House and Senate, when I was elected to that office, I knew that I was elected for the purpose of doing a job and doing it as well as I possibly can. And I want you to know that I have no intention whatever of ever walking away from the job that the people elected me to do for the people of the Untied States.[110]

Nixon stresses the legitimacy of his presidency by referring to his election, something held in common with the legislators. He would, however, not be able to carry through on his intentions to stay in the White House, and he resigned the presidency less than seven months later. Nevertheless, Nixon used the forum of the SUA in an attempt to rally forces around his beleaguered presidency.

Reagan's situation in 1987 was not as dire as Richard Nixon's was in 1974 when he delivered his SUA. However, Iran-Contra represented a serious crisis confronting the Reagan Administration. News reports in the fall of 1986 were relaying stories of an arms for hostages deal with Iran. Reagan gave a televised address to the nation on November 13, 1986, in which he denied a weapons for hostage scheme but did reveal a "secret diplomatic initiative to Iran."[111] By the end of the month, however, Reagan held a briefing in which he stated that a requested report from Attorney General Edwin Meese has "led me to conclude that I was not fully informed on the nature of one of the activities undertaken in connection with [policy toward Iran]. This action raises serious questions of propriety."[112] This action, although not specified by Reagan in the briefing, was the funneling of proceeds from weapons sales to the Contra rebels in Nicaragua.[113] The next day, Reagan appointed a special review board to be headed by former

Senator John Tower to investigate the matter.[114] Shortly thereafter, an independent counsel was named.[115] In this environment, Reagan delivers his 1987 SUA on January 27.

Reagan's rally-round-the-president SUA does not show increased levels of credit claiming; in fact, only about 8 percent of the speech is devoted to this activity, 2 percent below the median level for all SUAs and certainly below levels for most crisis SUAs. As is typical in a crisis SUA, Reagan has a low level of legislative requests, only 19. In this case, the relatively low level of requests is not due to more space being devoted to credit claiming. It is due, however, to space devoted to rhetoric Reagan uses to explain and justify his positions, especially his foreign policy goals. This particular crisis affects the 1987 SUA, though in a unique way.

In the 1987 SUA, Reagan uses a discussion of the Iran-Contra controversy as a lead in to the foreign policy section with which he begins his SUA. Modern presidents typically discuss domestic policy at the beginning of their SUA and leave foreign policy to the end. Reagan followed this practice in all of his SUAs, except the one in 1987. In this rally-round-the-president SUA, Reagan opens his foreign policy section at the beginning of the SUA with a statement about Iran-Contra.

> But though we've made much progress [in our position in the world], I have one major regret. I took a risk with regard to our action in Iran. It did not work, and for that I assume full responsibility.
>
> The goals were worthy. I do not believe it was wrong to try to establish contacts with a country of strategic importance or to try to save lives. And certainly it was not wrong to try to secure freedom for our citizens held in barbaric captivity. But we did not achieve what we wished, and serious mistakes were made in trying to do so. We will get to the bottom of this, and I will take whatever action is called for.[116]

As noted earlier, Reagan's SUAs have an educational tone; Reagan generally spoke very plainly and explained his reasons and rationales in a manner very much geared toward his public audience. His explanation above regarding Iran-Contra in the SUA, however, is quite vague (as was the previous statement from the briefing quoted earlier). He mentions only Iran and is not specific as to the mistakes that were made. This statement does serve, however, as a springboard that launches Reagan into a justification of his foreign policy, specifically relating to his anticommunist stances. Reagan's foreign policy was under extreme criticism, and he uses the SUA to defend it. He continues, "But in debating the past . . . , we must not deny ourselves the successes of the future. Let it never be said of this generation of Americans that we became so obsessed with failure that we refused to take risks that could further the cause of peace and freedom in the world."[117] He justifies presidential risk taking, which is how he began the statement on Iran. From here Reagan launches into an educational treatise on the state of communism in the world. He then criticizes Congress for cutting his foreign aid and defense requests. He invokes the Monroe Doctrine and quotes three Democratic presidents' statements on fighting communism in the Western Hemisphere. Finally, he arrives at a point where he addresses Nicaragua for several paragraphs. The section on Nicaragua ends with Reagan saying "Nicaraguan freedom fighters have never asked us to wage their battle, but I will fight any effort to shut off their lifeblood and consign them to death, defeat, or a life without freedom. There must be no Soviet beachhead in Central America."[118] Thus, at the beginning of the foreign policy section, Reagan accepts responsibility for the risk he took with respect to Iran; but, by the end of his foreign policy section, he addresses his feeling toward the Contras in such a way that can be read as a justification of administration actions in the pursuit of fighting communism. He uses the 1987 SUA in an attempt to rally the public around him and his foreign policy, especially the most controversial aspect of it tied to the crisis, support for the Contras.

Unlike Nixon's and Reagan's rally-round-the-president SUAs, Clinton does not mention the event responsible for the crisis confronting the president as he was giving his 1998 SUA. On January 17, 1998, Clinton gave a deposition in the Paula Jones sexual harassment case, the first time a sitting president had ever given testimony in his own defense.[119] Four days later, it was revealed independent counsel Kenneth Starr was investigating whether the president suborned perjury in the Jones case by denying an affair with former White House intern Monica Lewinsky, as well as urging her to lie about the affair to lawyers in the Jones case.[120] On that day, Clinton gave several media interviews in which he denied having a sexual relationship with Lewinsky.[121] The day before Clinton would give his SUA, he made a more forceful denial of an affair with the intern.

> But I want to say one thing to the American people. I want you to listen to me. I'm going to say this again. I did not have sexual relations with that woman, Miss Lewinsky. I never told anybody to lie, not a single time— never. These allegations are false. And I need to go back to work for the American people.[122]

When Clinton delivered his SUA on January 27, he did not address the allegations and ongoing investigation of his presidency. Nevertheless, the speech did attempt to rally audiences behind the president. Clinton, as the above quote makes clear, viewed the expanding Starr investigation as a distraction from governing. In the 1998 SUA, Clinton chooses to emphasize both what he had done in the past, through credit claiming, as well as what he hoped to do in the future, through his legislative recommendations.

While most presidents giving crisis SUAs will emphasize their past actions, Clinton is unique in the way he incorporates a high number of legislative requests in addition. Sixteen percent of the SUA is devoted to sentences claiming credit, the highest amount of Clinton's second term. Clinton also makes 52 requests for legislative action, which is only slightly above the median number of requests he makes in his SUAs (50.5), but is well above the number of requests of the other crisis SUAs. Because of the nature of the crisis Clinton was confronting, something he viewed as personal and a distraction to governing, he emphasized action—the administration's actions in the past as well as proposed ones for the future—as he sought to rally audiences to his presidency.

We should note that we did not classify Clinton's 1999 address as a crisis SUA, even though it was given in the midst of Clinton's impeachment trial in the Senate. As the *Washington Post* reported at the time of Clinton's acquittal in February, "For such a momentous occasion, though, the verdict was anticlimactic. The trial began five weeks ago with no suggestion that conviction was a realistic possibility."[123] Thus, rather than being an SUA focused on rallying audiences to support the president himself, it was a speech focused on Clinton's legacy. At the time of the 1999 SUA, Clinton had been impeached by the House of Representatives, something that would forever be noted in any assessment of his legacy. With conviction in the Senate being a remote possibility, Clinton could turn his attention to legacy concerns rather than mitigating the effects of the trial, the end result of which was virtually a foregone conclusion. The way he chose to do this was through an extraordinarily high level (77) of legislative requests through which he could emphasize the quantity of things he wanted to accomplish. He could also contrast the active nature of his agenda for the coming year with that of Congress's agenda for the last year, which had been focused on impeachment to the exclusion of much else.

There are differences among these three presidents in the way they used their policy substance in the rally-round-the-president SUAs. Nixon and Clinton had high levels of credit claiming, whereas Reagan did not. Nixon and Reagan had low levels of position taking, whereas Clinton did not. The nature of the crises the presidents were confronting varied, and the strategies used to deal with them varied as well. But, all used the SUA to try to affect the fallout of the scandal with which the administration was dealing. Crisis SUAs of all types still function as SUAs; in their policymaking rhetoric, presidents convey policy substance by claiming credit and recommending specific measures to Congress. The context of the crisis, however, affects what the president says in the SUA, just as the context of an election year or being a lame duck will affect the substantive rhetoric.

For contemporary presidents, the SUA represents an opportunity. All chief legislators appear before Congress near the beginning of the congressional session to engage in the very same activities. The attention of the nation, and even the world, is focused upon them. In this speech, where they fulfill their constitutional duties of reporting and recommending measures to Congress, they have substantial power to focus attention on accomplishments and proposals. All presidents claim credit for achievements and request legislative action from Congress. All SUAs are the same in this regard. The policy substance presidents convey in SUAs is tactical. By presenting things the way they do, they hope to gain an advantage in their ability to lead Congress. They use their substantive rhetoric to fulfill goals they have as chief legislator. Presidents employ tactics differently, and this is dictated by both the individual nature of the president as well as the political context in which the SUA occurs. Our examination of how presidents use SUAs has revealed that SUAs come in different types depending on the political environment confronting presidents.[124] The environments cause chief legislators to adapt their SUAs in similar ways. When chief legislators give what we call the inaugural SUA, they set the tone for their new administration and will particularly draw distinctions between themselves and the previous administration if there was a change in party. They engage in virtually no credit claiming, as there will be few accomplishments in the weeks-old administration. They must hit the ground running, however, so there will be relatively high levels of position taking. As presidents move into their second and third years, they give what we term intermediate SUAs. If there is a "typical" SUA, it is of this type. Both credit claiming and position taking occur at close to the median level. Election-year SUAs find presidents implicitly making their case for reelection. They want to stress their accomplishments, so they increase the level of credit claiming. They want to show they have an active agenda, so the level of legislative requests increase, as well. If they mention the election in their SUA, they will do so in a manner that stresses bipartisanship and the national interest, reflecting the fact they represent a national constituency. Presidents who give lame-duck SUAs are particularly focused on their legacy and engage in very high levels of credit claiming. While they have little reason to make legislative requests of a Congress they will not be leading, they still engage in a small amount of this activity; they do not abandon their goal of affecting public policy, even as they are on their way out the door. These SUAs also function as farewell addresses and tend to include sentimental and personal reflections from the president. Legacy SUAs occur in second terms, where presidents no longer need to focus on reelection goals, but can turn those energies toward securing a positive legacy. Both Reagan and Clinton differed in their levels of credit claiming and position taking in their second terms. Reagan's credit claiming and position taking decreased, whereas Clinton's position taking noticeably increased. Both presidents, however, gave more attention than they did in their first terms to legislative requests from the foreign and defense policy areas. Finally, crisis SUAs are the wild cards of SUAs. They tend to have unique characteristics, but all have the objective of using rhetoric to rally audiences around an object, which might be the flag, the presidency, or the president, himself. The way in which different presidents deal with the crises they confront in their SUAs depends on the president and the nature of the crisis.

Conclusion

American presidents operate in a system of shared powers. In addition to powers they have by virtue of being the head of the executive branch, they share a measure of legislative power with Congress. The Constitution gives presidents the qualified veto, the ability to give information and recommend measures to Congress, to call Congress into special session, and to set adjournment if Congress does not agree on a time. The legislative powers the Constitution gives presidents have not changed. Over time, however, presidents gained the role of chief legislator. The move to an orally delivered SUA before a joint session of Congress, later broadcast over the airwaves to the American public, was instrumental in the development of this role, enabling presidents to play an enhanced role at the beginning and middle of the legislative process. The contemporary SUA exemplifies why we call the president chief legislator. We see the president appear before Congress and his constituency, giving the appearance that he is the center of government. With his policymaking rhetoric, he offers leadership on policy solutions for national problems. The speech is a vital tool of political communication for the chief legislator.

As presidents don the hat of chief legislator in the SUA, they use the speech to help them fulfill goals they share with regular legislators, specifically goals to secure reelection and make public policy. The SUA extends the ability of presidents to promote their policy goals and cultivate public support, and it demonstrates that the chief legislator behaves in a manner similar to regular legislators. Presidents also have a desire to secure a positive legacy, and this is tied to the legislative victories they can secure. As part of the substantive rhetoric of SUAs, presidents claim credit for accomplishments and take positions on policy, two activities in which regular legislators engage for reelection purposes. For the chief legislator, these activities also aid them in securing a positive legacy and in their desire to make public policy.

In our analysis of how chief legislators use the SUA, we find that while all presidents engage in credit claiming and position taking in their SUAs to help them fulfill their goals as chief legislator, they individually differ in their use of these activities. Within a presidency, as well, there can be significant differences in the way a president uses these activities. As presidents confront different political circumstances, the activities of the SUA that help them fulfill their goals as chief legislator are adapted to fit the political time. Presidents tend to behave similarly when confronted with similar circumstances, as in their inaugural, intermediate, election, lameduck, or legacy SUAs. Crises, however, present unique circumstances for presidents to confront in their SUAs. With crisis SUAs, all presidents seek to use rhetoric to rally their audiences, but the rallying object varies depending on the nature of the crisis, and the means presidents use to rally audiences vary as well.

How do chief legislators utilize the substantive rhetoric of the SUA? They use it tactically, employing credit claiming and position taking to maximize their ability to influence public policy. Whereas legislators, as premised by Mayhew, primarily seek reelection, chief legislators seek three mutually reinforcing goals. The ultimate goal is to be successful with their policymaking rhetoric, that is, to get their wishes on their public policy preferences. They also want to be reelected to a second term; they can no longer make public policy if this goal is not attained. Presidents also want to secure a positive legacy for themselves; this is aided if they are both reelected and successful in making public policy. While these goals are mutually reinforcing, reelection and legacy both hinge on the policies with which the presidents are associated. Chief legislators want to lead Congress to accept their policy recommendations. Does Congress follow where a president leads?

Notes

1. US Constitution, Art. I, Sec. 7.

2. US Senate, *The Constitution of the United States of America: Analysis and Interpretation,* 103rd Cong., 1st Sess., 1992, S. Doc. 91, 540.

3. Truman labeled the Eightieth Congress the "do-nothing Congress" in his whistle-stop campaign in the fall, after they adjourned their special session failing to enact major legislation.

4. Byron W. Daynes, Raymond Tatalovich, and Dennis L. Soden, *To Govern a Nation: Presidential Power and Politics* (New York: St. Martin's Press, 1998), 152.

5. Robert J. Spitzer, *The Presidential Veto: Touchstone of the American Presidency* (Albany: State University of New York Press, 1988), 59.

6. Ibid., 62.

7. Ibid., 67.

8. Paul C. Light, *The President's Agenda: Domestic Policy Choice from Kennedy to Clinton,* 3rd ed. (Baltimore: Johns Hopkins University Press, 1999), 111.

9. Spitzer, *The Presidential Veto,* 33–59.

10. Richard E. Neustadt, "Presidency and Legislation: Planning the President's Program," *American Political Science Review* 49 (December 1955):1015.

11. Light, *The President's Agenda,* 111–115.

12. Stephen J. Wayne, *The Legislative Presidency* (New York: Harper & Row, 1978), 23.

13. Woodrow Wilson, *Constitutional Government in the United States* (New York: Columbia University Press, 1961), 68.

14. Jeffrey K. Tulis, *The Rhetorical Presidency* (Princeton: Princeton University Press, 1987).

15. Wayne, *The Legislative Presidency,* 13–15.

16. See Neustadt, "Presidency and Legislation," 999. This is also, not coincidentally, the time period in which the annual message on the state of the Union simply became known as the State of the Union address.

17. Truman was criticized in 1947 and Eisenhower in 1953 by some congressional actors for not offering the detailed program Congress had come to expect. See Neustadt, "Presidency and Legislation," 1015. For a detailed discussion of how presidential legislative programs became institutionalized, see Neustadt, "Presidency and Legislation," 982–1001.

18. Ibid., 992. He is comparing the budget message and the economic report with the SUA.

19. Michael Mezey, *Congress, the President, and Public Policy* (Boulder: Westview Press, 1989), 199.

20. The danger of using the hat metaphor is that one treats these various roles as separate entities, unconnected to others. One should recognize that these presidential functions coexist in the president and are not as discrete as the metaphor might imply.

21. Wilfred E. Binkley, "The President as Chief Legislator," *Annals of the American Academy of Political and Social Sciences* 307 (1956):92–105.

22. Tulis, *The Rhetorical Presidency,* 4; Samuel Kernell, *Going Public: New Strategies of Presidential Leadership*, 3rd ed. (Washington, DC: Congressional Quarterly Press, 1997).

23. On the general link between presidents' SUAs and the public, see Jeffrey E. Cohen, "Presidential Rhetoric and the Public Agenda," *American Journal of Political Science* 39 (February 1995):87–107; Kim Quaile Hill, "The Policy Agendas of the President and the Mass Public: A Research Validation and Extension," *American Journal of Political Science* 42 (October 1998):1328–1334.

24. George C. Edwards III, and B. Dan Wood, "Who Influences Whom? The President, Congress, and the Media," *American Political Science Review* 93 (1999):330.

25. Theodore J. Lowi, *The Personal President: Power Invested, Promise Unfulfilled* (Ithaca: Cornell University Press, 1985), 69, 112.

26. Richard F. Fenno Jr., *Congressmen in Committees* (Boston: Little, Brown and Company, 1973), 1, 139.

27. David R. Mayhew, *Congress: The Electoral Connection* (New Haven: Yale University Press, 1974), 17.

28. While Johnson does not run for reelection in 1968, when he gave the 1968 SUA, he had not yet dropped out of the race. The SUA would have been constructed at a time when Johnson was pursuing reelection. See Michael J. Towle, *Out of Touch: The Presidency and Public Opinion* (College Station: Texas A&M University Press, 2004), appendix. All other presidents studied ran for reelection, or in Ford's case, tried to win election in his own right. Nixon, Reagan, Clinton, and G. W. Bush were successful; Ford, Carter, and G. H. W. Bush were not.

29. We count Nixon, Reagan, Clinton, and G. W. Bush in this number, although only the 2001 and 2002 SUAs of Bush are included in our period of study.

Johnson is a special case because he served out the remainder of Kennedy's term and then was elected in his own right in 1964.

30. Light, *The President's Agenda*, 66–68.

31. Mayhew, *Congress: The Electoral Connection*, 73.

32. Ibid., 49.

33. Ibid.

34. Ibid., 53.

35. Ibid., 54.

36. Ronald W. Reagan, "Address Before a Joint Session of the Congress on the State of the Union," *Public Papers of the Presidents of the United States: Ronald W. Reagan, 1982*, vol. 1 (Washington, DC: GPO, 1983), 73.

37. George W. Bush, "Address Before a Joint Session of the Congress on the State of the Union," *Weekly Compilation of Presidential Documents* 38, no. 5 (4 February 2002):135.

38. Lyndon B. Johnson, "Address Before a Joint Session of the Congress on the State of the Union," *Public Papers of the Presidents of the United States: Lyndon B. Johnson, 1965*, vol.1 (Washington, DC: GPO, 1967), 8.

39. William J. Clinton, "Address Before a Joint Session of the Congress on the State of the Union," *Public Papers of the Presidents of the United States: William J. Clinton, 1995*, vol.1 (Washington, DC: GPO, 1996), 76.

40. Clinton, "Address Before a Joint Session of Congress on the State of the Union," *Public Papers, 1996,* 1: 83.

41. Ibid.

42. Mayhew, *Congress: The Electoral Connection*, 61.

43. Gerald Pomper's analysis of political party platforms identified three types of statements in those documents: statements of rhetoric and fact, evaluations of past performance, and statements of future policies. Pomper, *Elections in America: Control and Influence in Democratic Politics* (New York: Dodd, Mead & Co.,1968), 156–158. These three types of statements are also found in SUAs. For the credit-claiming portion of our analysis, we identify statements that are analogous to what Pomper termed evaluations of past performance. Each author independently coded each speech. Agreement on the sentences of credit claiming in each speech was achieved at 88 percent or higher. Discrepancies were dealt with on a case by case basis. The thirty-seven speeches included in this portion of our analysis include two lame-duck speeches given in 1969 and 1977 by Johnson and Ford, respectively. Also included are joint addresses given by Reagan, G. H. W. Bush, Clinton, and G. W. Bush shortly after taking office, although there will be few accomplishments for which these presidents' can claim credit at that early period in their presidencies.

44. We include everything for which a president may claim credit, such as executive and foreign policy actions, in addition to legislative successes. The goal of credit claiming is to show audiences that one is successful, and presidential successes will encompass more than just legislative actions.

45. George H. W. Bush, "Address Before a Joint Session of the Congress on the State of the Union," *Public Papers of the Presidents of the United States: George H. W. Bush, 1990*, vol. 1 (Washington, DC: GPO, 1991), 130.

46. Richard M. Nixon, "Address Before a Joint Session of the Congress on the State of the Union," *Public Papers of the Presidents of the United States: Richard M. Nixon, 1971*, vol. 1 (Washington, DC: GPO, 1973), 52.

47. Michael Nelson, "Bill Clinton and the Politics of Second Terms," *Presidential Studies Quarterly* 29 (Fall 1998). Michael B. Grossman, Martha Joynt

Kumar, and Francis E. Rourke, "Second-Term Presidencies: The Aging of Administrations," in *The Presidency and the Political System*, 6th ed., ed. Michael Nelson (Washington, DC: CQ Press, 2000), 223–247.

48. We do not include G. W. Bush in this number because his first term was not complete when the data were collected.

49. George C. Edwards III, "Campaigning Is Not Governing: Bill Clinton's Rhetorical Presidency," in *The Clinton Legacy*, eds. Colin Campbell and Bert A. Rockman (New York: Chatham House, 2000), 33–47; Corey Cook, "The Contemporary Presidency: The Permanence of the 'Permanent Campaign': George W. Bush's Public Presidency," *Presidential Studies Quarterly* 32 (December 2002):753–764.

50. Nixon's 1973 SUA was a series of written messages to Congress and therefore not included in our data.

51. We include neither Reagan's 1988 SUA, nor Clinton's 2000 SUA in our category of lame-duck SUAs. Each still had a year of governing left and would devote attention to policy recommendations in their final SUAs. Thus, our definition of lame-duck SUAs involves the two speeches in our data where the president gave a farewell SUA in the month that he was leaving office.

52. For example, Ford touted a tax proposal that had just been submitted "earlier this month." Gerald R. Ford, "Address Before a Joint Session of the Congress on the State of the Union," *Public Papers of the Presidents of the United States: Gerald R. Ford, 1976*, vol. 1 (Washington, DC: GPO, 1978), 2921. Johnson urged increasing Social Security benefits and increasing support for model cities. Johnson, "Address Before a Joint Session of the Congress on the State of the Union, *Public Papers, 1968*, 2:1265.

53. These statements correspond to what Pomper termed *statements of future policies* in his study of political party platforms and to the policy recommendation component of SUAs identified by Karlyn Kohrs Campbell and Kathleen Hall Jamieson. See Pomper, *Elections in America*, 156–158, and Campbell and Jamieson, *Deeds Done in Words: Presidential Rhetoric and the Genres of Governance* (Chicago: University of Chicago Press, 1990), 54. In examining the president as chief legislator, we limit ourselves to statements in which the president is requesting congressional action. Each author independently coded each speech and identified specific legislative requests. Agreement was achieved at 93 percent or higher and discrepancies dealt with on a case by case basis. Thirty-five speeches are utilized for this analysis. We do not include the two lame-duck addresses of Johnson in 1969 and Ford in 1977. In addition, Nixon's 1973 SUAs that were not delivered orally to a joint session of Congress are excluded.

54. We are interested in all of the legislative requests the president communicates in the SUA. We should note that this will be different from Light's computations of presidential requests for legislation in SUAs (see Light, *The President's Agenda*, Table 2, 42). Light's calculation of presidential agendas involved items that were both mentioned in an SUA and cleared as being in accordance with the president's program through the Office of Management and Budget (see Light, *The President's Agenda*, 9). Furthermore, our measure of legislative requests encompasses the president touting legislation that may not be of his own initiative, that may already be in the congressional pipeline, and that might benefit from presidential attention.

55. Clinton, "Address Before a Joint Session of the Congress on Administration Goals," *Public Papers, 1993*, 1:114.

56. Ibid., 1:115.

57. Clinton, "Address Before a Joint Session of the Congress on the State of the Union," *Public Papers, 1996,* 1:83.

58. Nixon, "Address Before a Joint Session of the Congress on the State of the Union," *Public Papers, 1970,* 1:8.

59. Reagan, "Address Before a Joint Session of the Congress on the State of the Union," *Public Papers, 1982,* 1:73–74.

60. We will nevertheless refer to these initial addresses to a joint session of Congress as inaugural SUAs to avoid confusion with inaugural addresses.

61. Reagan, "Address Before a Joint Session of the Congress on the Program for Economic Recovery," *Public Papers, 1981,* 1:114.

62. Clinton, "Address Before a Joint Session of the Congress on Administration Goals," *Public Papers, 1993,* 1:114.

63. G. W. Bush, "Address Before a Joint Session of the Congress on Administration Goals," *Public Papers, 2001,* 1:140.

64. G. H. W. Bush, "Address on Administration Goals Before a Joint Session of the Congress," *Public Papers, 1989,* 1:75.

65. Reagan, "Address Before a Joint Session of the Congress on the Program for Economic Recovery," *Public Papers, 1981,* 1:113.

66. Light, *The President's Agenda,* 41–43.

67. Included in this classification are LBJ's 1965 and 1967, Nixon's 1970 and 1971, Carter's 1978 and 1979, Reagan's 1982 and 1983, G. H. W. Bush's 1990, and Clinton's 1994 and 1995 SUAs. We include LBJ's 1965 SUA because, while it is the first year of his first term in his own right, it is not an inaugural SUA, as he had given an SUA in 1964 when finishing Kennedy's term. Not included are G. H. W. Bush's 1991 SUA and G. W. Bush's 2002 SUA, as both of these classify as crisis SUAs.

68. The overall median for credit claiming in all SUAs is 10.7 percent.

69. These SUAs are LBJ's 1968, Nixon's 1972, Ford's 1976, Reagan's 1984, Bush's 1992, and Clinton's 1996. LBJ's 1968 SUA is included here as he was pursuing reelection at the time it was given, even though he would later withdraw from the race. See Towle, *Out of Touch,* appendix. Carter's 1980 SUA is not included, as it is classified as a crisis SUA.

70. Johnson, "Address Before a Joint Session of the Congress on the State of the Union," *Public Papers, 1968,* 1:33.

71. Nixon, "Address Before a Joint Session of the Congress on the State of the Union," *Public Papers, 1972,* 1:35.

72. G. H. W. Bush, "Address Before a Joint Session of the Congress on the State of the Union," *Public Papers, 1992,* 1:160.

73. Carter sent a written one in 1981. Carter, "State of the Union Annual Message to the Congress, *"Public Papers, 1980,* 3:2931–2997.

74. Nixon's 1974, Reagan's 1987, and Clinton's 1998 SUAs all fall into the category of crisis SUAs.

75. Clinton, "Address Before a Joint Session of the Congress on the State of the Union," *Public Papers, 1995,* 1:85.

76. Clinton, "Address Before a Joint Session of the Congress on the State of the Union," *Public Papers, 1996,* 1:82.

77. Clinton, "Address Before a Joint Session of the Congress on the State of the Union," *Public Papers, 1997,* 1:113.

78. Clinton, "Address Before a Joint Session of the Congress on the State of the Union," *Public Papers, 1998,* 1:116; *Public Papers, 1999,* 1:65; *Public Papers, 2000,* 1:132.

79. Clinton, "Address Before a Joint Session of the Congress on the State of the Union," *Public Papers, 1999,* 1:66.

80. John Mueller defines a rally-round-the-flag effect as it pertains to the effect of international events on presidential popularity. John E. Mueller, *War, Presidents, and Public Opinion* (New York: John Wiley & Sons, 1973), 205.

81. James E. Carter, "Address Before a Joint Session of the Congress on the State of the Union," *Public Papers of the Presidents of the United States: James E. Carter, 1980,* vol. 1 (Washington, DC: GPO, 1981), 1:195.

82. Ibid.

83. Ibid., 197.

84. Ibid., 200.

85. Michael R. Gordon, "Iraq Army Invades Capital of Kuwait in Fierce Fighting," *New York Times,* 2 August 1990, A1.

86. G. H. W. Bush, "Address to the Nation Announcing Allied Military Action in the Persian Gulf," *Public Papers, 1991,* 1:42–44.

87. G. H. W. Bush, "Address Before a Joint Session of the Congress on the State of the Union," *Public Papers, 1991,* 1:74.

88. Ibid.

89. Ibid., 79.

90. G. W. Bush, "Address Before a Joint Session of the Congress on the State of the Union," *Weekly Compilation of Presidential Documents* 38, no. 5 (4 February 2002):137.

91. Ibid., 134.

92. Clifton Daniel, "Ford's Gallup Rating off 21 Points After Pardon," *New York Times,* 13 October 1974, 1.

93. James M. Naughton, "Senate and House Margins Are Substantially Enlarged," *New York Times,* 6 November 1974, 93.

94. Gerald R. Ford, "Address Before a Joint Session of the Congress on the State of the Union," *Public Papers, 1975,* 1:36.

95. Ibid., 1:37.

96. Ibid., 1:40.

97. Ibid., 1:41.

98. Ibid.

99. Ibid.

100. Ibid., 1:38.

101. Light, *The President's Agenda,* 112.

102. Ford, "Address Before a Joint Session of the Congress on the State of the Union," *Public Papers, 1975,* 1:37.

103. Ibid., 1:45.

104. Ibid., 1:42.

105. Ibid., 1:45.

106. Carroll Kilpatrick, "Nixon Forces Firing of Cox; Richardson, Ruckelshaus Quit," *Washington Post,* 21 October 1973, A1.

107. Richard M. Nixon, "Letter to the Chairman of the Senate Select Committee on Presidential Campaign Activities Responding to Subpoenas Requiring Production of Presidential Tape Recordings and Documents," *Public Papers, 1974,* 1:5–6. A narrower subpoena had been issued by the committee in July 1973, and Nixon responded to it in a similar fashion by maintaining the tapes were privileged.

108. Nixon, "Address Before a Joint Session of the Congress on the State of the Union," *Public Papers, 1974,* 1:54.

109. Ibid., 1:55.

110. Ibid.

111. Reagan "Address to the Nation on the Iran Arms and Contra Aid Controversy," *Public Papers, 1986*, 2:1546.

112. Reagan "Remarks Announcing the Review of the National Security Council's Role in the Iran Arms and Contra Aid Controversy," *Public Papers, 1986*, 2:1587.

113. Stephen Engelberg, "Reagan Reportedly Sat In on Briefings by Meese," *New York Times*, 30 November 1986, A24.

114. Reagan, "Statement on the Special Review Board for the National Security Council," *Public Papers, 1986*, 2:1588.

115. Reagan, "Statement on the Appointment of an Independent Counsel to Investigate the Iran Arms and Contra Aid Controversy," *Public Papers, 1986*, 2:1636.

116. Reagan, "Address Before a Joint Session of the Congress on the State of the Union," *Public Papers, 1987*, 1:56.

117. Ibid.

118. Ibid., 1:57–58.

119. Peter Baker, "President Faces His Accuser; Clinton Questioned Under Oath for Six Hours on Allegations of Harassment," *Washington Post,* 18 January 1998, A1.

120. Susan Schmidt, Peter Baker, and Toni Locy, "Clinton Accused of Urging Aide to Lie; Starr Probes Whether President Told Woman to Deny Alleged Affair to Jones's Lawyers," *Washington Post*, 21 January 1998, A1.

121. Clinton, "Interview with Jim Lehrer," *Public Papers, 1998,* 1:89–99.

122. Clinton, "Remarks on the After-School Child Care Initiative," *Public Papers, 1998*, 1:111.

123. Peter Baker and Helen Dewar, "Clinton Acquitted," *Washington Post*, 13 February 1999, A1.

124. One difficulty with presidential research of this type is the small number of observations available. We should note, therefore, that the patterns we have identified in SUAs should be treated tentatively.

5

Ask and Ye Shall Receive?

In the realm of legislative actors, the president is *chief* legislator. The reporting and recommending done by chief legislators in the SUA facilitate leadership of Congress and are a means to an end: making the public policy presidents desire. Presidents make legislative requests with the ultimate goal of seeing them enacted, enabling them to fulfill their mutually reinforcing goals of making policy, getting reelected, and securing a positive legacy. Position taking is not an end unto itself for the chief legislator, as it often may be for regular legislators. We now turn to an examination of the end result of the process a president begins, or tries to further, each time he gives his SUA. Do presidents get the legislative requests they ask for in the SUA?

In the legislative arena, the relationship between the president and Congress must at some point be cooperative if anything is to be accomplished. As Peterson notes, "In a strict legal sense, the chief executive and Capitol Hill are a partnership to the degree that they must jointly engage in the activity of the legislative process if there are to be statutory responses to policy issues."[1] Yet, the public looks to the president, not Congress, to provide leadership, guidance, and initiative. Nowhere is this more evident than in a State of the Union address. The chief legislator captures attention unlike any member of Congress, and the SUA is a forum that provides a stage unlike anything to be had by a member of Congress. The speech giver, setting, and rhetoric of the SUA encourage a notion of president-centered government. Whether a president is ultimately viewed as successful is tied to his policy accomplishments. Therefore, the stakes for presidents are high when they choose to take positions with legislative requests in the SUA. The president very publicly signals what he wants Congress to do; failure on the part of Congress to act can signal an ineffective chief legislator.

With their policymaking rhetoric, chief legislators address problems and detail the courses of action that they believe will fix those problems. The policymaking rhetoric of the SUA, in which presidents use symbolism and convey policy substance, furthers the chief legislators' goal of making public policy. By making legislative requests in the SUA, they signal to their audiences their priorities at that point in time. By using both symbolism and credit claiming for past achievements, presidents hope to convince their audiences to follow them. While Campbell and Jamieson identify the overall form of "deliberative, policy making rhetoric" in SUAs and also identify one component of the speech as being devoted to policy recommendations,[2] they do not attempt to address whether or not the president's policymaking rhetoric is successful, nor do they ask what the ultimate result of this type of rhetoric might be.

Policymaking rhetoric is structured to enable policy leadership. If presidents present their audiences with problems and their proposed solutions, do their audiences, specifically Congress, follow their leadership and give them their requests?

Legislative Success

The legislative requests in the SUA indicate the highlights of the president's legislative agenda at the beginning of each congressional session.[3] Once we identified the legislative requests presidents made in SUAs, we determined whether the president's policymaking rhetoric was successful in the congressional session in which the president gave his address; that is, did he get what he wanted, some version of what he wanted, or was his request unsuccessful? Beginning with every SUA and new congressional session, we start anew with requests and the actions (or inactions) that follow in that session. This time frame is justified for two reasons. One, SUAs are annual events. While policy proposals may take more than one congressional session, or even more than one Congress, to be enacted, we are interested in the speech as political communication, what the president says in the speech and to what extent he gets his requests fulfilled. Often, presidents made repeat requests from one SUA to the next, indicating that previously unsuccessful requests were continuing priorities for them. Sometimes, requests that were not successful in the previous session were absent in the next year's speech, indicating waning priority. Since these previous requests were not reemphasized in the next SUA, they do not carry over in our analysis. In addition, presidents will often request actions in the SUA that pertain to the federal budget. The SUA typically precedes the deadline for the president's budget submission to Congress by a few weeks, the beginning of a yearly process that is to be completed within the session.[4] It is not unusual for the president to address specific items from his upcoming budget and urge congressional action. For the session following the SUA, we determine success by using the relevant year of the *Congressional Quarterly Almanac*.[5]

How do presidents fare with their legislative requests from SUAs? Previous research on presidential agendas found that 42 percent of presidents' legislative initiatives once on the agenda were enacted in the period 1953 to 1996.[6] While we are not studying the whole of the president's agenda, only what the president chooses to rhetorically highlight in SUAs, this finding can guide our expectations. We expect, however, that legislative requests in SUAs would garner higher success than presidential initiatives in general, since the requests in SUAs represent policy items that were chosen to be publicly highlighted. In addition, legislative requests in SUAs are not limited to just presidential initiatives, but also include instances where presidents take positions on congressional initiatives that may already have a place on the agenda. This may entail the president jumping on the congressional bandwagon, taking a position on legislation that is already headed for passage. Finally, a legislative request can also involve presidents urging Congress *not* to act, a prospect generally easier than getting Congress to act.

We previously found the policy substance in SUAs (levels of credit claiming and position taking) to be affected by both individual presidents and the context in which the SUA is taking place. When examining the outcome of the legislative requests, we would similarly expect different results depending upon both the president and the political context of the year following the requests. The types of SUAs identified in Chapter 4 reflect conditions affecting the input of the SUA's policy substance. Likewise, there are particular conditions that should affect the outcome of legislative requests made in SUAs, such as the year following an election, second terms, crises, and the presence of divided government.

In inaugural years, as well as in a year following reelection, presidents ought to obtain higher levels of success with their legislative requests given that they are fresh off an election. In election returns, Congress has tangible evidence of where the president stands with the public. This election effect should manifest itself in success rates for first- and fifth-year SUAs, although we expect fifth-year successes not to match first-year ones, as presidents confront the "cycle of decreasing influence" which Light identified affecting presidential domestic agendas.[7] In addition, we would expect overall success rates in second terms to decline after the fifth-year SUA, given that second terms tend to be less successful.[8]

The crises that presidents confront are varied. On one hand, we might expect that years in which presidents gave rally-round-the-flag SUAs would be relatively successful ones for presidential legislative requests, given that international crises boost popularity, which might inhibit opposition. Rally events, as defined by John Mueller and affecting presidential popularity, tend to be of relatively short duration, however.[9] We expect successes for presidents in years they gave this type of crisis SUA to vary depending on the nature of the crisis, as well as how they linked the crisis to their legislative requests. In years presidents gave SUAs as they were confronting a personal crisis (the rally-round-the-president SUAs), we would expect presidents to have low levels of success on their legislative requests, as each of these crises was characterized by a conflict between the president and Congress. A similar result is expected with the one rally-round-the-presidency SUA in our time period.

Some presidents will be more successful than others with their initiatives, and George Edwards and Andrew Barrett found that the presence of unified or divided government made a difference in a president's success rate with his initiatives on the agenda.[10] We would similarly expect the condition of government to affect the success of presidents with the items they highlight in their SUAs.[11] Chief legislators leading a Congress controlled by their own party should have higher levels of success than chief legislators leading a Congress in which at least one chamber is controlled by the opposition. Presidents who encounter a Congress with only one chamber controlled by the opposition party ought to fare marginally better than those who confront a Congress with both chambers controlled by the opposition. Furthermore, presidents leading a Congress that their party controls ought to have higher levels of success in getting their full requests than those leading divided Congresses, as the party they are leading and the Congress they are leading coincide.

Findings

When presidents ask for congressional action in their SUAs, do they receive it? Table 5.1 shows a summary of individual presidents' successes, as well as the success rate of all presidents. Requests are deemed fully successful if the president was granted his request by Congress; if the president received some version of his request, then it is deemed partially successful. The most comprehensive way to view presidential success is by combining requests that were either fully or partially enacted by Congress. Legislative requests that failed to be enacted during the session are deemed unsuccessful. There is substantial variation among presidents with the successfulness of their SUA requests. Ford's legislative requests are the least successful with Congress, with a median of almost 72 percent of Ford's requests failing. Johnson's are the most successful, with a median of 57.5 percent of his requests being fully or partially successful. He is the only president who obtains a median success rate that is above 50 percent. On the whole, the median success rate for all presidents is 43.3 percent, not substantially dif-

Table 5.1 Summary of Presidential Requests for Congressional Action in State of the Union Addresses

		Median Percentage of Requests per SUA	
	Median Number of Requests per SUA	Fully/Partially Successful	Not Successful
Johnson (1965–1968)	36.0	57.5	42.5
Nixon	18.0	37.7	62.4
Ford	31.5	28.5	71.5
Carter	18.0	50.0	50.0
Reagan	21.0	44.9	55.2
Bush, G. H. W.	33.5	38.8	61.2
Clinton	50.5	49.6	50.5
Bush, G. W. (2001–2002)	31.5	48.9	51.1
Overall	31.0	43.3	56.7

ferent from previous research on the success of presidential initiatives, which found a 42 percent success rate.[12] Whereas we had expected presidents to be somewhat more successful with their SUA requests than they were with presidential initiatives in general, this was not the case. Being chief legislator does not mean getting everything one wants out of Congress. SUA requests do not have high levels of enactment.

Table 5.2 shows the results of our analysis by year. There is tremendous variability in the number of successes and failures presidents have during their time in office. Reagan has one of the best success rates in 1981, getting 70 percent of his SUA requests either fully or partially enacted; six years later, he has the worst year of any president, failing to get congressional enactment on 95 percent of his SUA requests. Every president has good years and bad. Only Johnson has more "good" years, in which he achieves a majority of his requests being fully or partially enacted by Congress, than "bad" ones, having a majority be unsuccessful. Nixon, Ford, and G. H. W. Bush have more bad years than good. Nixon does obtain the highest level of success, however, receiving 70.6 percent of his SUA requests in full or part in 1970. In nineteen of the thirty-five SUAs we examine, the president was unsuccessful with a majority of his requests for congressional action.

In only three years did presidents succeed in getting more than half of their *full* requests enacted, Johnson in 1965, Nixon in 1970, and Clinton in 1996. Johnson was successful in getting almost 67 percent of his SUA requests fully enacted in 1965 following his landslide election victory in 1964. Nixon, in 1970, had considerable success with his requests, the bulk of which were environmental and crime policy. With the urban riots of the

Table 5.2   Presidential Requests for Congressional Action, by Number and Success Rate, in State of the Union Addresses

	Number of Requests	Percentage of Requests			
		Fully Successful	Partially Successful	Fully/Partially Successful	Not Successful
Johnson					
1965	36	66.7	2.8	69.4	30.6
1966	36	50.0	2.8	52.8	47.2
1967	36	19.4	5.6	25.0	75.0
1968	45	44.4	17.8	62.2	37.8
Nixon					
1970	17	58.8	11.8	70.6	29.4
1971	21	19.0	0.0	19.0	81.0
1972	19	21.1	15.8	36.8	63.2
1974	13	23.1	15.4	38.5	61.5
Ford					
1975	29	24.1	3.4	27.6	72.4
1976	34	20.6	8.8	29.4	70.6
Carter					
1978	18	33.3	16.7	50.0	50.0
1979	20	15.0	10.0	25.0	75.0
1980	9	33.3	22.2	55.6	44.4
Reagan					
1981	27	37.0	33.3	70.4	29.6
1982	22	9.1	22.7	31.8	68.2
1983	31	12.9	12.9	25.8	74.2
1984	19	21.1	36.8	57.9	42.1
1985	35	8.6	11.4	20.0	80.0
1986	20	50.0	10.0	60.0	40.0
1987	19	0.0	5.3	5.3	94.7
1988	18	44.4	16.7	61.1	38.9
Bush, G. H. W.					
1989	43	16.3	23.3	39.5	60.5
1990	29	17.2	41.1	58.6	41.4
1991	21	9.5	28.6	38.1	61.9
1992	38	13.2	13.2	26.3	73.7
Clinton					
1993	49	34.7	16.3	51.0	49.0
1994	47	38.3	14.9	53.2	46.8
1995	44	25.0	5.0	29.5	70.5
1996	42	54.8	9.5	64.3	35.7
1997	57	33.3	24.6	57.9	42.1
1998	52	30.8	17.3	48.1	51.9
1999	77	22.1	13.0	35.1	64.9
2000	87	11.5	19.5	31.0	69.0
Bush, G. W.					
2001	33	30.3	24.2	54.5	45.5
2002	30	36.7	6.7	43.3	56.7
Total (N)	1,173	28.0 (328)	15.3 (179)	43.2 (507)	56.8 (666)

Note: N is the number of requests.
Percentage of requests rows may not add to 100 percent due to rounding.

late 1960s and growing awareness of the environmental movement, fueled by such things as Rachel Carson's 1962 publication of *Silent Spring* and the Cuyahoga River catching fire in 1969, Nixon chose to focus his SUA requests in these policy areas, requests to which a Democratic Congress was receptive. Clinton in 1996, after he gained some leverage with Congress as a result of the government shutdown of 1995–1996, also had a majority of his requests fully enacted. Reagan, on the other hand, got none of the 19 requests he made in 1987 fully enacted. In November 1986, elections returned the Senate to Democratic party control, and the Iran-Contra revelations came to light, which were damaging to the administration's standing with Congress.

Table 5.3 represents the successes presidents had with legislative requests in years following presidential elections. There is evidence of presidents having higher levels of success with their SUA requests in their inaugural year, as we expected. Of the four presidents who gave joint addresses in their first year of office (Reagan through G. W. Bush), three are granted a majority of the policy requests they make in that year in full or part. G. H. W. Bush is the exception; he gets only 40 percent of his initial requests either fully or partially enacted. For the three SUAs that occurred after either a successful reelection campaign (Reagan and Clinton), or in Johnson's case, an election where the sitting president wins election in his own right, two of the three have levels of success well over the median level, and a majority of requests were

Table 5.3 Postelection Success

	Number of Requests	Percentage of Requests			
		Fully Successful	Partially Successful	Fully/Partially Successful	Not Successful
Johnson					
1965	36	66.7	2.8	69.4	30.6
Reagan					
1981	27	37.0	33.3	70.4	29.6
1985	35	8.6	11.4	20.0	80.0
Bush, G. H. W.					
1989	43	16.3	23.3	39.5	60.5
Clinton					
1993	49	34.7	16.3	51.0	49.0
1997	57	33.3	24.6	57.9	42.1
Bush, G. W.					
2001	33	30.3	24.2	54.5	45.5
Total (N)	280	32.1 (90)	19.3 (54)	51.4 (144)	48.6 (136)

Note: N is the number of requests.
Percentage of requests rows may not add to 100 percent due to rounding.

enacted in each case. Reagan does not meet our expectations for success after reelection. His fifth-year success rate is poor—80 percent of his requests fail. Despite having won reelection handily over Walter Mondale, Reagan had used up much of his "political capital" with Congress in 1981, when he was very successful with his main initiatives.[13] Johnson's 1965 SUA occurs on the heels of a presidential election won by a landslide. Not only does he succeed (in full and part) with almost 70 percent of his requests, but he also is fully successful with 67 percent, the highest level of any president. The 1964 elections also returned large majorities of Democrats to Congress, and Johnson was able to get them to deliver his requests with little compromise. Clinton's fifth-year SUA requests are also quite successful. On the whole, Clinton's requests are even more successful than his inaugural year requests, when Democrats controlled the Congress. Notably, Clinton got higher enactment of his full requests in 1993, with his party controlling Congress, than in 1997, when Republicans controlled. His partial successes, where the president got some but not all of what he wanted, boost his overall success rate in 1997 to a level above that of his inaugural year.

Only Reagan and Clinton serve out two complete second terms in our data (Table 5.4). Once again, Reagan confounds our expectation; he has two very unsuccessful years, each followed by a very successful year. Following his dismal successes in 1985 with his SUA requests, Reagan's fortunes improve in 1986. He is able to get a major success in tax code reform, and

Table 5.4   Second-Term Success

| | Number of Requests | Percentage of Requests | | | |
		Fully Successful	Partially Successful	Fully/Partially Successful	Not Successful
Nixon					
1974	13	23.1	15.4	38.5	61.5
Reagan					
1985	35	8.6	11.4	20.0	80.0
1986	20	50.0	10.0	60.0	40.0
1987	19	0.0	5.3	5.3	94.7
1988	18	44.4	16.7	61.1	38.9
Clinton					
1997	57	33.3	24.6	57.9	42.1
1998	52	30.8	17.3	48.1	51.9
1999	77	22.1	13.0	35.1	64.9
2000	87	11.5	19.5	31.0	69.0
Total (N)	378	22.8 (86)	15.9 (60)	38.6 (146)	61.4 (232)

Note: N is the number of requests.
Percentage of requests rows may not add to 100 percent due to rounding.

several of his SUA requests in 1986 relate to that policy. The year following, however, is dominated by the Iran-Contra scandal, and Reagan gets
very few of the things he requested from Congress. His fortunes improve as
the fallout from Iran-Contra subsides in his final year. Clinton does meet
our expectations of second terms, and his success levels steadily fall in his
final four years in office.

What is remarkable about Clinton's second-term successes, however, is
that his percentages are as high as they are in his final three years. At the
beginning of 1998, the Lewinsky revelations came to light, and by the end
of the year, Clinton would be only the second president to be impeached by
the House of Representatives. Yet, in that year, he got 48 percent of his
SUA requests either in full or part, a rate above the median level of success
for all presidents. Table 5.5 shows the successes of presidents in the year
following their delivery of a crisis SUA. As expected, successes vary as
presidents confront different crises during their tenure and have different
strategies for dealing with those crises in their SUAs.

In the year following an SUA involving a rally-round-the-flag crisis,

Table 5.5 Crisis Success

		Percentage of Requests			
	Number of Requests	Fully Successful	Partially Successful	Fully/Partially Successful	Not Successful
Rally-Round-the-Flag Crisis					
Carter					
1980	9	33.3	22.2	55.6	44.4
Bush, G. H. W.					
1991	21	9.5	28.6	38.1	61.9
Bush, G. W.					
2002	30	36.7	6.7	43.3	56.7
Total (N)	60	26.7 (16)	16.7(10)	43.3 (26)	56.7 (34)
Rally-Round-the Presidency/Rally-Round-the-President Crises					
Nixon					
1974	13	23.1	15.4	38.5	61.5
Ford					
1975	29	24.1	3.4	27.6	72.4
Reagan					
1987	19	0.0	5.3	5.3	94.7
Clinton					
1998	52	30.8	17.3	48.1	51.9
Total (N)	113	23.0 (26)	11.5 (13)	34.5 (39)	65.5 (74)

Note: N is the number of requests.
Percentage of requests rows may not add to 100 percent due to rounding.

where events that were international in scope affected a president's SUA activities, we do see varying levels of success. Carter's most successful year with his legislative requests occurs in 1980, also the year he would lose his reelection bid. Of all the SUAs we examine, the 1980 SUA is the most unique. Carter's reactions to the invasion of Afghanistan (embargoes of grain to the Soviets and Olympic athletes to the Moscow Olympics) and the taking of American hostages in Iran (failed rescue attempt), all executive actions, would prove to erode Carter's support leading up to the election in November, yet 55.6 percent of his SUA requests in 1980 would succeed with Congress. His success rate was substantially higher than the median success for presidents as a whole and also was the highest in his term. This high level of success for Carter was due to the fact he had very few requests in the 1980 SUA, and they were largely drawn from policy areas related to the crises he confronted. On these requests, Congress was more likely to follow because of the requests' connection to the crises.

In the case of both presidents Bush, their rally-round-the-flag SUAs included requests related to the crisis, but also included requests related to the larger domestic agenda. The crisis did not overwhelmingly dominate the legislative requests in the SUA, as was the case with Carter's SUA. The Democratic Congress gave G. H. W. Bush only about 38 percent of his SUA requests in 1991. Bush's popularity peaked in early 1991 at what was then the highest level of presidential popularity ever recorded, but then continually declined over the course of the year.[14] G. W. Bush's legislative requests in the 2002 SUA fared much better than his father's; Congress gave Bush more than one-third of his requests fully. When his partial successes are considered, he garnered a 43 percent success rate. After the terrorist attacks of September 11, 2001, G. W. Bush received the highest approval rating ever, at 90 percent.[15] He would sustain a high level of popularity for the rest of the year and into the following one.[16] Bush faced, however, a Senate controlled by the Democrats, albeit by the smallest of margins.

Presidents who faced crises within their own presidencies also claimed varying degrees of success with SUA proposals. Nixon in 1974, with an opposition Congress and facing impeachment, had the same level of success as G. H. W. Bush did in 1991, who had an opposition Congress, but historically high public approval. However, Nixon had only 13 requests in his 1974 SUA, so in sheer number, his successes were slight. Clinton, in the year he was impeached by the House, had almost half of his requests either fully or partially enacted. This is even more impressive given the number of requests Clinton had that year. Many of Clinton's requests, after the defeat of comprehensive healthcare reform and a Republican takeover of Congress, were small in scope, and he turned his focus to incremental policy change. The only SUA request Reagan got out of Congress in the year of the Iran-Contra investigation was a request for Congress to continue funding the Strategic Defense Initiative, better known as the "Star Wars" program. This was only a partial success, as Congress did fund it, but not at the level the president requested. Finally, the hapless Ford received about 28 percent of his SUA requests in 1975 following his rally-round-the-presidency SUA. The Congress that convened after the 1974 midterm elections, in which the Democrats increased their margin of control, did not follow Ford on most of his requests concerning the economy and energy policy.

Table 5.6 ranks presidential success rates on SUA requests from most successful to least successful and reports the condition of government the presidents confronted during their term of office. For presidents Clinton and Reagan, the condition of government changed in the midst of their time in office, necessitating two entries for them.[17] Table 5.6 indicates that Johnson's term, Clinton's first two years, and Carter's term, all under unified government, obtain the highest levels of median success, being successful (in full and part) with half or more of their SUA requests. Presidents with unified government also have higher median levels of getting their full requests from Congress. Presidents who confronted both chambers controlled by the opposition party—Clinton (1995–2000), G. H. W. Bush, Nixon, Reagan (1987–1988), and Ford—were the least successful with their congressional requests. The two presidents who encountered periods in which only one of the chambers was held by the opposition, G. W. Bush (2001–2002) and Reagan (1981–1986), had median success rates (full and partial) that were situated between those with unified government and a

Table 5.6 Ranking of Presidential Success and Condition of Government

President	Condition	Median Yearly Success Rate (percent)	
		Full and Partial	Full
Johnson (1965–1968)	Unified	57.5	47.2
Clinton (1993–1994)	Unified	52.1	36.5
Carter	Unified	50.0	33.3
Bush, G. W. (2001–2002)[a]	Divided (Senate)	48.9	33.5
Reagan (1981–1986)	Divided (House)	44.9	17.0
Clinton (1995–2000)	Divided (Both)	41.6	27.9
Bush, G. H. W.	Divided (Both)	38.8	14.8
Nixon	Divided (Both)	37.7	22.1
Reagan (1987–1988)	Divided (Both)	33.2	22.2
Ford	Divided (Both)	28.5	22.4

Note: a. The first five months of 2001 were unified government, but the Senate was evenly divided at 50-50. The Republicans controlled the chamber by virtue of Vice President Cheney's status as President of the Senate, and there was an unprecedented power-sharing arrangement. Senator Jim Jeffords switched from Republican to Independent in June 2001, and control of the Senate shifted to the Democrats; thus the remainder of the 107th Congress was divided.

fully divided Congress. A difference-of-medians test, however, indicates that the median success rates (full and partial) between presidents confronting unified government and those confronting divided government are not statistically significant.[18] Statistical significance is obtained when a difference-of-medians test is conducted on the rates of only the full successes presidents confronting unified or divided government achieve.[19] Thus, presidents who lead a Congress of their own party are more likely to get the full measure of the things they want than presidents who attempt leadership of a Congress in which the opposition controls at least one chamber.

While the president is no ordinary legislator and has the extraordinary platform of the SUA, this does not ensure he will always get his legislative requests. It does not mean he will receive even a bare majority of the things for which he asks. Generally, about two in five requests will have some level of success with Congress. While the president can utilize the SUA as a tool of political communication, its power is limited by the system of government in which it functions, where legislative power is shared. Simply looking at success rates for SUA requests, however, does not illuminate what role the SUA played in the eventual result of a president's legislative request. We turn now to four case studies, each with differing outcomes, to examine the role the SUA played in the outcome of each legislative request.

Four Legislative Requests
from State of the Union Addresses

Teddy Roosevelt once remarked, "Oh, if only I could be President and Congress too for just ten minutes."[20] All presidents have surely had the same sentiment. In a system where governmental functions are divided and powers are shared, in Richard Neustadt's classic formulation of "separated institutions *sharing* powers,"[21] if anything is to be accomplished legislatively, a president needs Congress, and Congress needs the president. How presidents go about dealing with Congress will vary. The experience and skill they bring to this relationship will differ. One must always keep in mind that "the highly personalized nature of the modern presidency makes the strengths and weaknesses of the White House incumbent of the utmost importance. It places a premium on the ability of chief executives to get the most out of their strong points and compensate for their limitations."[22] The political context in which the president governs will affect the relationship, as well as his standing with the public. While the president uses the SUA as a tool of political communication, its power is limited. Simply asking does not ensure a request will be fulfilled, but asking is generally a prerequisite for a desired action. As has been shown, presidents, despite being a *chief* legislator, are not particularly successful in getting Congress to accept their

SUA requests for legislative action. Yet, presidents do have successes; Congress typically enacts two of every five requests they make. Some presidents are more successful than others, and a whole host of factors affect their success. We turn now to an examination of the role the SUA played in four cases from our data. Each case has a different outcome. In each, we discuss what role the president's SUA communication played in the result, as well as the primary goal(s) that appear to have motivated the president's SUA request.

The four cases we discuss represent four different outcomes: an unsuccessful request, a request that was fully successful, a request that was partially successful, and a request that multiple presidents made that was eventually successful. The first case is an example in which the most successful president in the period we study, Johnson, is unable to get Congress to propose a constitutional amendment providing for four-year terms for House members. However, the SUA plays a key role in advancing a debate that had been stalled on Capitol Hill, even though the debate would not be a successful one for the president. The second case examines Reagan's request for a new space initiative in 1984, a permanently manned space station. This request was made in an election year and at a time when rising budget deficits were putting a severe strain on new spending. Even though many within the administration were opposed to the initiative, Reagan forged ahead and succeeded in getting his request. The SUA was a vital part of this process. The third case examines Carter's push for civil service reform in 1978, typically not an issue on which the public clamors for action absent a presidential assassination.[23] Yet, Carter used the SUA to discuss why he thought civil service reform was a necessity. He would be successful in not only getting reform on the agenda, but also obtaining most of what he wanted in the way of civil service reform. The example of the line-item veto is our final case. Every president from Reagan to Clinton asked for this power in their SUAs at least twice. During the Clinton administration, the reform finally succeeded, although the Supreme Court would later invalidate it. Multiple presidents' use of the SUA to talk about the line-item veto kept the issue in front of Congress and the public. The effect of rising budget deficits and growing awareness of this reform eventually moved Congress to expand the president's fiscal power.

It Seemed Like a Good Idea at the Time: Johnson's Request for Four-Year House Terms

On January 12, 1966, Johnson gave his third SUA. In his introductory remarks, he summarized the various recommendations he would be discussing, which included a call for a constitutional amendment to extend the term of House members to four years. "I will ask you to make it possible for

Members of the House of Representatives to work more effectively in the
service of the Nation through a constitutional amendment extending the
term of a Congressman to 4 years, concurrent with that of the President."[24]
In the body of the SUA, Johnson would include more detail and explanation
of why he believed the reform was necessary.

> To strengthen the work of Congress, I strongly urge an amendment to pro-
> vide a 4-year term for Members of the House of Representatives—which
> should not begin before 1972.
>   The present 2-year term requires most Members of Congress to divert
> enormous energies to an almost constant process of campaigning—depriv-
> ing this Nation of the fullest measure of both their skill and their wisdom.
> Today, too, the work of government is far more complex than in our early
> years, requiring more time to learn and more time to master the technical
> tasks of legislating. And a longer term will serve to attract more men of the
> highest quality to political life. The Nation, the principle of democracy,
> and I think, each congressional district, will all be better served by a 4-
> year term for Members of the House. And I urge your swift action.[25]

The Constitution stipulates that "the House of Representatives shall be composed of Members chosen every second Year."[26] Johnson's request, therefore,
would take a constitutional amendment, and the typical way amendments are
proposed is by a two-thirds vote in each chamber of Congress.[27] The president plays no formal role in the amendment process, but in this instance,
Johnson used his SUA as an occasion to urge Congress to act. He refers to the
changed nature of modern elections and governing, necessitating longer
terms. Reflecting Johnson's role as chief legislator, the reform is couched in
terms of the national interest. Too-frequent elections deprive the nation of
representatives' attention, as well as serving to detract some qualified individuals who otherwise might run if they could serve a four-year term.

In the next day's *New York Times,* there was an entire article devoted to
the president's "surprise proposal."[28] It was noted that it "was greeted by
prolonged applause and cheers. Then as the applause died down, many
members of Congress turned in their seats and whispered excitedly."[29] The
1966 SUA marked the first time the president had ever publicly weighed in
on this particular issue.[30]

The length of House terms was a subject of debate at the Constitutional
Convention in Philadelphia in 1787. In *Federalist 52* and *53*, Madison gave
justification for biennial elections for members of the House. One year was
too short to induce people to serve, and more than two years would not provide sufficient responsiveness. House terms again became a subject of
debate in the twentieth century. In 1950, the American Political Science
Association's Committee on Political Parties issued "Toward a More
Responsible Two-Party System," a lengthy report that gave specific policy
recommendations for the American political system.[31] One of the reforms

suggested was lengthening House terms to four years. "The present term is so short that a freshman member is involved in a campaign for renomination before he knows his job or has had much opportunity to prove his worth to his constituents or his party."[32] A few years later, President Eisenhower voiced support for four-year terms in 1955.[33] At the time of Johnson's SUA in 1966, there were resolutions pending in both the House and the Senate to move House members to four-year terms, but no hearings had been held in the first session of the Eighty-ninth Congress (1965).[34] A Gallup Poll, conducted in December 1965, reported that 61 percent of the public favored extending House terms to four years, 24 percent opposed, and 15 percent had no opinion.[35] Therefore, prior to announcing his desire to amend the Constitution to allow four-year House terms, there was support emanating from both the Hill, as well as from the public. Charles Jones speculated in his book *Every Second Year* that this support may have been why Johnson included this request in his 1966 SUA, as "it seemed at that moment that the necessary conditions existed for an important change in the House of Representatives."[36]

The attention Johnson brought to this issue by devoting a portion of his 1966 SUA to it provided the necessary impetus for action in Congress. After the speech, Senator Birch Bayh (D-IN), chair of the Senate Judiciary's Subcommittee on Constitutional Amendments, stated that "every effort will be made" to hold hearings soon.[37] This would be in line with Johnson's call for "swift action." Johnson followed up his SUA with a written message to Congress on January 20.[38] This message was devoted entirely to two Constitutional reforms Johnson was seeking. The first was the change to four-year terms for House members Johnson had advocated in his 1966 SUA, and the other was a reform of the electoral college system.[39] The bulk of this message was devoted to explaining Johnson's proposal for House terms, and it was accompanied by the administration's text for the proposed resolution.

On January 20, Senator Bayh introduced a resolution that proposed amending the Constitution consistent with the president's recommendation.[40] Days later, Representative Frank Chelf (D-KY) followed suit in the House.[41] Chelf had introduced a resolution in 1965, on which action was still pending, that would have extended the length of terms, but set the elections in midterm years, not coinciding with presidential elections as the president wanted.[42] Thus, Chelf had two resolutions before the House Judiciary committee—both extended House terms, but one set the elections to coincide with presidential elections and the other put them in midterm election years. The House Judiciary committee began hearings on February 8, 1966, on the administration's and related proposals.[43] It was clear very quickly, however, that support for the measure was not as strong as initially surmised. The first day of hearings, Emanuel Celler (D-NY), the committee's chair, gave his support to two-year terms, not the four-year terms the president wanted.[44] Celler professed that "it is campaigning that keeps a member alive to the issues. . . . It keeps members of the House where they belong—on their toes."[45] Celler noted that "two House members went insane while in office and would have been immune from removal by the voters for two extra years under the amendment."[46] To this, Robert T. Ashmore (D-SC) responded "maybe they were driven insane worrying about the next election."[47] When Attorney General Nicholas Katzenbach testified before the committee on February 15, he encountered opposition to the president's proposal. One of the arguments Katzenbach gave was that having members of the House elected at the same time as the president "would produce executive-legislative solidarity."[48] This immediately caused Richard Poff (R-VA) to declare, "I can't imagine a better argument against the proposal than that."[49] The *New York Times* reported, "When President Johnson first made the proposal in his State of the Union Message last month, the committee was believed to favor it by a big majority. As its hearings have progressed, however, enthusiasm has waned."[50] The House Judiciary Committee would conclude hearings on March 1.[51] The Senate Judiciary Committee's Subcommittee on Constitutional Amendments would subsequently hold hearings on the president's proposal, but they, too, would not act further.[52] The resolution stalled and it never saw floor action.

Johnson's attention to this issue would be fleeting. After the special message sent January 20, 1966, he would devote no further communications to the issue. It became clear very quickly the proposal did not have the requisite support on the committees that held hearings, let alone the support necessary to secure the favorable vote of two-thirds of each chamber needed to advance the proposal to the states for ratification. Johnson's attention was increasingly occupied by Vietnam in 1966, and the issue became a dead letter for the administration.

As is the case with most of the policymaking rhetoric in the SUA, when the president details the situation and gives his recommendation, he does not seriously discuss the cons to his proposals. In the case of Johnson's touting of four-year terms, he mentions reasons for changing the tenure of representatives but does not mention any drawbacks, not even to explain why they should be dismissed. This exemplifies the one-sided nature of the president's policymaking rhetoric. The initial reaction to the president's proposal was viewed as positive. Quickly, however, as Congress began to do what it is supposed to do—that is, deliberate—it became evident that the drawbacks to the president's request were serious ones. While it seemed like a desirable reform that House terms should be changed when Johnson spoke of them in his SUA, once deliberation began, the congressional tide turned against the president's request. Johnson did not exert any more leadership on the issue and it subsequently died.

In 1966, Johnson got a majority of his SUA requests. A constitutional amendment to extend House terms, however, would not be one of them. The SUA played a very important role concerning this particular issue. While the request was not a successful one for Johnson, his mention of it in the SUA prompted congressional hearings. Once they took place, however, it was clear that support for the president's proposal was not substantial enough. The issue was not a new one; debate over the length of House terms extended back to the earliest days of the Republic. Even in the twentieth century, the idea had been discussed as a possible reform since the 1950s. Johnson believed that the time was right and that he had sufficient political capital to move the issue. What role did the SUA play in the outcome of this request? It sufficiently advanced an issue that had been languishing on Capitol Hill. Hearings were held in both chambers. That, however, was not sufficient to move the issue any further. It is important to note that Johnson did not devote time or attention to the issue once it became clear that there was significant opposition. The time and attention of the president are scarce resources, and Johnson quickly realized the momentum was not significant enough for an amendment to be proposed. Johnson, who went into the 1966 SUA with enormous political capital, saw the potential to advance an issue that seemed ripe and one that he had not indicated a preference on previously. The Democratic Congress followed the president to a point, but not blindly. They held hearings on his request, something that likely would not have occurred absent presidential attention, but his request lacked the momentum to get it to the floor of either chamber.

In advocating a constitutional amendment on House terms, Johnson's primary goal was to make public policy, specifically a reform he believed would make government work better. As a former member of the House, Johnson understood the way elections impacted the House, and in the interest of "good government" he advocated a change. Johnson supported tying four-year terms to presidential elections, strengthening the connection presidents would potentially have to House members. This reform was not likely to be a reelection issue for the president. While public opinion polls showed support for this reform, procedural issues rarely excite the public. One difficulty with polls is that they do not measure the intensity of public support for an issue. In advocating a change to House terms, the president undoubtedly considered his legacy; getting Congress to act on a constitutional amendment is no small feat, although the legacy goal was secondary, at best, to the goal of making public policy.

Reagan's Quest to Fund a Manned Space Station

In his 1984 SUA, Reagan requested the development of a permanently manned space station. If his request was to be successful, Congress would need to authorize and appropriate the funds for this program. While the National Aeronautics and Space Administration (NASA) had been developing plans for such an endeavor for some time, there had been significant opposition to the plan from within the administration. Budget deficits were spiraling upward, constraining the ability of the administration to offer new initiatives. Furthermore, Reagan had not weighed in on the matter. That would change on January 25, 1984, when Reagan would devote a substantial amount of the SUA to the space station.

> Our second great goal is to build on America's pioneer spirit—[laughter]—I said something funny? [Laughter] I said America's next frontier—and that's to develop that frontier. A sparkling economy spurs initiatives, sunrise industries, and makes older ones more competitive.
>
> Nowhere is this more important than our next frontier: space. Nowhere do we so effectively demonstrate our technological leadership and ability to make life better on Earth. The Space Age is barely a quarter of a century old. But already we've pushed civilization forward with our advances in science and technology. Opportunities and jobs will multiply as we cross new thresholds of knowledge and reach deeper into the unknown.
>
> Our progress in space—taking giant steps for all mankind—is a tribute to American teamwork and excellence. Our finest minds in government, industry, and academia have all pulled together. And we can be proud to say: We are first; we are the best; and we are so because we're free.
>
> America has always been greatest when we dared to be great. We can reach for greatness again. We can follow our dreams to distant stars, living and working in space for peaceful, economic, and scientific gain. Tonight, I am directing NASA to develop a permanently manned space station and to do it within a decade.
>
> A space station will permit quantum leaps in our research in science, communications, in metals, and in lifesaving medicines which could be manufactured only in space. We want our friends to help us meet these challenges and share in their benefits. NASA will invite other countries to participate so we can strengthen peace, build prosperity, and expand freedom for all who share our goals.
>
> Just as the oceans opened up a new world for clipper ships and Yankee traders, space holds enormous potential for commerce today. The market for space transportation could surpass our capacity to develop it. Companies interested in putting payloads into space must have ready access to private sector launch services. The Department of Transportation will help an expendable launch services industry to get off the ground. We'll soon implement a number of executive initiatives, develop proposals to ease regulatory constraints, and, with NASA's help, promote private sector investment in space.[53]

As discussed in Chapter 3, the symbolic language presidents use in SUAs often portrays specific policy requests as embodying common, shared experiences and values. Requests will be addressed in such a manner that reinforces the common ideals and history Americans share. If legislative requests can be painted as being consonant with commonly agreed upon values, ideals, and shared experiences, as opposed to merely partisan proposals, they stand a better chance of acceptance.

Policymaking rhetoric often looks backward, and the theme of Americans' pioneering, frontier spirit is frequently used by presidents to set the stage for their recommendations. This was certainly the case in 1984 when Reagan used the SUA to promote a permanent and continually manned space station orbiting the earth, a request that Congress would have to authorize and fund. Reagan refers to the "clipper ships and Yankee traders" of America's past; space represents the "next frontier" for conquering. Reagan also evokes Kennedy with his call to build a space station "within a decade," echoing Kennedy's 1961 challenge to put a man on the moon "before this decade is out."[54] In addition, the space race with the Soviets is conjured when Reagan says, "And we can be proud to say: We are first; we are the best; and we are so because we're free." This legislative request is perfectly in line with Reagan's larger mission of restoring the preeminence of the United States; the space station is another way to "reach for greatness again" and beat the Soviets.

The political context is key in understanding this particular case, Reagan's inclusion of this request in the SUA, and the request's success with Congress. In the 1960s, the race to the moon captured the attention and broadened the imagination of a nation. By 1984, fifteen years had passed since Neil Armstrong landed on the moon and the age of space exploration reached its peak. The development of the space shuttle in the 1970s and 1980s did not hold as much appeal for the American public. Getting to the moon, and getting there first, was a significant and inspiring goal. The space shuttles did not have a comparable one; they were orbiters. Furthermore, by 1984 shuttle flights were becoming a bit routine. Being the first country to actually have people living in space for extended periods of time in a permanent structure, however, potentially held more appeal as a goal.

In January 1984, the month Reagan would give his SUA, he was preparing for a reelection campaign. The time was right for Reagan to advocate new initiatives, especially ones that would exemplify Reagan as a visionary leader. The attention of the public was also being drawn to space. Senator John Glenn (D-OH), the former astronaut who was the first American to orbit the earth, was vying for the Democratic nomination for president and had voiced support for a space station.[55] Just days before the 1984 SUA, Glenn reiterated his strong support for the project during a campaign appearance, and he also stressed that one of his opponents for the nomination, Walter Mondale, had been against the space shuttle in the 1970s.[56] In addition, the Soviets had long signaled their intent for a space station that would be permanently manned.[57] Therefore, an element of the 1950s and 1960s space race was also part of the mix of events that brought public attention to the issue of space.

Within the Reagan administration, however, there was significant opposition to a space station. The Department of Defense (DOD) did not support the NASA project, which it viewed as having no military value, especially in the 1980s budget environment where "every dollar spent on a space station would be one dollar less for their space budget."[58] The Office of Management and Budget (OMB) was against spending money for a space station, as was the president's science advisor, who preferred NASA's attention be focused on the shuttle program.[59] The Central Intelligence Agency was not in favor of the project either, for basically the same reasons as the DOD.[60] Rounding out the opposition, the National Academy of Sciences issued a report in the fall of 1983 that said it saw no scientific need for a permanent space station.[61] How is it, then, that Reagan would include a legislative request for the development of a space station in his SUA and be successful in getting Congress to approve funds for the project?

What seems to have captured Reagan's attention was a meeting on space commercialization and the space station that was arranged by Craig L. Fuller, assistant to the president for cabinet affairs, in August 1983.[62] After this meeting, it was clear to participants that "Reagan was enthralled."[63] Reagan did not, however, use the opportunity of an address on NASA's twenty-five-year anniversary in October 1983 to call for funds for the NASA initiative, even though agency officials had predicted he would.[64] In December, NASA provided the president with a briefing specifically on the space station. "Afterward, OMB director David Stockman talked about deficits. Reagan mentioned Ferdinand, Isabella, and Columbus."[65] Clearly, a permanently manned space station appealed to the visionary in Reagan, but did it have enough appeal for Reagan to successfully request funds for it in a time of rising deficits?

On December 14, the *New York Times* carried a front-page article titled, "President Seems Near Commitment on Space Station." Administration officials dropped hints that a new initiative would be proposed soon.[66] Given the environment, what better platform from which to announce a new initiative than the upcoming election-year SUA? Reagan took advantage of the opportunity the SUA provided and discussed his proposal at some length.

The day following the SUA, another front-page *New York Times* headline proclaimed, "President Backs U.S. Space Station as Next Key Goal."[67] Emphasizing the importance of this new program, Reagan continued to press the issue as he sought to convince Congress to appropriate funds in the midst of rising budget deficits and increased military spending. On January 28, three days after the SUA, Reagan devoted his

Saturday radio address to the proposed new space program. In the address, Reagan provided more information on the initiative. He explained that a permanently manned space station would be built within ten years, science and industry would both benefit from the station, and it would be a "stepping stone for further goals."[68] The one thing Reagan did not share with the public in either the SUA or the radio address was the expected cost of the program.

With the president setting the stage with his request, NASA presented the plans for the manned space station to the public the day after the SUA. The new station would be constructed in parts and would cost approximately $8 billion over ten years.[69] Despite the cost and the opposition within the administration, in the end Reagan endorsed the idea, according to one official because "[he] loves it. You don't have to look much farther than that."[70] That explains why Reagan made the request of Congress, but how did Reagan get Congress to accept his request, and what role did the SUA play?

In the president's budget sent to Congress in February, the request for funds in NASA's budget devoted to the development of the space station was $150 million. This represented 2 percent of NASA's proposed budget of $7.5 billion for fiscal year 1985. The initial outlay of $150 million for the $8 billion, ten-year project was slight, less than 2 percent of the total estimated cost of development.[71] The space station development, however, captured headlines and attention because of the president's SUA.

The initial congressional reaction to Reagan's space station request was positive.[72] The first hurdle for funding was cleared when the House's Science and Technology Subcommittee on Space Science and Applications approved the amount requested by Reagan in the FY1985 authorization bill for NASA.[73] The remainder of the authorization process would present no problems for Reagan's request for a manned space station in either the House or Senate.[74] Reagan would sign the bill authorizing $150 million for NASA to begin the development of the space station on July 16, 1984.[75] The appropriations process also moved relatively smoothly. The House Appropriations subcommittee with jurisdiction over NASA, however, did earmark $15 million of the $150 million to be devoted to research for an unmanned station, a slight alteration of Reagan's request.[76] Representative Bill Green (R-NY), the ranking Republican on the subcommittee, wanted NASA to explore options that were not specifically for a manned station. His rationale was that in a survey of scientists he had conducted, many feared a large amount of funds devoted to the space station might "put the squeeze on other vital scientific programs."[77] When the appropriations bill moved to the floor of the House, there was an attempt to remove this particular requirement, but it was defeated.[78] The Senate Appropriations Committee, however, dropped the earmark the House had inserted and approved the full $150 million for manned space station development.[79]

Earmarking $15 million of the $150 million was not a provision included in the conference committee report at the end of June.[80]

As the authorization and appropriations for the space station were working their way through Congress, Reagan continued to press for the space station during various public appearances, including his commencement address on May 30, 1984, at the Air Force Academy.

> Your generation stands on the verge of greater advances than humankind has ever known. America's future will be determined by your dreams and your vision. This past January, in my State of the Union Address, I challenged our nation to develop a permanently manned space station and to do so within a decade. And now we are moving forward with a strategy that will chart the future course of the U.S. space program.[81]

It was clear by this time that Congress was going to give its blessing to Reagan's proposal, and it had encountered very little resistance. When Reagan signed the appropriations bill that funded NASA for the coming fiscal year, he got exactly what he had requested from Congress for the development of a manned space station.

As Reagan began to make campaign appearances in the fall, he often mentioned the space station and his success, echoing the language he had used in the SUA. "That's why I directed NASA to develop a permanently manned space station, and to do it in a decade."[82] Furthermore, he frequently tied space station support references to criticisms of his Democratic opponent, Walter Mondale.

> But my opponent, in the Senate, led the fight against the entire shuttle program and called it a horrible waste. Well, we support the space shuttle, and we've committed America to meet a great challenge—to build a permanently manned space station and to do so within a decade.[83]

Reagan's quest for a permanently manned space station began with the 1984 SUA. NASA was successful in getting the president behind a project they had wanted to develop for some time, primarily because it appealed to Reagan-the-visionary. Space station development could also serve several other purposes for Reagan, by being an outlet for US "greatness" and ingenuity, giving the United States a leg up on the Soviet's space program, and providing a potential achievement on which Reagan could campaign. Not only did the president get on board, but he also used a significant portion of his SUA to discuss this initiative and why it should be pursued. This attention was necessary to propel the issue onto the front pages. Getting Congress to fund the proposal at the level Reagan requested in his budget did not prove to be too difficult, even in a time of rising budget deficits. The acceptance of Reagan's budget request was aided by the fact it was a fraction of the total cost of the ten-year development. Nevertheless, Reagan's attention to this issue, as well as the way he framed it in the SUA as being one more stage of exploration in the United States' pioneering history, was vital to the program's acceptance. Furthermore, its presence in an election-year SUA was also important. Once his request was successful, Reagan could tout his success as further proof that "America is back," a component of Reagan's reelection campaign.

Reagan's request for the development of a manned space station served all three of the goals chief legislators have. Reagan lent his support to the issue because of his desire to make public policy, particularly this policy, which would exemplify so many of the characteristics and values of Americans Reagan admired. Few policy proposals Reagan would support would be more in line with Reagan-the-dreamer. At the same time, backing a manned space station would give Reagan a new initiative as he was entering his reelection campaign, a campaign in which space exploration was an issue. If Glenn was his opponent, Reagan's support would neutralize Glenn's support for a space station as an issue. If Mondale was his opponent, Reagan could use his support for space exploration and contrast it with Mondale's past stance on killing the space shuttle program. Concerns about his legacy were certainly a factor; if successful, Reagan would be remembered as the president who started the country on the next stage of space exploration, but the legacy goal was secondary to the others.

Battling Entrenched Interests and Courting Congress: Carter and Civil Service Reform

Jimmy Carter became president, in part, because he was a Washington outsider and campaigned on that very fact. In the mid-1970s, his message of bringing a different ethic to Washington resonated with voters dissatisfied with the culture of Washington as it had been displayed in recent events such as Vietnam and Watergate. Once elected, however, an assertive Congress (controlled by his own party) was not all that amenable to Carter's leadership. In his campaign, Carter had vowed to improve the workings of the federal government. He echoed this theme in his inaugural address.

> Let our recent mistakes bring a resurgent commitment to the basic principles of our Nation, for we know that if we despise our own government, we have no future. We recall in special times when we have stood briefly, but magnificently, united. In those times no prize was beyond our grasp.
>
> But we cannot dwell upon remembered glory. We cannot afford to drift. We reject the prospect of failure or mediocrity or an inferior quality of life for any person. Our Government must at the same time be both competent and compassionate.[84]

In seeking to make government "competent," Carter picked an ambitious goal. The federal bureaucracy had not seen major reform in the almost 100 years since the Pendleton Act was adopted to insert merit principles into the civil service. Carter clearly thought the time was right for reform of the civil service, but it would not prove an easy task. In his first SUA in 1978, Carter would call for government reform. In the end, Carter was successful in getting Congress to adopt most of his civil service reform proposal, but it was a particularly arduous task.

The groundwork for Carter's proposal was laid in his first year in office. A task force was formed in 1977 composed of about 100 civil servants, academics, and business experts to study changes in the civil service.[85] The Carter Administration, in recognizing the difficulty of reform in this area, sought to forestall opposition to any plan by involving all the various parties that would be affected or have a role in the reform, including employees' unions and Congress, in the development of their proposal.[86]

On January 19, Carter delivered his 1978 SUA and emphasized government reform in general.

> During these past years, Americans have seen our Government grow far from us. For some citizens, the Government has almost become like a foreign country, so strange and distant that we've often had to deal with it through trained ambassadors who have sometimes become too powerful and too influential, lawyers, accountants, and lobbyists. This cannot go on. We must have what Abraham Lincoln wanted, a government for the people.[87]

Significantly, Carter does not identify himself as part of government with his rhetoric, but as one of the American people. Even after being president for one year, Carter puts himself in the role of outside reformer. From the pantheon of great US presidents, Carter reminds audiences of Lincoln; civil service reform can restore the ideal of government for the people.

After detailing things already accomplished in the area of government reform, such as various reorganizations, the elimination of some commissions and boards, paperwork reduction, putting federal regulations into plain English, and the creation of the Department of Energy, Carter arrives at a discussion of his proposal for the civil service.

> But even the best organized Government will only be as effective as the people who carry out its policies. For this reason, I consider civil service reform to be absolutely vital. Worked out with the civil servants themselves, this reorganization plan will restore the merit principle to a system which has grown into a bureaucratic maze. It will provide greater management flexibility and better rewards for better performance without compromising job security.
> Then and only then can we have a government that is efficient, open,

and truly worthy of our people's understanding and respect. I have promised that we will have such a government, and I intend to keep that promise.[88]

With his rhetoric, Carter places himself as part of the government, using
"our people's understanding," only *after* reform is complete. Despite
Carter's belief in the "absolutely vital" nature of civil service reform, it is
not the type of issue likely to resonate with the public, even in a era of dissatisfaction with government. Headlines the day after Carter's speech neither hailed, nor even mentioned, this Carter priority.

On the day of the SUA, Carter also sent a more detailed written message to Congress on the state of the Union that further indicated civil service reform was a major goal of the president.

> The Civil Service System is too often a bureaucratic maze which stifles the
> initiative of our dedicated Government employees while inadequately pro-
> tecting their rights. Our 2.8 million civil servants are governed by outdated
> rules and institutions that keep them from being as efficient as they would
> like to be. No one is more frustrated by this system than hard-working
> public servants. Therefore, one of my major priorities in 1978 will be to
> ensure passage of the first comprehensive reform of the system since its
> creation nearly a century ago—reforms developed with the direct involve-
> ment of civil servants.[89]

While the written message did provide a bit more detail regarding the
reform than the oral address provided, it would take the Carter
Administration another six weeks to actually get its civil service reform
proposal to Congress. On March 2, Carter announced at the National Press
Club that he was sending his proposal to Congress that day and outlined his
plan for civil service reform. Carter explained the rationale behind his proposal.

> The simple concept of a merit system has grown into a tangled web of
> complicated rules and regulations. Managers are weakened in their ability
> to reward the best and most talented people and to fire those few who are
> unwilling to work.
>   The sad fact is that it is easier to promote and to transfer incompetent
> employees than it is to get rid of them. It may take as long as 3 years mere-
> ly to fire someone for a just cause, and at the same time the protection of
> legitimate rights is costly and time-consuming for the employee.[90]

Improving the merit system under which bureaucrats were hired and pro-
moted was the major goal. The main components of the Civil Service
Reform Bill would construct a Senior Executive Service for the highest levels of the bureaucracy, offer incentive pay and pay for performance for
midlevel grades, and eliminate automatic raises linked to length of service.

Furthermore, Carter proposed to make modifications to hiring preferences for nondisabled military veterans, reducing a lifetime preference to ten years.[91] With this proposal, Carter potentially faced opposition from federal employee unions, veterans groups, and members of Congress who had large numbers of federal employees in their districts and states.

Support for Carter's reform in Congress was generally favorable in the beginning, although some members expressed doubts about a change in preferences for veterans, and the American Legion quickly came out against the reform.[92] The largest federal employee union, the American Federation of Government Employees (AFGE), affiliated with the American Federation of Labor–Congress of Industrial Organizations (AFL-CIO), supported the reform initially, although some other unions were expected to oppose the plan.[93] To get his plan enacted, Carter would have to exercise some significant legislative leadership, something he had not excelled at in the past.[94]

Unfortunately for Carter, some of the initial support for his proposal dissipated rather quickly. In April 1978, due to continuing inflationary pressure, Carter announced he would propose capping federal pay raises at 5.5 percent.[95] This caused AFGE to back away from their previous support of Carter's civil service reform.[96]

Faced with growing opposition from affected groups and the indifference of much of the public, Carter attempted to mobilize his resources. He started by hosting his top aides and all of his Cabinet at Camp David, during which time the president castigated them for the way they were mishandling key elements of his agenda. "[Participants] agreed that it was an extraordinary performance from a man who normally is loathe to show emotion or criticize his subordinates."[97] A few days later, Carter gave a press conference in which his opening statement dealt entirely with civil service reform. He began his remarks by saying,

> Before I became President I realized and was warned that dealing with the Federal bureaucracy would be one of the worst problems I would have to face. It's been even worse than I had anticipated. Of all the steps that we can take to make government more efficient and effective, reforming the civil service system is the most important of all.[98]

Carter was frustrated with the opposition his reform legislation was encountering on Capitol Hill. In May, the *New York Times* reported, "The entire Cabinet has been enlisted to lobby for the Civil Service bill with the Congressmen they deal with on substantive issues."[99] In addition, Carter took the issue to the public. At a press conference held in Oregon, Carter's opening statement is, again, entirely devoted to the issue of civil service reform. Before taking questions, Carter stated,

> I think the American people in the West and all across the country are going to be watching how the Congress handles this very difficult but very important assignment to reform the bureaucracy of our Government, the keystone of which is to make the civil service work better.[100]

The problem with this strategy was that civil service reform, even though Carter framed it as a way to restore government for the people, never really resonated with the public, something Carter's chairman of the Civil Service Commission, Alan Campbell, acknowledged.[101] Campbell also indicated the proposal faced a difficult path through Congress.[102]

The piece of Carter's reform that was the most problematic was the change in veteran hiring preferences. In June, the Governmental Affairs Committee in the Senate accepted the major tenets of Carter's reforms, except for the change in preferences for veterans.[103] About the same time as the Senate committee was defeating the provision, Carter sent a letter to Robert Nix (D-PA), chair of the House Post Office and Civil Service Committee, whose committee would soon take up the civil service reform bill. The letter's purpose was solely to reiterate Carter's strong support for the change in preferences for veterans. He stressed the reasons why he wanted this change.

> We owe veterans our deep gratitude for serving their country, and they more than deserve special treatment from our government. However, veterans preference as it presently operates severely interferes with employment opportunities for women and other minorities, discriminates against younger veterans who are outnumbered by veterans who served before, and greatly hampers managerial flexibility.[104]

However, Carter also signaled the components of the change in veterans preferences on which he was willing to compromise.[105] This package of compromises had specifically been rejected by the Senate Governmental Affairs Committee. In the House committee, however, the administration-backed compromises on veterans hiring preferences were accepted.[106] The committee altered a few other aspects of Carter's original proposal and added several amendments, but Carter issued a statement after the committee voted saying, "The bill reported from committee carries forward the major thrust of my civil service reform proposal, though there were some amendments added by the committee that I opposed."[107]

Carter continued to heavily push for civil service reform and continued to remind anyone who would listen that civil service reform was, as he put it in a July 20 news conference, "a burning issue in the minds of the American people, to finally do something about waste and control of the federal bureaucracy."[108] In an interview he gave to editors and news directors at the end of July, Carter discussed civil service reform first as he opened the interview.[109] A few days later, Carter held a roundtable discussion in Virginia with civil servants focused entirely on his reform and reorganization proposals, which was carried live on television. The bill was reaching a critical juncture in Congress, and Carter continued to try to build public support. As he opened the roundtable, he asserted, "I spent 2 years campaigning for the office that I hold, and one of the most intense desires of the American people is to have a government, a bureaucracy, that's effective and efficient, and which serves them well."[110] Carter identified the cynicism and dissatisfaction he had encountered while on the campaign trail as the rationale behind his civil service reform.

Carter also continued to press members of Congress to advance his reform. "Like the suitor of a reluctant maiden, Jimmy Carter has been pursuing Congress in recent weeks with everything from flattery to invitations to the White House."[111] Carter, whose first year in office had been marked by poor congressional relations, was learning from his previous mistakes. As he would comment in an interview conducted the day before he was to sign the Civil Service Reform Act in October, "We had an overly optimistic impression that I could present a bill to the Congress which to me seemed patently in the best interests of our country and that the Congress would take it and pretty well pass it. I have been disabused of that expectation."[112] With civil service reform, the White House not only lobbied members of Congress, but also was willing to compromise, something for which Carter had previously shown distaste.

In the Senate, compromises had to be made to bring the bill to the floor. The White House accepted the compromises as the price of getting reform, which Carter desperately wanted. On August 24, the Senate approved the measure with an 87-1 vote. While several amendments were accepted, the basic aspects of the bill were in line with what the administration had proposed, except for the change in hiring preferences for veterans Carter had sought, which was not included in the Senate reform bill.[113] The House, however, was mired in procedural delays brought by two Democrats, who wanted some expanded union provisions. The tactics used to cause delay included a call for the 261-page bill to be read aloud before continuing debate.[114] Carter was able to aid getting the bill to a vote in the House by writing a letter to one of the delaying congressmen in which Carter signaled his support of another bill.[115] Finally, on September 13, after a barrage of attempts to amend, the House passed the civil service reform by a vote of 385-10. The compromise provision Carter had backed on veterans preferences in committee was stripped out of the bill on the House floor. While the bill would go to conference committee to hammer out House and Senate differences without this aspect of Carter's proposal, there were no other major changes to what Carter had proposed.

The conference reached agreement after Senator Ted Stevens (R-AK) threatened to scuttle things over "a minor provision to assure some military reserve officers that they could get high-paying civil service jobs and still draw full military retirement pay."[116] Conference chair Mo Udall (D-AZ) recommended the conference give in to Stevens's demands and "Udall finally got to bang his gavel."[117] After the Senate passed the conference report by voice vote and the House voted 365-8, Carter signed the Civil Service Reform Act of 1978 on October 13.[118]

Civil service reform would end up being one of the significant domestic achievements of Carter's presidency. In his first SUA, he signaled to audiences that it was a very important issue for him. He saw it as a way to respond to public disaffection with government and, whenever speaking about the issue, always framed it as such. In acting as chief legislator and pushing this particular issue, Carter's main goal was not reelection, as this rather arcane issue was not likely to win him lots of votes with the public, nor was it likely to be an issue upon which to construct a great legacy; rather Carter truly desired to make public policy he thought was in the best interest of the nation. Civil service reform was not an issue Congress would take up on its own; a chief legislator would have to spur congressional action. Carter was able to do this with the attention he brought to the issue, and the SUA was a part of that strategy. While his devotion of a portion of the SUA to this topic did not make much of a media splash following the SUA, Congress did take the issue up once Carter sent his proposal. Carter continued to press for his reforms and was a much more effective chief legislator than he had been previously; he talked to the public about the issue, lobbied members of Congress, and was willing to compromise. Eight months from the time the administration submitted its proposal to Congress, Carter got most of what he wanted out of Congress with his civil service reform initiative.

The Long, Strange Trip of the Line-Item Veto

Multiple presidents have used the policymaking rhetoric of the SUA to ask Congress for a line-item veto that would enable them to cancel individual spending items, or "lines," in annual appropriations bills, while accepting other items. In the 1980s and 1990s, as budget deficits spiraled ever upward, presidents advocated this reform giving them expanded power over appropriations as a way of reigning in wasteful (i.e., pork barrel) spending. Members of Congress want to "bring home the bacon," so to speak, to their states and districts. Individual members will frequently advocate, and often get, money appropriated to their pet projects in their individual states or districts. One person's pork, however, is another's vital economic development or research program. There is little incentive for Congress to rein in this type of spending; an individual member of Congress supports another's pet project with the expectation of reciprocity. Chief legislators have often argued, however, that they would effectively be able to correct wasteful spending if they had an item veto.

Presidents have long exercised power to impound funds, refusing to spend monies appropriated by Congress. In the nineteenth century, Jackson, John Tyler, James Buchanan, Ulysses Grant, and Grover Cleveland were all presidents who impounded funds associated with public works projects.[119] Military programs were the target of impoundments by Franklin Roosevelt, Truman, Eisenhower, and Kennedy. Johnson continued this practice and extended it to domestic programs until the states and Congress raised objections.[120] In 1974, as a result of Nixon's impoundments, which "set a precedent in terms of magnitude, severity, and belligerence," Congress passed the Budget and Impoundment Control Act of 1974 in order to limit a president's ability to impound funds and to allow Congress the opportunity to either accept or reject the president's request.[121] The act allows presidents to use both deferrals and rescissions. A deferral merely delays the spending of appropriated funds, whereas a rescission is a permanent cancellation. Rescissions are proposed to Congress by the president and unless both chambers act to approve the rescission, money is released after 45 days.[122] Since the passage of the Impoundment Control Act of 1974, most of the action taken in Congress regarding line-item veto powers has centered on expanding rescission authority. The Line-Item Veto Act of 1996, despite the name, was not a pure line-item veto, which would take a constitutional amendment, but a statutory means of giving the president an item veto by enhancing his rescission powers. Under the Impoundment Control Act, Congress needed to accept the rescissions made by the president; no action on the part of Congress meant the rescissions did not take effect. With the Line-Item Veto Act, however, and the enhanced rescission authority it gave to the president, Congress would have to pass legislation in 30 days to overturn a rescission, which could be vetoed by the president; no action on the part of Congress meant the president's rescission took effect.[123]

Discussions in the last two decades of the twentieth century over whether the line-item veto should be adopted were specifically linked to balancing the budget. Those who argued in favor of the line-item veto saw it as something that would allow the president to exercise fiscal discipline where Congress cannot. Those who argued against the reform believed that Congress would be giving power to the president in violation of the Constitution, which requires a president to accept or reject bills in whole, not selectively. From 1984 to 1996, all three presidents asked for the line-item veto in multiple SUAs. The line-item veto was finally passed by the 104th Congress, twelve years after Reagan first asked for it in an SUA. In every SUA from 1984 to 1988, Reagan requested the line-item veto power be given to him. George H. W. Bush asked for the power in his 1989 and 1992 SUAs, and Clinton asked for the power in both 1995 and 1996. Clinton's request was successful in 1996, and the 104th Congress approved the Line-Item Veto Act. The law took effect January 1, 1997. Clinton was the only president to ever exercise this power, however, as the Supreme Court would rule the act unconstitutional in 1998.

The path the line-item veto took in becoming law was a long one. Reagan would advocate most forcefully for the power, repeating in SUA after SUA that it was a power he needed. G. H. W. Bush and Clinton were more selective in the way they used their SUAs to request action from Congress. It would take a combination of presidential, congressional, and public support, as well as rising deficits over twelve years, for the power to become a reality.

As Reagan was gearing up for reelection in 1984, the budget deficit was looming as an issue that threatened Reagan's reelection prospects. The first policy topic Reagan discussed in his 1984 SUA was budget deficits. One of the things he advocated was a constitutional amendment to provide the president with the line-item veto. He reminded his audiences that he had the power as governor of California and that many other governors also wielded this power. "As Governor, I found this line-item veto was a powerful tool against wasteful or extravagant spending. It works in 43 states. Let's put it to work in Washington for all the people."[124]

Early in his presidency, Reagan had occasionally voiced his support for a line-item veto in his public appearances, but he had never done so in an SUA, or any other major speech.[125] After the January 1984 SUA, Reagan would mention the line-item veto an average of five times each month until the election.[126] A few months later, in April, the Senate Judiciary Committee's Subcommittee on the Constitution held hearings on two proposals to amend the Constitution to give the president the line-item veto, but the proposals did not advance.[127] In May 1984, the Republican-controlled Senate rejected a proposal to give the president, through legislation, an item-veto.[128] In September, the issue would return again to the Senate in a slightly different form, but the end result was the same.[129] Reagan's attention, however, increased the level of awareness about the issue. Before raising it in the 1984 SUA, there had been scant attention paid to the issue in Congress.[130] The day of his reelection, Reagan signaled getting the line-item veto would be a top priority in his second term.[131]

In the two years following his reelection, Reagan would mention the item veto less frequently in his public appearances than in 1984, but he would include the request in every subsequent SUA. In 1985's SUA, Reagan expressed hope that Congress would make his request a reality when he told his audiences that "Senator Mattingly has introduced a bill permitting a 2-year trial run of the line-item veto. I hope you'll pass and send that legislation to my desk."[132] Unfortunately for Reagan, in July 1985 the Senate could not end a week-long filibuster on the bill.[133]

In the 1986 SUA, Reagan said,

> And tonight I ask you to give me what 43 Governors have: Give me a line-item veto this year. Give me the authority to veto waste, and I'll take the responsibility, I'll make the cuts, I'll take the heat. This authority would not give me any monopoly power, but simply prevent spending measures from sneaking through that could not pass on their own merit. And you can sustain or override my veto; that's the way the system should work.[134]

He made very similar requests in the 1987 and 1988 SUAs, but from 1985 to the end of Reagan's term, the line-item veto would be virtually dropped in the halls of Congress.[135]

Reagan's SUA requests on the line-item veto were initially successful in 1984 and 1985 in propelling the issue onto Congress's agenda. The Senate did consider both a constitutional amendment and a statutory means of giving the president this power, but these attempts were unsuccessful. By 1987, Iran-Contra was occupying Washington, and the Senate was once again in Democratic hands. Even though budget deficits continued to climb, Congress would not follow Reagan by giving him this power he very much wanted; the official debate over the item veto largely ceased.

When George H. W. Bush took office in 1989, the budgetary situation was not improving. In his first joint address to the Congress in February 1989, Bush began by addressing budgetary matters, and one of the first legislative requests he had was for the line-item veto. Bush, however, did not devote very much of his rhetoric to this particular issue and used the same general phrasing as Reagan had done. "Forty-three Governors have the line-item veto. Presidents should have it, too. And at the very least, when a President proposes to rescind Federal spending, the Congress should be required to vote on that proposal instead of killing it by inaction."[136] Bush signaled that he preferred a constitutional amendment giving him this power, but he would settle for "expedited rescission" authority given through legislation, a weaker alternative than even the "enhanced rescission" approach.[137] In 1989, the Senate Judiciary Committee's Subcommittee on the Constitution held hearings on a line-item veto amendment, and reported two resolutions regarding the matter to the full committee.[138] There was also an attempt to add a line-item veto through legislative means as an amendment to a bill in the Senate, but the attempt was unsuccessful.[139] Finally, the Bush Administration contemplated testing the president's veto power by exercising a line-item veto on the claim that the president has veto power and could define how he wields it.[140] In other words, he would claim it as an existing part of the veto power, and it could then be tested in the courts. The administration did not carry through on this action, however.

Bush would not mention the line-item veto in his 1990 SUA, but there was some action in Congress. In the second session of the 101st Congress, there was another attempt to add the line-item veto through legislative means as an amendment to bills in the Senate.[141] The Senate Judiciary committee took up the two measures approved the year before by the subcommittee and reported them favorably to the Senate.[142] The Senate would not take up the issue, however, and no other action was taken in the 101st Congress.

The 1991 SUA also did not contain mention of the line-item veto, and there was virtually no action in Congress on the matter. As the election neared in 1992, the federal budget deficit continued to loom as an issue, threatening Bush and his reelection. Bush would again request the line-item veto in his 1992 SUA, and his remarks were much more explanatory than they had been in 1989.

> You know, it's time we rediscovered a home truth the American people have never forgotten: This Government is too big and spends too much. And I call upon Congress to adopt a measure that will help put an end to the annual ritual of filling the budget with pork barrel appropriations. Every year, the press has a field day making fun of outrageous examples: a Lawrence Welk museum, research grants for Belgian endive. We all know how these things get into the budget, and maybe you need someone to help you say no. I know how to say it, and I know what I need to make it stick. Give me the same thing 43 Governors have, the line-item veto, and let me help you control spending.[143]

Following Bush's address, he advocated the line-item veto at numerous campaign appearances; mention of it became standard in his stump speech. In October 1992 alone, Bush mentioned the issue at thirty-six separate campaign appearances. Congress returned to the issue of the line-item veto, as well, and for the first time, the House considered it. The House had success on the issue and on October 3, 1992, passed an expedited rescissions bill by a vote of 312-97.[144] The bill would not have a chance, however, in the Senate, largely because of the adamant opposition of Senator Robert Byrd (D-WV), who had been behind the 1985 filibuster of a similar measure.

Thus, when Bush left the presidency in 1993, the line-item veto had not advanced much in the four years he had been president. However, Bush's rhetoric in the 1992 SUA was much more forceful, it became an election issue, and Congress chose to consider it, whereas they had not in 1991 when Bush had not included a request in the SUA.

As governor of Arkansas, Bill Clinton had the line-item veto, and as president he supported an enhanced rescission measure that would require two-thirds majorities in Congress to override.[145] After the election, both Clinton and Speaker of the House Tom Foley (D-WA) indicated they believed the line-item veto should be addressed. Senator Bill Bradley (D-NJ) had recently written a prominent opinion piece in the *Wall Street Journal* in which he explained why he had reversed his previous opposition to the line-item veto.[146] Senate Majority Leader George Mitchell (D-ME), however, as well as long-time opponent Senator Byrd, did not lend their support.[147] Democrats were divided on the issue. Although Clinton had talked about the line-item veto in his campaign, he did not include mention of it in his first joint address to Congress as president in 1993, nor would he discuss it in his 1994 SUA. While the Democrats controlled the Congress in 1993–1994, the House would pass an expedited rescissions measure twice, but there would be little action in the Senate. There was one unsuccessful attempt to attach an enhanced rescissions measure to the Motor Voter Bill in the Senate, but that was the extent of the action.[148]

In the Fall of 1994, Republicans in the House of Representatives were embarking on a fierce public relations campaign that sought to vault their party to victory in the November elections. Dubbed the "Contract with America," this document was a pledge by Republicans to bring certain items up for votes in the first 100 days should they be elected to the majority. At the top of the list was a call for legislation on a presidential line-item veto.[149]

After the Republican takeover of Congress in the 1994 elections, the new House majority was eager to get to work on their "Contract." Even though there was some debate about giving a Democratic president the line-item veto, Republicans in the House pressed the issue. A Gallup Poll taken in December 1994 after the Republican victory and specifically focused on points in the Contract found that 77 percent supported the line-item veto.[150]

President Clinton suffered a major setback to his presidency when Republicans captured control of both the House and the Senate in the 1994 elections. He opened his 1995 SUA by saying,

> Again we are here in the sanctuary of democracy, and once again our democracy has spoken. So let me begin by congratulating all of you here in the 104th Congress and congratulating you, Mr. Speaker. If we agree on nothing else tonight, we must agree that the American people certainly voted for change in 1992 and 1994. And as I look out at you, I know how some of you must have felt in 1992.[151]

Clinton supported the line-item veto but had refrained from pushing the issue too much in the 103rd Congress because Democrats were divided and he had other major priorities. For the first time, Clinton requested a line-item veto in his 1995 SUA.

> For years, Congress concealed in the budget scores of pet spending projects. Last year was no different. There was . . . $1 million to study stress in

plants and $12 million for a tick removal program that didn't work. It's hard to remove ticks. Those of us who have had them know. But I'll tell you something, if you'll give me line-item veto, I'll remove some of that unnecessary spending.[152]

Clinton took the opportunity to voice his support for the line-item veto knowing full well that it was a plank in the Republican Contract. Clinton's support did not deter Republicans, at least initially, and in early 1995, House Republicans passed a bill 294-134 to give the president enhanced rescission power. In a symbolic gesture, the House acted on February 6, Ronald Reagan's eighty-fourth birthday.[153]

Clinton supported the House bill, but the Senate was still a potential roadblock for this particular measure. At the time, Republican control of the Senate was 54-46 and Senator Byrd was threatening a filibuster. Republicans did not know if they would be able to muster the necessary sixty votes to invoke cloture, but they promised to blame the Democrats if the bill failed. Public support for the line-item veto was strong, and Majority Whip Trent Lott (R-MS) said, "it's up to the President" to secure Democratic support for the legislation.[154] Senate Majority Leader Robert Dole (R-KS) continued to set the stage for blaming the Democrats if the bill was defeated by a filibuster. He urged Clinton to voice his support and added, "I guess [if] it's a choice between passing something he always supported or denying Republicans a legislative victory, then the line-item veto will probably be sacrificed on the altar of politics."[155] On March 20, Clinton would issue a statement on the line-item veto.

The Senate is now debating the line-item veto legislation which passed last month in the House. I urge the Senate to pass the strongest possible line-item veto and to make it effective immediately. If the Members of Congress from both parties are serious about cutting the deficit, give me this line-item veto, and I will get started right away. This is one area where both parties can and should come together.[156]

Clinton needed to persuade enough Democratic Senators to join the Republicans in order to reach the sixty votes needed to invoke cloture if a filibuster occurred. Dole promised to be able to make sure all fifty-four Republicans would vote together, leaving Clinton to find six Democrats to vote with them. Even though Clinton wanted the line-item veto, he avoided specifically stating exactly what type of power he wanted; his statement urged "the strongest possible" measure. Each party produced different versions. As much as he wanted a strong item veto he knew that many Democrats would not support the Republican version, because many felt it gave too much authority to the president. Senator John McCain (R-AZ), however, voiced that the president's statement "left no doubt" which version he favored: "give me a break . . . if the Democratic version is the strongest possible version, then fish fly."[157] On March 23, the Senate passed a version of the line-item veto that was different from the House version by a vote of 69-29. Instead of taking the enhanced rescission path, the Senate passed a version that broke up appropriations bills, new entitlements, or targeted tax breaks after passage into individually enrolled measures that the president could then selectively veto.[158] Senator Byrd, ever the opponent, claimed this approach created a "logistical nightmare" where there would be "hundreds of little orphan bills" each requiring the president's signature. Senator McCain reassured Byrd that with modern technology and computers this would not be a problem.[159] The version passed by the House and the one passed by the Senate were quite far apart. Representative Cardiss Collins (D-IL) summed up the two versions by calling the House version "unconstitutional" and the Senate version "patently absurd."[160] A conference committee would need to iron out the differences.

After Senate passage, Clinton had issued another statement in support of the line-item veto but still urged the "strongest possible bill" rather than taking a stand on one version or the other.[161] Two days later in his weekly radio address, Clinton specifically asked "members of both parties to resolve their differences" so that "the line-item veto can put people ahead of pork."[162] Clinton would continue to press for further congressional action, but weeks turned into months and a conference committee was not scheduled.

Clinton continued his public statements. In April, he addressed the American Society of Newspaper Editors.

> Let's talk about the line-item veto. As I said before, that was in the Republican contract, and I campaigned for President on it in 1992. I appeal to Congress to pass it in its strongest form. I appeal to members of my own party who have reservations about it to support it as well. The line-item veto has now passed both the Senate and the House.
>
> If you look at how it passed the Senate, that's an example of how we can make this system work. I strongly supported it. I campaigned to Democratic Senators and asked them to support it. They worked out their differences, and it passed overwhelmingly in the Senate.
>
> The President and the Congress both need the power to cut spending. If you doubt it—if you doubt it—look at the bill that Congress recently passed to restore to 3.2 million self-employed Americans, farmers, small businesspeople, professionals and all their family members, the 25 percent deduction for the cost of their health insurance.
>
> That was a part of my health care plan. I desperately want to do that. We ought to do more. They ought to be treated just like corporations. It is imperative to sign it. But hidden in that bill was a special tax break for people who did not need it. If I had the Senate version of the line-item veto, I could sign the bill and help the people who are entitled to it, and veto the special break. This is the kind of thing that's been hidden in bills

of Congress forever. We can now do something about it, and we ought to do it.[163]

By June there was still no conference scheduled on the line-item measure. In a Rose Garden ceremony, Clinton stated,

> I have now seen two separate news reports in which the majority in Congress, according to some of their members, say that they have decided not to pass the line-item veto after all, after campaigning on it for a dozen years now. This line-item veto is a tool that would permit the President to single out special pork projects, veto them, send them back to Congress, and Congress would be able to override the veto. But they would have to vote on these projects separately instead of burying them in big bills that a President cannot in good conscience veto.
>
> Now, that line-item veto was part of their Contract With America and a part that I embraced. President Reagan was for it. President Bush was for it. The House passed it on President Reagan's birthday. They talked about what an urgent thing it was. Now they say they don't think they ought to give it to me this year because I might use it.[164]

The same day, Clinton sent a letter to congressional leaders that conveyed his concerns about the status of the line-item veto and reminded Republicans of their pledge to cut the deficit and reduce spending.[165] Many Republican lawmakers did not want to give a Democratic president the line-item veto power. Even though both houses passed versions of the line-item veto with strong support, there was no indication when a conference committee would convene to work out the differences. On June 20, 1995, the Senate named their conferees, but the House would not follow until September 7; the first meeting of the conference would take place September 27.[166] One other meeting was held in November, the only other meeting for the year.[167]

Clinton would be able to take the stage during the SUA in 1996 and press once again for action on the line-item veto. In the 1996 SUA, however, Clinton's legislative request was limited to one sentence. He said, "I also appeal to Congress to pass the line-item veto."[168] As Clinton began to make campaign appearances after the 1996 SUA, he frequently mentioned the line-item veto and chastised the Republican Congress for not delivering. The conference committee did finally agree to an enhanced rescissions version of the line-item veto in March 1996. The Senate agreed to the conference report on March 27, and the House followed the next day. President Clinton signed the Line-Item Veto Act of 1996 into law on April 9. With this new law that took effect January 1, 1997, the president could rescind appropriations, new entitlement spending, and some targeted tax breaks. Congress would have thirty days to pass a disapproval bill if they disagreed with the president's actions, which could in turn be vetoed by the president.[169]

The line-item veto is a power many presidents have called for, but that Congress had been reluctant to give to presidents. Even with divided government and in an election year, a Democratic president and a Republican Congress passed a piece of legislation that seemed, at times, very unlikely to find its way out of the congressional policymaking labyrinth. Through the combination of presidential leadership, favorable public opinion, pressure from budget deficits, and congressional support, the Line-Item Veto Act emerged. Upon signing the bill into law, Clinton reminded the public,

> This new law shows what we can achieve when we put our partisan differences aside and work together for the Nation. Members of both parties have fought for this legislation because they believed that no matter which party has control of the White House or the Congress, the line item veto would be good for the country.[170]

The Supreme Court, however, would not agree that the Line-Item Veto Act was good for the country. In June 1998, the Act was ruled as a violation of the presentment clause in Article I, section 7 of the Constitution.[171]

Presidents Reagan, Bush, and Clinton kept the line-item veto issue alive for twelve years as it slowly gained support. Asking Congress for this power in multiple SUAs kept the issue in front of the public and Congress. The presidents' vocal support for the line-item veto was a significant factor. The way each president framed the line-item issue in their SUAs was virtually identical. Reagan highlighted the "boondoggles" of cranberry, blueberry, and crawfish research in his 1988 SUA; Bush pointed to a Welk museum; and Clinton brought attention to a tick removal program—all things that received federal funds. The public tends to have a visceral reaction against pork, and the presidents used particularly egregious examples to tap into this public feeling. Each president also stressed that they could be responsible when Congress could not bring itself to be. Reagan said, "I'll take the heat." Bush said, I'll "help you say no." Clinton pledged, "I'll remove" waste. The SUA usage by these presidents with regard to the line-item veto was instrumental in keeping the issue alive until conditions were favorable for action. Rising budget deficits were also an important factor. What finally tipped the balance in favor of the line-item veto was the election of a Republican Congress. Every recent president, regardless of party, has wanted the line-item veto. Democratic Congresses in the 1970s and 1980s were unwilling to bestow it on the president. The right combination of factors occurred in the mid-1990s.

This particular case also exemplifies the mutually reinforcing nature of the chief legislator's goals. Presidents advocated the line-item veto because they had a desire to make public policy, and in this case it was a policy that would give the chief legislator enhanced power, uniting presidents of different parties, styles, and ideologies behind the same policy for institutional reasons. Reelection goals were also important. Both Reagan and Bush gave attention to the line-item veto in their 1984 and 1992 SUAs, and it became a reelection issue for each. At the time of the 1996 SUA, the measure was in conference and Clinton devoted only one sentence to the line-item in the SUA. But, in the handful of election events, and even official events Clinton had before passage in March, he reminded audiences of Republican stalling on the issue. Had the measure not passed, the lack of follow-through would have been a large issue for the president to hold over the heads of congressional Republicans, and particularly his opponent Senator Dole. Finally, legacy considerations were also important for these presidents as they requested action on the line-item veto. As Clinton noted in his signing statement, presidents going back to Grant had wanted this power.[172] That it was approved under his leadership, and that he would be the first (and only) to exercise the power, potentially carried significance for his legacy, just as the inability of Reagan and Bush to secure the power was also of significance.

Conclusion

In this chapter, we have examined the outcomes of the policymaking rhetoric of the SUA. With policymaking rhetoric, chief legislators want to lead Congress to accept their legislative requests. Does Congress follow where they lead? Congress generally does not enact most of the SUA requests in a given year following the SUA. When presidents use an SUA to ask Congress for enactment of their policy priorities in the coming year, they typically receive about two in five of their requests, either in full or in part. Success rates, however, vary from president to president; as one would expect, Johnson was much more successful than Ford. Presidents also have varying levels of success within their presidencies. Addresses presidents give following either their initial election or their reelection tend to have success rates that are higher than the median. Crisis SUAs also have very different levels of success depending upon the nature of the particular crisis and to what extent presidents tie their requests to the crisis. Finally, whether presidents are in office at a time of divided or unified government makes a significant difference in their success in getting their full requests, although not when one considers both full and partial successes.

Case studies allowed us to examine what role the SUA played in the outcome of four different legislative requests. In all of the cases, the SUA played an integral role, although this did not always mean the president was successful in getting his request enacted or that the SUA was the most important factor. In addition, these four requests, to varying degrees, were included in the SUA to further the mutually reinforcing goals presidents have as chief legislator.

Johnson has been described as "one of the most gifted practitioners in American history of the art of coaxing decisions out of a political system that makes it easier to block initiatives than bring them to fruition."[173] Johnson is the most successful with his SUA requests of all our presidents. Being both a former member of the House and a very effective Senate Majority Leader, Johnson understood like few chief legislators what it took to lead Congress. Even so, Johnson was unable to get Congress to propose a constitutional amendment for four-year terms for House members. Johnson's SUA request, however, was largely responsible for getting Congress to hold hearings on the matter, although the action would go no further and Johnson's attention to the issue would be brief. The primary goal Johnson was pursuing with this request was the goal of making public policy.

As Reagan entered his reelection year, he pushed a new space initiative: building a permanently manned space station. NASA was successful in getting the president's support because the project appealed to Reagan's vision of the greatness and inventiveness of America. Reagan, in turn, was successful in convincing Congress. Congress would need to fund this project, and Reagan was successful in convincing them to authorize and appropriate the exact amount he requested, despite the opposition of many within his own administration and rising budget deficits. Reagan was no doubt aided by the relatively small amount he requested for the first year of this ten-year project, but that should not diminish his accomplishment. The way Reagan discussed this initiative in his SUA was instrumental in getting his request. It became front page news and a part of his reelection campaign. For Reagan as chief legislator, this request served primarily the goals of making public policy and reelection, although legacy considerations were also a factor.

Jimmy Carter's relationship with his Democratic Congress was often strained, but he was able to correct some of his past mistakes in his dealings with them and achieve significant civil service reform, getting the bulk of what he requested from Congress. He made government reform a key theme of his campaign, and as president, he viewed civil service reform as vital in addressing the public's dissatisfaction with Washington. In his SUA, he framed the issue as one of restoring the government to its people. His attention to the issue in the SUA and subsequent actions placed it on Congress's agenda. Absent Carter's attention, Congress was not likely to take up the issue on its own. It was not easy for Carter to get his request. Many federal employee unions were against aspects of it, as were veterans groups. Carter compromised and lobbied Congress to get what he wanted, two things he had been reluctant to do in his first year. The main goal Carter was pursuing with this SUA request was to make public policy. Civil service reform, despite Carter's belief to the contrary, was not a "burning issue" with the public, but Carter pursued it because he believed it was in the best interest of the nation and would help restore citizens' faith in government. It did not significantly contribute to his goal for reelection. While civil service reform is one of the significant domestic achievements of Carter's presidency, his legacy is generally dominated by his foreign policy successes and failures.

Finally, we considered multiple presidents' requests in multiple SUAs for the line-item veto. Each president discussed the need for the line-item veto in a similar fashion. All conveyed it was the president who was situated to be fiscally responsible and eliminate wasteful spending, whereas Congress was not positioned to do so. Each president also drew from examples of pork to incite public reaction against such "wastefulness." The steady stream of requests for this initiative over twelve years was eventually successful. SUAs played an important part in continually signaling this desire. Combined with increased attention to rising deficits and a change in the partisan composition of Congress, the SUA would help President Clinton receive what he and other presidents had long desired. All three goals of the chief legislator—making public policy, working toward reelection, and obtaining a positive legacy—were factors in why presidents made this particular request.

Thus, the SUA played an important role in the outcome of each of the four cases we examined. In the cases of extending House terms, the development of a space station, and civil service reform, the president's attention to the issue in the SUA placed the request on Congress's agenda. Getting on the agenda, however, does not mean the president's request will ultimately be successful, but it is a prerequisite for the request to be fulfilled. With the line-item veto, a presidential mention did not always get the issue on the agenda. Despite asking for a line-item veto in every year from 1984 to the end of his presidency, Reagan was successful only in 1984 and 1985 at getting much consideration in Congress on the issue. Eventually, continual presidential attention to the issue, rising deficits, and a change in the partisan composition of Congress did mean success for the presidential request.

The SUA is a marvelous tool of political communication for chief legislators. With it, they can further the goals of making public policy, winning reelection, and securing a positive legacy. The policymaking rhetoric of the SUA, however, is one-sided and incorporates symbolic and emotional appeals, making it a perfect forum for a demagogue. The attention given to chief legislators as they deliver this speech encourages a view of a president-centered political system. The public hones in on the president, and the setting in which the SUA is delivered promotes this view. These impressions, however, are misleading. The speech is not without its limitations. An examination of the legislative requests in SUAs shows that presidents do not get Congressional enactment on a substantial number of the highlighted policies in the year following the speech. The chief legislators' increase in rhetorical powers represented in the SUA did give them an advantage over regular legislators, but it did not unduly increase their power over the legislature. The system of shared legislative powers continues to check the president. Presidents have power to recommend measures and regularly do so with their SUAs. Their position in the political system as chief legislator makes it much more likely Congress will give consideration to their requests, but it does not guarantee they will receive a substantial amount of their requests. The evidence from SUAs does not depict contemporary chief legislators as "superepresenators" who, "empowered by popular support . . . reign over the people's representatives in Congress."[174] The role of chief legislator is not one of an ordinary legislator, but neither does it empower the president with an arsenal with which to assault Congress. The SUA is a tool the chief legislator can use to facilitate congressional leadership, but it is not a weapon.

Notes

1. Mark A. Peterson, *Legislating Together: The White House and Capitol Hill from Eisenhower to Reagan* (Cambridge: Harvard University Press, 1990), 8.

2. Karlyn Kohrs Campbell and Kathleen Hall Jamieson, *Deeds Done in Words: Presidential Rhetoric and the Genres of Governance* (Chicago: University of Chicago Press, 1990), 54.

3. We do not distinguish between major and minor legislation precisely because we are interested in what the president requests in the SUA, regardless of whether it might be considered major or minor. If the president requests it, it is in the speech for a particular reason. For example, Clinton excelled at requesting large amounts of things in the SUA. Some of them would be considered major, but some of them (such as V-chips) would be considered relatively minor. However, the way Clinton utilized the sheer number of requests served a particular purpose for him. Furthermore, in a speech in which he assessed his legacy, Clinton emphasized both major and minor accomplishments, as he claimed credit for an array of successes. William J. Clinton, *Clinton Presidential Legacy*, speech given November 10, 2005, at Hofstra University, Hempstead, New York, 11th Presidential Conference, "William Jefferson Clinton: The 'New' Democrat from Hope," C-SPAN National Cable Satellite Corporation, 2005, DVD.

4. If Congress and the president did not complete the budget process in that session, any relevant legislative requests from the president's SUA are unsuccessful.

5. In most cases, the *Almanac* provided sufficient information. In instances where it did not, other more specialized sources were used, typically *Congressional Quarterly Weekly Reports* and/or appropriations acts.

6. George C. Edwards III and Andrew Barrett, "Presidential Agenda Setting in Congress," in *Polarized Politics: Congress and the President in a Partisan Era*, ed. Jon R. Bond and Richard Fleisher (Washington, DC: CQ Press, 2000), 109–133.

7. Paul C. Light, *The President's Agenda: Domestic Policy Choice from Kennedy to Clinton*, 3rd ed. (Baltimore: Johns Hopkins University Press, 1999), 36.

8. Michael Nelson, "Bill Clinton and the Politics of Second Terms,"

Presidential Studies Quarterly 29 (1998); Michael Grossman, Martha Joynt Kumar, and Francis E. Rourke, "Second-Term Presidencies: The Aging of Administration," in *The Presidency and the Political System*, 6th ed., ed. Michael Nelson (Washington, DC: CQ Press, 2000).

9. John E. Mueller, *War, Presidents, and Public Opinion* (New York: John Wiley & Sons, 1973), 205.

10. Edwards and Barrett, "Presidential Agenda Setting," 127–132.

11. Unlike Edwards and Barrett's study, which examined presidential and congressional initiatives separately, the president's legislative requests in the SUA will include both presidential initiatives as well as congressional initiatives on which he chooses to advertise a position.

12. Edwards and Barrett, "Presidential Agenda Setting."

13. Light, *The President's Agenda*, 248–249.

14. Michael Kagay, "Approval of Bush Soars," *New York Times*, 19 January 1991, 9; Samuel Kernell, *Going Public: New Strategies of Presidential Leadership*, 3rd ed. (Washington, DC: CQ Press, 1997), 181.

15. "A Snapshot Gives Bush 90% Approval," *New York Times*, 24 September 2001, B6.

16. Gary C. Jacobson, "The Bush Presidency and the American Electorate," *Presidential Studies Quarterly* 33 (December 2003):701–731.

17. Condition of government also changed in the midst of the first two years of George W. Bush's administration. However, the majority of the 107th Congress occurred under divided government, and that is how we classify it.

18. Mann-Whitney U test indicates $z = -.34$ ($p \geq 0.75$).

19. Mann-Whitney U test indicates $z = -1.9$ ($p \leq 0.10$).

20. Quoted in Robert E. DiClerico, *The American President*, 5th ed. (New Jersey: Prentice Hall, 2000), 67.

21. Emphasis original, Richard E. Neustadt, *Presidential Power and the Modern Presidents*, rev. ed. (New York: Free Press, 1990), 29.

22. Fred Greenstein, *The Presidential Difference: Leadership Style from FDR to Clinton* (New York: Free Press, 2000), 189.

23. The last time significant civil service reform took place was after President Garfield was assassinated by a man who is invariably referred to as "a disaffected job seeker," which produced the Pendleton Act of 1883.

24. Lyndon Johnson, "Address Before a Joint Session of the Congress on the State of the Union," *Public Papers of the Presidents of the United States: Lyndon B. Johnson, 1966*, vol. 1 (Washington, DC: GPO, 1967), 7.

25. Ibid.

26. US Constitution, Art. I, Sec. 2.

27. The Constitution also allows for amendments to be proposed by a convention requested by two-thirds of the state legislatures, but this method of proposal has never been used.

28. Marjorie Hunter, "President Calls for 4-Year Terms in the House," *New York Times*, 13 January 1966, A15.

29. Ibid.

30. "LBJ Election Law Proposals Surprise, Delight Reformers," *Congressional Quarterly Weekly Report*, 21 January 1966, 246.

31. "Toward a More Responsible Two-Party System: A Report of the Committee on Political Parties, American Political Science Association," *American Political Science Review*, Supplement, 44 (September 1950).

32. Ibid., 75.

33. Dwight D. Eisenhower, "The President's News Conference of March 2,

1955," *Public Papers of the Presidents of the United States: Dwight D. Eisenhower, 1955*, vol. 1 (Washington, DC: GPO, 1961), 313.

34. "LBJ Election Law Proposals," 247.

35. Charles O. Jones, *Every Second Year: Congressional Behavior and the Two-Year Term* (Washington, DC: Brookings Institution, 1967), 23.

36. Ibid., 24.

37. Quoted in Marjorie Hunter, "President Calls for 4-year Terms in the House," *New York Times*, 13 January 1966, A15.

38. Johnson, "Special Message to the Congress Proposing Constitutional Amendments Relating to Terms for House Members and the Electoral College System," *Public Papers, 1966*, 1:36–40.

39. Johnson had mentioned this reform in his 1965 SUA, but it was not repeated in the 1966 SUA.

40. "Committee Roundup: Four-Year House Term," *Congressional Quarterly Weekly Report*, 18 February 1966, 429.

41. Ibid., 428.

42. "LBJ Election Law Proposals," 247.

43. "Committee Roundup," 18 February 1966, 428.

44. Ibid., 429.

45. Quoted in "Celler and Some Republicans Oppose 4-Year Terms in House," *New York Times*, 9 February 1966, A25.

46. Ibid.

47. Ibid.

48. Quoted in "Katzenbach Challenged on 4-Year House Terms," *New York Times*, 16 February 1966, A18.

49. Ibid.

50. Ibid.

51. "Committee Roundup: Four-Year House Term," *Congressional Quarterly Weekly Report*, 4 March 1966, 495.

52. "Election Reforms," *Congressional Quarterly Weekly Report*, 15 April 1966, 782.

53. Ronald W. Reagan, "Address Before a Joint Session of the Congress on the State of the Union," *Public Papers of the Presidents of the United States: Ronald W. Reagan, 1984*, vol. 1 (Washington, DC: GPO, 1985), 90.

54. John F. Kennedy, "Special Message to the Congress on Urgent National Needs," *Public Papers of the Presidents of the United States: John F. Kennedy, 1961*, vol. 1 (Washington, DC: GPO, 1963), 404.

55. John Noble Wilford, "Political Aides Urge Reagan to Back Space Station," *New York Times*, 21 September 1983, D26.

56. David Shribman, "Glenn Urges Commitment to 'Permanent Presence in Space,'" *New York Times*, 19 January 1984, A21.

57. John Noble Wilford, "Satellite Linked to Space Station as Russians Aim for Larger Craft," *New York Times*, 11 March 1983, A12.

58. M. Mitchell Waldrop, "The Selling of the Space Station," *Science*, 24 February 1984, 793.

59. Ibid. George A. Keyworth II, the president's science advisor, would eventually get behind the space shuttle project. See "A Station in Space Predicted," *New York Times*, 19 July 1983, C3.

60. Wilford, "Political Aides Urge Reagan," D26.

61. Philip J. Hilts, "The Federal Report: The Science Agencies," *Washington Post*, 26 December 1983, A19.

62. Waldrop, "Selling of the Space Station," 794.

63. Ibid.

64. "Reagan Hails NASA but Does Not Offer Space Station Funds," *New York Times*, 20 October 1983, B11.

65. Waldrop, "Selling of the Space Station," 794.

66. Philip M. Boffey, "President Seems Near Commitment on Space Station," *New York Times*, 14 December 1983, A1.

67. Philip M. Boffey, "President Backs U.S. Space Station as Next Key Goal," *New York Times*, 26 January 1984, A1.

68. Reagan, "Radio Address to the Nation on the Space Program," *Public Papers, 1984*, 1:108.

69. Philip M. Boffey, "Many Voices Oppose Space Station but White House Listens to NASA," *New York Times,* 29 January 1984, D2.

70. Quoted in Boffey, "Many Voices," D2.

71. Robert Rothman, "1985 Budget: $8 Billion Total Cost Expected: Planning Funds Requested for Manned Space Station," *Congressional Quarterly Weekly Report*, 4 February 1984, 192.

72. Ibid.

73. Robert Rothman, "NASA Authorization Approved: Manned Space Station Wins House Panel's Endorsement," *Congressional Quarterly Weekly Report*, 17 March 1984, 614.

74. The authorization process grants authority for a government program to exist and sets a funding ceiling for that program, but it does not actually fund the program. That is done in the appropriations process, where actual funds are allocated. Appropriations are not always at the same level as the authorization. Robert Rothman, "Space Station Funds Included: House Committee Authorizes $7.5 Billion for NASA Programs," *Congressional Quarterly Weekly Report*, 24 March 1984, 670; Rothman, "NASA Authorization, Landsat Sale," *Congressional Quarterly Weekly Report*, 12 May 1984, 1151.

75. Robert Rothman, "President Signs NASA Authorization Measure," *Congressional Quarterly Weekly Report*, 28 July 1984, 1865.

76. Robert Rothman, "$14 Billion Approved for HUD," *Congressional Quarterly Weekly Report*, 19 May 1984, 1199.

77. Quoted in "Space Station Usefulness Questioned," *New York Times*, 1 May 1984, C2.

78. Robert Rothman, "EPA, Veterans Included: House Passes $58.4 Billion HUD/Agency Bill," *Congressional Quarterly Weekly Report*, 2 June 1984, 1327.

79. Robert Rothman, "Trims $2.4 Billion from House Bill: Panel Votes $56.1 Billion for HUD, Agencies," *Congressional Quarterly Weekly Report*, 9 June 1984, 1393.

80. Robert Rothman, "HUD Appropriations Cleared for President," *Congressional Quarterly Weekly Report*, 30 June 1984, 1588.

81. Reagan, "Commencement Address to the United States Air Force Academy," *Public Papers, 1984*, 1:760.

82. Reagan, "Remarks at a Reagan-Bush Rally in Fountain Valley, California," *Public Papers, 1984*, 2:1223.

83. Reagan, "Remarks at a Reagan-Bush Rally in Millersville, Pennsylvania," *Public Papers, 1984*, 2:10–19.

84. Jimmy Carter, "Inaugural Address of President Jimmy Carter," *Public Papers of the Presidents of the United States: James E. Carter, 1977*, vol. 1

(Washington, DC: Office of the Federal Register, National Archives and Records Service, 1981), 2.

85. Ann Cooper, "Carter Plan to Streamline Civil Service Moves Slowly Toward Senate, House Votes," *Congressional Quarterly Weekly Report,* 15 July 1978, 1777.

86. Barry M. Hager, "Unions Await Carter Plan to Base Promotions on Merit," *Congressional Quarterly Weekly Report,* 10 December 1977, 2567.

87. Carter, "Address Before a Joint Session of the Congress on the State of the Union," *Public Papers, 1978,* 1:94.

88. Ibid., 95.

89. Carter, "The State of the Union Annual Message to Congress," *Public Papers, 1978,* 1:107.

90. Carter, "Federal Civil Service Reform Remarks Announcing the Administration's Proposals to the Congress," *Public Papers, 1978,* 1:435.

91. Barry M. Hager, "Carter Proposes Civil Service Reform," *Congressional Quarterly Weekly,* 4 March 1978, 562.

92. Ibid.

93. Ibid.

94. Light, *The President's Agenda,* 49.

95. Carter, "Anti-Inflation Policy Remarks to Members of the American Society of Newspaper Editors Announcing the Administration's Policy," *Public Papers, 1978,* 1:724.

96. Jerry Flint, "Labor Chiefs Skeptical of Carter Wage-Restraint Plan," *New York Times,* 14 April 1978, A13. Later in the year, AFGE held a "funeral" in Chicago for Carter's "broken promises," specifically ones to equalize pay between business and government, and they emphasized their change in support for Carter's civil service reform as a result. Mike Causey, "Union Holds 'Carter Funeral,'" *Washington Post,* 9 August 1978, C2.

97. Terence Smith, "Capt. Carter Tells Crew to Tighten Their Lips," *New York Times,* 23 April 1978, E4.

98. Carter, "The President's News Conference of April 25, 1978," *Public Papers, 1978,* 1:775.

99. "Vance Joins Lobbying on Civil Service Bill," *New York Times,* 4 May 1978, A21.

100. Carter, "The President's News Conference of May 4, 1978," *Public Papers, 1978,* 1:845.

101. "Vets Job Preference Rule Hurts Women, Minorities," *Congressional Quarterly Weekly Report,* 15 July 1978, 1780.

102. Cooper, "Carter Plan to Streamline," 1777.

103. Ibid., 1783.

104. Carter, "Veterans Preference in Civil Service Reform Letter to Chairman Robert N. C. Nix of the House Post Office and Civil Service Committee," *Public Papers, 1978,* 1:1138.

105. Ibid.

106. Cooper, "Carter Plan to Streamline," 1784.

107. Carter, "Federal Civil Service Reform Statement on the House Post Office and Civil Service Committee's Action on Legislation," *Public Papers, 1978,* 1:8.

108. Carter, "The President's News Conference of July 20, 1978," *Public Papers, 1978,* 2:1324.

109. Carter, "Interview with the President, Remarks and a Question-and-

Answer Session with a Group of Editors and News Directors," *Public Papers, 1978,* 2:1347.

110. Carter, "Federal Civil Service Reform and Reorganization Remarks and a Question-and-Answer Session at a Roundtable Discussion," *Public Papers, 1978,* 2:1361.

111. Terence Smith, "Carter Striving to Ease Strains with Congress," *New York Times,* 4 August 1978, A1.

112. "Transcript of Carter Remarks in an Interview on His Presidency and the Nation," *New York Times,* 6 November 1978, 38.

113. Ann Cooper, "Senate Approves Carter Civil Service Reforms," *Congressional Quarterly Weekly Report,* 26 August 1978, 2239.

114. Ann Cooper, "House Civil Service Debate Slowed by Bill Opponents," *Congressional Quarterly Weekly Report,* 9 September 1978, 2441.

115. Ann Cooper, "Civil Service Reforms Likely This Year," *Congressional Quarterly Weekly Report,* 16 September 1978, 2458.

116. Ann Cooper, "Enactment of Civil Service Reform Nears," *Congressional Quarterly Weekly Report,* 7 October 1978, 2736.

117. Ibid.

118. Ann Cooper, "Congress Approves Civil Service Reforms," *Congressional Quarterly Weekly Report,* 14 October 1978, 2945.

119. Louis Fisher, *Constitutional Conflicts Between the President and Congress* (Lawrence: University of Kansas Press, 1991), 128–129.

120. Ibid., 129.

121. Ibid., 196.

122. The 45 days are 45 days of "continuous session," not counting recesses of more than 3 days, in practice generally 60–75 calendar days. Virginia McMurtry, "Item Veto and Expanded Impoundment Proposals" (Congressional Research Service, Issue Brief IB89148, 2001). Deferrals have caused both controversy and confusion over the years as a deferral is approved unless one chamber disallows it. Legislative vetoes of this sort were declared unconstitutional in *INS v. Chadha* (1983). Fisher, *Constitutional Conflicts,* 197; Christopher Wlezien, "The Politics of Impoundment," *Political Research Quarterly* 42 (March 1994):61.

123. The Line-Item Veto Act gave presidents the ability to cancel appropriations items, as well as new entitlements, and narrowly targeted tax cuts. Andrew Taylor, "Line-Item Veto Bill Becomes Law," *Congressional Quarterly Weekly Report,* 13 April 1996, 984.

124. Reagan, "Address Before a Joint Session of Congress on the State of the Union," *Public Papers, 1984,* 1:89.

125. See for example, Reagan, "Remarks and a Question-and-Answer Session at a Working Lunch with Out-of-Town Editors," *Public Papers, 1981,* 1:947–960; "Interview with Jeremiah O'Leary of the *Washington Times* on Federal Tax and Budget Reconciliation Legislation," *Public Papers, 1982,* 2:1044–1048. Reagan did, however, bring up the line-item veto frequently in meetings with Members of Congress. Martin Tolchin, "Line-Item Veto: A Surrender, or Deficit Remedy?" *Washington Post,* 3 January 1984, A16.

126. Reagan, *Public Papers, 1984.*

127. "Legislative History of P.L. 104-130," available from LexisNexis Congressional [Online] (Bethesda, MD: Congressional Information Service, 1996).

128. Helen Dewar, "Senate Rejects Line-Item Veto Idea," *Washington Post,* 5 May 1984, A1.

129. Helen Dewar, "51 Senators Press Measure for Trial of Line-Item Veto," *Washington Post,* 27 September 1984, A6.

130. The Republican Senate had voted on a constitutional amendment to give the president the line-item veto in 1983, but it did not obtain the necessary two-thirds vote. Helen Dewar, "Senate Marks Time as Debt Deadline Nears," *Washington Post,* 30 October 1983, A4.

131. Lou Cannon, "Reagan Predicts Serious Talks On Arms Curbs in Next Term; Balanced Budget, Line-Item Veto To Be Pushed," *Washington Post,* 7 November 1984, A1.

132. Reagan, "Address to a Joint Session of Congress on the State of the Union," *Public Papers, 1985,* 1:132.

133. Helen Dewar, "Line-Item Veto Falters in Senate," *Washington Post,* 24 July 1985, A5.

134. Reagan, "Address to a Joint Session of Congress on the State of the Union," *Public Papers, 1986,* 1:127.

135. There were three attempts in the Senate to provide the president with the line-item veto through amendments to other legislation in 1986 and 1987, but no congressional hearings were held in 1986, 1987, or 1988. "Legislative History of P.L. 104-130."

136. George H. W. Bush, "Address on Administration Goals Before a Joint Session of the Congress," *Public Papers of the Presidents of the United States: George H. W. Bush, 1989,* vol. 1 (Washington, DC: GPO), 75.

137. "Expedited rescissions" refer to measures that "supplement rather than supplant the existing framework for rescissions. Under expedited rescission, congressional approval would still be necessary to cancel the funding. However, by expediting an up-or-down vote on the President's message, it likely would become more difficult to ignore proposed rescissions and hence to reject them by inaction. . . . On the other hand, enhanced rescission proposals typically seek to reverse the "burden of action" regarding rescissions and thereby create a presumption favoring the President. Such proposals usually stipulate that budget authority identified in a rescission message from the President is to be permanently canceled unless Congress acts to disapprove the request within a prescribed period." McMurtry, "Item Veto." See also Mary Jacoby, "White House, Democratic Leaders Support Rep. Stenholms' 'Expedited Rescission' Idea," *Roll Call,* 11 March 1993.

138. McMurtry, "Item Veto."

139. "Legislative History of P.L. 104-130," and "Section Notes: Senate Action Stalled on Transportation Bill," *Congressional Quarterly Weekly Report,* 11 November 1989, 3054.

140. Mark Mashek, "White House Retreats on Line-Item Veto," *Boston Globe,* 25 October 1989, 24; Alyson Pytte, "Fairness Doctrine, Dial-a-Porn Coupled on House Measure," *Congressional Quarterly Weekly Report,* 7 October 1989, 2629.

141. "Legislative History of P.L. 104-130."

142. McMurtry, "Item Veto."

143. George H. W. Bush, "Address Before a Joint Session of the Congress on the State of the Union," *Public Papers, 1992,* 1:162.

144. George Hager, "Carper's Compromise," *Congressional Quarterly Weekly Report,* 10 October 1992, 3136.

145. Kenneth Cooper and Helen Dewar, "House Democrats Draft Limited Line-Item Veto Proposal for Clinton," *Washington Post,* 27 March 1993, A11.

146. Bill Bradley, "Line-Item Veto: Why I Changed My Mind," *Wall Street Journal,* 13 January 1993, A14.

147. Jerry Gray, "Bradley Would Give Clinton Line-Item Veto," *Washington Post*, 14 January 1993, B5.

148. "Fight Flares Over Line-Item Veto," *Congressional Quarterly Weekly Report*, 13 March 1993, 590.

149. Andrew Taylor, "Judge Voids Line-Item Veto Law; Backers Look to High Court," *Congressional Quarterly Weekly Report*, 12 April 1997, 833–834.

150. Charles E. Cook, "With Right Message, Republicans Succeed Even if Contract Fails," *Roll Call*, 8 December 1994.

151. Clinton, "Address Before a Joint Session of the Congress on the State of the Union," *Public Papers, 1995*, 1:75.

152. Ibid., 1:78.

153. Taylor, "Judge Voids Line-Item Veto Law," 834.

154. Quoted in Helen Dewar, "Senate Republicans Agree on Strategy for Line-Item Veto," *Washington Post*, 17 March 1995, A7.

155. Quoted in Helen Dewar, "Dole Pressures Clinton on Line-Item Veto Bill," *Washington Post*, 18 March 1995.

156. Clinton, "Statement on Proposed Line-Item Veto Legislation," *Public Papers, 1995*, 1:374.

157. Helen Dewar, "President Urges Passage of Strong Line-Item Veto," *Washington Post*, 21 March 1995.

158. McMurtry, "Item Veto."

159. Edwin Chen, "Senate Votes to Give President Line-Item Veto," *Los Angeles Times*, 24 March 1995, A1.

160. Dewar, "Line-Item Veto Strategy," *Washington Post*, 28 September 1995, A14.

161. Clinton, "Statement on Action in the Senate on the Line-Item Veto," *Public Papers, 1995*, 1:374.

162. Clinton, "The President's Radio Address, March 25, 1995," *Public Papers, 1995*, 1:396.

163. Clinton, "Remarks and a Question-and-Answer Session with the American Society of Newspaper Editors in Dallas, Texas," *Public Papers, 1995*, 1:478.

164. Clinton, "Remarks at the Safe and Drug-Free Schools Recognition Program," *Public Papers, 1995*, 1:826–827.

165. Clinton, "Letter to Congressional Leaders on Line-Item Veto Legislation," *Public Papers, 1995*, 1:829–830.

166. McMurtry, "Item Veto."

167. Ibid.

168. Clinton, "Address Before a Joint Session of the Congress on the State of the Union," *Public Papers, 1996*, 1:85.

169. McMurtry, "Item Veto."

170. Clinton, "Statement on the Signing of the Line-Item Veto Act," *Public Papers, 1996*, 1:559.

171. McMurtry, "Item Veto"; Andrew Taylor, "Few in Congress Grieve as Justices Give Line-Item Veto the Ax," *Congressional Quarterly Weekly Report*, 27 June 1998, 1747.

172. Clinton, "Statement on the Signing of the Line-Item Veto Act," 559.

173. Greenstein, 76.

174. Patricia Lee Sykes, "The President as Legislator: A 'Superepresenator,'" *Presidential Studies Quarterly* 19 (1989):313.

6

Conclusion:
Making Deeds Follow Words

As Rossiter pointed out when discussing the president's chief legislator role,

> Congress still has its strong men, but the complexity of the problems it is asked to solve by a people who assume that all problems are solvable has made *external* leadership a requisite of effective operation. . . . [T]he chief responsibility for bridging the constitutional gulf between executive and legislature now rests irrevocably with the president. His tasks as leader of Congress are difficult and delicate, yet he must bend to them steadily or be judged a failure.[1]

Presidents enter office with ambitious plans and policy goals. Articulating these goals is essential, not just at the beginning of their term, but also throughout their presidency. The SUA allows presidents an opportunity to initiate and/or accelerate the discussion with Congress and the public about policy on which they seek to lead. An analysis of SUAs provides a systematic look at both presidential rhetoric and the outcomes of presidential attempts at policy leadership of Congress. The task of presidents seeking to lead Congress is to make actions follow their rhetoric.

A chief legislator has a distinct advantage over a regular legislator, and the SUA is no small part of this advantage. Being chief legislator, however, has not meant that the president has come to dominate the legislature. The built-in sharing of legislative powers between the legislative and executive branches, despite the fact that the legislative power of the president has expanded over the course of American history, still constrains the president. There are, however, other effects of the policymaking rhetoric of the SUA. We now turn to assessing the ultimate result of the type of rhetoric the president uses in the speech.

When the president's role as chief legislator emerged, in which the oral SUA was instrumental, a perception of presidential government became dominant. The attention given to the president in the political system, nicely represented by the attention given to the president on the occasion of the SUA, encourages this perception. When giving an SUA, the president stands in the center of the only chamber originally designed to directly represent the people. The president does not stand in the well of the House, where deliberation takes place, but stands at the pulpit-like rostrum. He publicly pronounces his preferred solutions for the policy dilemmas on which he wishes Congress to act in the coming year. Debate, if it is to occur, takes place at another time. The president appears as the dominant actor. The executive, however, is not the dominant institution in the legislative process, as power is shared with the legislative branch.

Presidents want to solve policy problems, but they can be stymied by the political system in which they operate, a key goal of the system's design. As the president gained the role of chief legislator and became much more involved in the legislative process, the public and Congress came to expect not just administration from the president, but also real follow-through on the legislative items he would publicly proclaim he wanted to accomplish. Constituents care about outcomes and they have come to expect the president to deliver on his rhetoric. The public, however, often fails to fully recognize the nature of the president's shared power with Congress. When presidents frame the situation, claim credit for past actions, and propose solutions in the SUA, they encourage a view that they can easily solve policy problems. If presidents cannot deliver, which typically happens on three of five requests, and expectations are not met, cynicism may result.

The policymaking rhetoric presidents engage in as chief legislator tends to exacerbate what has become known as the expectations gap. This refers to the chasm that occurs between what the public expects presidents to do, and what they actually are able to accomplish given their limited powers.[2] With the SUA, the public expects presidents to lead Congress in solving the problems they highlight, but the political system in which they function constrains their ability to get what they want. Performance, therefore, often does not meet expectations as "the expectations of the masses have grown faster than the capacity of presidential government to meet them."[3] Thus, there occurs a gap between what the public *expects* the president to accomplish, and what the president actually *can* accomplish in a system of government that divides power in order to make it difficult to wield. The rhetoric that modern presidents use exacerbates this gap. Nowhere is this more evident than in the SUA, where presidents are on display primarily as chief legislators and discuss the key agenda items on which they are seeking to lead Congress in the coming session. The form of policymaking rhetoric with its symbolic and substantive elements, which includes the activities of credit claiming and position taking, encourages the public to believe presidents have the answers to the problems discussed in the SUA.

Furthermore, public evaluations are shaped by the expectations the public holds.[4] Presidents who do not meet expectations may negatively impact their effectiveness as leaders, their reelection prospects, and their legacy. Therefore, it is in the interest of presidents to be mindful of the expectations they may set with the policymaking rhetoric of the SUA.

Occasionally in their SUAs, presidents recognize the problem that high expectations can present. In his very first joint address to Congress, Clinton challenged his congressional audience.

> Our people will be watching and wondering, not to see whether you disagree with me on a particular issue but just to see whether this is going to be business as usual or a real new day, whether we're all going to conduct ourselves as if we know we're working for them. We must scale the walls of the people's skepticisms, not with our words but with our deeds.[5]

With this challenge, Clinton recognized a fundamental problem contemporary presidents confront with their SUAs. Expectations not being met can cause public cynicism. He asserts that the president and Congress must work together to "scale the walls of the people's skepticisms." He attributes this public skepticism to a lack of action, a reliance on words, not deeds. Words raise the expectations; deeds can fulfill them.

Presidents and Their Words

Several characteristics of the SUA result in the president fueling the expectations gap. The president is to report on the state of the Union; few presidents want to represent the state of the Union in a negative light, especially if they, or their party has been in control for the past year. The SUA has evolved into a speech that is to be positive, visionary, and one in which the president wants to exhibit leadership of Congress. The SUA has large, multiple audiences, and this encourages a president to target his requests to appeal as broadly as possible. The very essence of policymaking rhetoric, as Campbell and Jamieson discussed, "exudes the reassurance that problems can be solved."[6]

There are many examples of contemporary presidents using sweeping rhetoric in their SUAs that raise expectations. Gerald Ford, in his 1976 SUA, presented his audiences with the following vision:

> The time has now come for a fundamentally different approach for a new realism that is true to the great principles upon which this Nation was founded.

> We must introduce a new balance to our economy—a balance that favors not only sound, active government but also a much more vigorous, healthy economy that can create new jobs and hold down prices.
>
> We must introduce a new balance in the relationship between the individual and the government—a balance that favors greater individual freedom and self-reliance.
>
> We must strike a new balance in our system of federalism—a balance that favors greater responsibility and freedom for the leaders of our State and local governments.
>
> We must introduce a new balance between the spending on domestic programs and spending on defense—a balance that ensures we will fully meet our obligation to the needy while also protecting our security in a world that is still hostile to freedom.
>
> And in all that we do, we must be more honest with the American people, promising them no more than we can deliver and delivering all that we promise.[7]

Ford's rhetoric from the above passage paints with very broad strokes his vision for America. He juxtaposes the sweeping language about all that government *must* do with a final statement in which he says (ironically, after encouraging an expectations gap with his own words), that government must guard against promising more than can be delivered.

George H. W. Bush in his first joint address sought to inspire Congress to solve policy problems with sweeping references to human ability.

> And let all Americans remember that no problem of human making is too great to be overcome by human ingenuity, human energy, and the untiring hope of the human spirit. I believe this. I would not have asked to be your President if I didn't. And tomorrow the debate on the plan I've put forward begins, and I ask the Congress to come forward with your own proposals. Let's not question each other's motives. Let's debate, let's negotiate; but let us solve the problem.[8]

Similarly, Johnson, in the election year of 1964, opened his SUA by challenging Congress with lofty goals.

> Let this session of Congress be known as the session which did more for civil rights than the last hundred sessions combined; as the session which enacted the most far-reaching tax cut of our time; as the session which declared all-out war on human poverty and unemployment in these United States; as the session which finally recognized the health needs of all our older citizens; as the session which reformed our tangled transportation and transit policies; as the session which achieved the most effective, efficient foreign aid program ever; and as the session which helped to build more homes, more schools, more libraries, and more hospitals than any single session of Congress in the history of our Republic.[9]

Johnson was, in fact, able to lead Congress in the completion of several of these goals, most notably the Civil Rights Act of 1964, which was the most far-reaching civil rights legislation that Congress had ever passed.

Part of effective leadership is inspiring people to reach deep within themselves and achieve things they otherwise might not. In detailing the paradoxes of the presidency, Thomas Cronin addresses a particular one that is applicable to the SUA; we want presidents to inspire but at the same time not promise more than they can deliver.[10] The rhetoric presidents use to inspire their audiences, however, naturally raises expectations. Sometimes presidents can fulfill these expectations, but often they cannot. Policy problems are complex, continuous, and multifaceted; they typically defy the seemingly easy fixes presidents advocate with their policymaking rhetoric.

This paradox captures the catch-22 contemporary presidents confront in their political communications, especially the SUA. If they are visionary and inspirational, they will surely raise expectations. More often than not, presidents will be unable to meet the inflated expectations, which may negatively affect their ability to lead, their reelection prospects, and the future evaluations of their presidency. If they use rhetoric that guards against raising expectations, they will be cited as lacking leadership, which could hurt their ability to secure future accomplishments and their future evaluations.[11] Presidents tend to favor the soaring rhetoric side of this particular paradox in their SUAs. Because it is not particularly inspiring, contemporary presidents generally do not characterize the state of the Union as bad, especially if the Union has been under their or their party's stewardship for the past year.[12] The state of the Union may not be rosy, but even so, a tone of hopefulness and optimism for the future will be struck in SUAs. The audiences want to see a president exhibit leadership traits that will lead them out of a crisis, or sustain them in good times. The point is that the public expects presidents to look to the future with hope, not with doom, and they expect presidents to lead them into a better future. The nature of the SUA is such that it is virtually inevitable that it will raise expectations given its subject matter, current format, deliverer, and the setting in which it takes place.

Presidents and Their Deeds

The policymaking rhetoric of the SUA highlights for audiences the legislative deeds presidents would like to accomplish in the coming year. Making deeds follow words, however, is difficult for chief legislators because they exist in the American political system in which legislative power is shared between two separate branches. Despite the fact the president became chief legislator, rather than being originally designated chief legislator, the fundamental structure of government was not altered. Even though the SUA provides the president with a megaphone and the rhetorical powers the president has are substantial, they are still limited. These limitations are brought into focus by examining the way presidents utilize SUAs and the outcomes of their requests.

There are consistencies and patterns evident in the SUAs that we examine. All SUAs have the same form, which is dictated by the two constitutional provisions at its root. The policymaking rhetoric of the SUA enables chief legislators to report and recommend measures to Congress. Each SUA we examine in the 1965 to 2002 time period also has the same format. They are oral addresses given before a joint session of Congress, generally given in the evening and broadcast to the public. All presidents utilize symbolic language and convey policy substance in their SUAs, so that they might further the mutually reinforcing goals they have as chief legislator: making public policy, securing reelection, and securing a positive legacy. SUAs can be classified by different types that are contingent upon the time frame and level of activities presidents engage in with their substantive rhetoric. Despite these similarities, presidents have varying levels of success with the legislative requests they make of Congress in their SUAs. Some presidents, like Johnson, are relatively successful, while others, such as Ford, are less so. Even within a presidency, presidential successes vary from year to year. An examination of the outcomes of the chief legislator's requests of Congress reveals that presidents typically have only modest success in getting their requests fulfilled, receiving about 43 percent of their requests, in full or in part. Our four case studies, however, reveal the SUA to be important in each case for getting Congress to consider the president's request, but this does not always translate into continuous attention or enactment of the president's request.

As the SUA developed into a significant presidential power, it became a tool presidents could use to assist them in their legislative endeavors, but it did not become a weapon. What has been illustrated in the previous chapters is that while chief legislators do hold an advantage over regular legislators in the legislative process, they do not hold a similar advantage over the legislature. Despite having gained significant rhetorical powers, presidents remain anchored in a political system where legislative powers are shared. Unfortunately, their constituents often fail to recognize the limited nature of their powers as chief legislator, and the SUA contributes to this perception.

With their SUAs, presidents communicate with Congress as well as their constituents. The attention given to presidents on the occasion of the SUA captures the view many of their constituents have regarding the political system—that it is one centered on the president. The SUA contributes to the gap in expectations and abilities that plague modern presidents. This gap fosters cynicism in the public about government in general, and presidents specifically. Therefore, while the SUA can aid the stewardship of chief legislators by showcasing their policy priorities, it can also inhibit their leadership as well. Expectations not being met can affect evaluations of presidents, which can negatively impact the likelihood of the chief legislators being able to fulfill their goals of making public policy and securing both reelection as well as a positive legacy. This is the challenge of leadership presidents confront in the US political system. They must utilize this tool of political communication without raising expectations to the point where they make their job even more difficult; expectations not fulfilled make for poor evaluations, affecting the president's ability to lead. At the same time, presidents must inspire their audiences to accept their policy leadership as they strive to make deeds follow their words.

Notes

1. Emphasis original, Clinton Rossiter, *The American Presidency* (New York: Harcourt, Brace and Company, 1956), 14–15.

2. James E. Ceaser, et al., "The Rise of the Rhetorical Presidency," in *Rethinking the Presidency*, ed. Thomas E. Cronin (Boston: Little, Brown & Co., 1982); Theodore J. Lowi, *The Personal President: Power Invested, Promise Unfulfilled* (Ithaca, NY: Cornell University Press, 1985), 115; Richard W. Waterman, Hank C. Jenkins-Smith, and Carol L. Silva, "The Expectations Gap Thesis: Public Attitudes Toward an Incumbent President," *Journal of Politics* 61:944–966.

3. Lowi, *The Personal President,* xii.

4. Waterman, Jenkins-Smith, and Silva, "The Expectations Gap Thesis," 945.

5. William J. Clinton, "Address Before a Joint Session of Congress on Administration Goals," *Public Papers of the Presidents of the United States: William J. Clinton, 1993*, vol. 1 (Washington, DC: GPO, 1994), 121.

6. Karlyn Kohrs Campbell and Kathleen Hall Jamieson, *Deeds Done in Words: Presidential Rhetoric and the Genres of Governance* (Chicago: University of Chicago Press, 1990), 74.

7. Gerald R. Ford, "Address Before a Joint Session of the Congress on the State of the Union," *Public Papers of the Presidents of the United States: Gerald R. Ford, 1976,* vol. 1 (Washington, DC: GPO, 1977), 32.

8. G. H. W. Bush, "Address on Administration Goals Before a Joint Session of the Congress," *Public Papers of the Presidents of the United States: G. H. W. Bush, 1989,* vol. 1 (Washington, DC: GPO, 1993), 80.

9. Lyndon B. Johnson, "Annual Message to the Congress on the State of the Union," *Public Papers of the Presidents of the United States: Lyndon B. Johnson, 1963–1964,* vol. 1 (Washington, DC: GPO, 1965), 112.

10. Thomas C. Cronin, "The Paradoxes of the Presidency," in *Analyzing the Presidency*, 2nd ed., ed. Robert E. DiClerico (Guilford, CT: Dushkin, 1990), 58–59.

11. One need only consider what is popularly known as Carter's "malaise" speech if there is any doubt about presidents finding themselves in this situation. While not an SUA (and also not a speech that used the term *malaise*), the speech is notable precisely because Carter addresses the "crisis of confidence" he saw pervading America. This particular speech contributed to the dourness and pessimism that permeated the final years of the Carter presidency and enabled Ronald Reagan to contrast his sunny optimism with Carter's outlook and leadership. The public

responded much better to Reagan's optimism. James E. Carter, "Energy and National Goals Address to the Nation," *Public Papers of the Presidents of the United States: James E. Carter, 1979,* vol. 2 (Washington, DC: GPO, 1981), 1235–1241.

12. The one exception is Ford's 1975 SUA, which did proclaim that "the state of the Union is not good." Ford did confront a unique crisis in this SUA, and he does go on to state, "from adversity, let us seize opportunity." Gerald R. Ford, "Address Before a Joint Session of the Congress Reporting on the State of the Union," *Public Papers of the Presidents of the United States: Gerald R. Ford, 1975,* vol. 1 (Washington, DC: GPO, 1977), 36, 42.

Appendix:
Criteria for Policy Areas

The following terms and descriptions were used to categorize sentences within the State of the Union addresses into policy areas.

Foreign Policy

diplomacy, United Nations, foreign aid, collective security agreements (unless exclusively military in nature), policy toward specific nations, trade

Defense

conduct of war and military strategy, draft, living conditions of military personnel, weapons systems, military research, civil defense, United Nations armed forces, disarmament, testing of nuclear weapons, intelligence, international terrorism

Economic Policy

control of business cycles, federal fiscal policy and taxation, regulation of business, distribution of military procurement contracts, science and nonmilitary research, transportation (including mass transit and rivers and harbors), depressed areas, infrastructure, technology, space (unless defense oriented)

Labor

regulation of labor unions, employment conditions, minimum wage, retraining programs, employment services, farm workers, standards in government contracts other than nondiscrimination

Agriculture

farm commodity, storage, loan, and income policies; food reserves; foreign distribution of agricultural surpluses; agricultural research; production and marketing controls; rural electrification

Resources

policies relating to minerals, fuels, and other raw materials; depletion allowances; water, forest, and game policy; air and water pollution; conservation and recreation; atomic energy for domestic purposes; regional development; electrical and hydroelectric power policy (excluding rural electrification); fisheries

Social Welfare

all programs related to health, hospitals, education, and social welfare; social security; unemployment insurance; programs for the aged and handicapped; consumer protection; housing; urban planning and renewal (other than transportation); Department of Urban Affairs; veterans; rent control; food stamp programs; school lunches

Government

administration, loyalty programs, management of the civil service, federalism (including programs of federal-state tax adjustment), federal budgeting and spending levels apart from particular programs, the national debt, statehood, government of territories and District of Columbia, regulation of elections, legislative apportionment, congressional procedures (other than Senate cloture), crime (administration of justice)

Civil Rights/Civil Liberties

all provisions related to discrimination against minorities (including segregation in the armed forces, schools, etc.); social welfare programs specifically designed to deal with racial discrimination; Senate cloture; immigration policy; American Indians; discrimination against women, sexual minorities, and disabled; civil liberties

Note

Policy areas with minor modifications are from Gerald M. Pomper with Susan S. Lederman, *Elections in America*, 2nd ed. (New York: Longman, 1980).

Bibliography

Adams, Willi Paul. *The First American Constitutions: Republican Ideology and the Making of the State Constitutions in the Revolutionary Era*. Chapel Hill: University of North Carolina Press, 1980.

Andrade, Lydia, and Garry Young. "Presidential Agenda Setting: Influences on the Emphasis of Foreign Policy." *Political Research Quarterly* 49 (1996):591–605.

Annals of the Congress of the United States, 1789–1824. 42 vols. Washington, DC, 1834–1856.

Aristotle. *On Rhetoric*, trans. George A. Kennedy. New York: Oxford University Press, 1991.

Barber, James David. *The Presidential Character: Predicting Performance in the White House*. New Jersey: Prentice Hall, 1992.

Barrett, Andrew W. "Gone Public: The Impact of Going Public on Presidential Legislative Success." *American Politics Research* 32 (May 2004):338–370.

Beasley, Vanessa B. *You, the People: American National Identity in Presidential Rhetoric*. College Station: Texas A&M University Press, 2004.

Binkley, Wilfred E. "The President as Chief Legislator." *Annals of the American Academy of Political and Social Sciences*, 307 (1956):92–105.

Bond, Jon R., and Richard Fleisher. *The President in the Legislative Arena*. Chicago: University of Chicago Press, 1990.

Bowles, Nigel. *The White House and Capitol Hill: The Politics of Presidential Persuasion*. Oxford: Clarendon Press, 1987.

Burns, James MacGregor. *The Power to Lead*. New York: Simon and Schuster, 1984.

Bush, George H. W. *Public Papers of the Presidents of the United States: George H. W. Bush, 1989–1993*. 8 vols. Washington, DC: GPO, 1993.

Bush, George W. *Public Papers of the Presidents of the United States: George W. Bush, 2001–2002*. 3 vols. Washington, DC: GPO, 2002.

Bush, George W. "Address Before a Joint Session of the Congress on the State of the Union." *Weekly Compilation of Presidential Documents* 38, no. 5 (4 February 2002):133–139.

Campbell, Karlyn Kohrs, and Kathleen Hall Jamieson. *Deeds Done in Words: Presidential Rhetoric and the Genres of Governance*. Chicago: University of Chicago Press, 1990.

Canes-Wrone, Brandice. "The President's Legislative Influence from Public Appeals." *American Journal of Political Science* 45 (April 2001):313–329.

Carter, James E. *Public Papers of the Presidents of the United States: James E. Carter, 1977–1981*, 9 vols. Washington, DC: Office of the Federal Register, National Archives and Records Service, 1981.

Ceaser, James W., Glen E. Thurow, Jeffrey Tulis, and Joseph M. Bessette. "The Rise of the Rhetorical Presidency." *Presidential Studies Quarterly* 11 (Spring 1981):158–171.

Clinton, William J. *Public Papers of the Presidents of the United States: William J. Clinton, 1993–2001*, 17 vols. Washington, DC: GPO, 2001.

———. *Clinton Presidential Legacy*. Speech given November 10, 2005, at Hofstra University, Hempstead, New York. 11th Presidential Conference, "William Jefferson Clinton: The 'New' Democrat from Hope." C-SPAN National Cable Satellite Corporation, 2005. DVD.

Cohen, Jeffrey E. "A Historical Reassessment of Wildavsky's 'Two Presidencies' Thesis." In *The Two Presidencies: A Quarter Century Assessment,* ed. Steven A. Shull. Chicago: Nelson-Hall, 1991.

———. "Presidential Rhetoric and the Public Agenda." *American Journal of Political Science* 39 (1995):87–107.

———. *Presidential Responsiveness and Public Policy-making: The Public and the Policies that Presidents Choose*. Ann Arbor: University of Michigan Press, 1997.

Cohen, Jeffrey E., and John A. Hamman. "The Polls: Can Presidential Rhetoric Affect the Public's Economic Perceptions?" *Presidential Studies Quarterly* 33 (2003):408–422.

"Committee Roundup: Four-Year House Term." *Congressional Quarterly Weekly Report*, 18 February 1966, 428–429.

"Committee Roundup: Four-Year House Term." *Congressional Quarterly Weekly Report*, 4 March 1966, 495.

Congressional Globe. 46 vols. Washington, DC: Blair & Rives, 1834–1873.

Constitution of New York. 1777. Avalon Project of Yale University Law School [online]. Available from http://www.yale.edu/lawweb/avalon/states/ny01.htm#1 [15 December 2004].

Cook, Charles E. "With Right Measure, Republicans Succeed Even if Contract Fails." *Roll Call,* 8 December 1994.

Cook, Corey. "The Contemporary Presidency: The Permanence of the 'Permanent Campaign': George W. Bush's Public Presidency." *Presidential Studies Quarterly* 32 (2002):753–764.

Cooper, Ann. "Carter Plan to Streamline Civil Service Moves Slowly Toward Senate, House Votes." *Congressional Quarterly Weekly Report*, 15 July 1978, 1777–1784.

———. "Carter Civil Service Plan: Battered but Alive." *Congressional Quarterly Weekly Report*, 22 July 1978, 1839–1841.

———. "Civil Service Reorganization Plan Approved." *Congressional Quarterly Weekly Report*, 12 August 1978, 2125.

———. "Senate Approves Carter Civil Service Reforms." *Congressional Quarterly Weekly Report*, 26 August 1978, 2239, 2299.

———. "House Civil Service Debate Slowed by Bill Opponents." *Congressional Quarterly Weekly Report*, 9 September 1978, 2441.

———. "Civil Service Reforms Likely This Year." *Congressional Quarterly Weekly Report*, 16 September 1978, 2458–2462.

———. "Enactment of Civil Service Reforms Nears." *Congressional Quarterly Weekly Report*, 7 October 1978, 2735–2736.

———. "Congress Approves Civil Service Reforms." *Congressional Quarterly Weekly Report*, 14 October 1978, 2945.

Cronin, Thomas E., and Michael Genovese. *The Paradoxes of the American Presidency*. New York: Oxford University Press, 2004.

Daynes, Byron W., Raymond Tatalovich, and Denis L. Soden. *To Govern a Nation: Presidential Power and Politics*. New York: St. Martin's Press, 1998.

Dealy, James Quayle. *Growth of American State Constitutions from 1776 to the End of the Year 1914*. Boston: Ginn and Company, 1915.

DiClerico, Robert E. *The American President*. New Jersey: Prentice Hall, 2000.

DiClerico, Robert E., ed. *Analyzing the Presidency*, 2nd ed. Guilford, CT: Dushkin, 1990.

Dorsey, Leroy G. "Introduction." In *The Presidency and Rhetorical Leadership*, ed. Leroy G. Dorsey. College Station: Texas A&M University Press, 2002.

Edelman, Murray. *The Symbolic Uses of Politics*. Urbana: University of Illinois Press, 1985.

Edwards, George C., III. *At the Margins: Presidential Leadership of Congress*. New Haven, CT: Yale University Press, 1989.

———. "Building Coalitions." *Presidential Studies Quarterly* 30 (2000):47–78.

———. "Campaigning Is Not Governing: Bill Clinton's Rhetorical Presidency." In *The Clinton Legacy*, ed. Colin Campbell and Bert A. Rockman. New York: Chatham House, 2000.

———. "Presidential Rhetoric: What Difference Does It Make?" In *The Future of the Rhetorical Presidency*, ed. Martin J. Medhurst. College Station: Texas A&M University Press, 1996.

Edwards, George C., III, and Andrew Barrett. "Presidential Agenda Setting in Congress." In *Polarized Politics: Congress and the President in a Partisan Era*, ed. Jon R. Bond and Richard Fleisher. Washington, DC: CQ Press, 2000.

Edwards, George C., III, and B. Dan Wood. "Who Influences Whom? The President, Congress, and the Media." *American Political Science Review* 93 (1999):327–344.

Eisenhower, Dwight D. *Public Papers of the Presidents of the United States: Dwight D. Eisenhower, 1953–1961*. 8 vols. Washington, DC: GPO, 1961.

"Election Reforms." *Congressional Quarterly Weekly Report,* 15 April 1966, 782.

Fenno, Richard F., Jr. *Congressmen in Committees*. Boston: Little, Brown and Company, 1973.

———. *Home Style: House Members in Their Districts*. Boston: Little, Brown and Company, 1978.

Fersh, Seymour H. *The View from the White House: A Study of the Presidential State of the Union Messages*. Washington, DC: Public Affairs Press, 1961.

Fett, Patrick J. "Truth in Advertising: The Revelation of Presidential Legislative Priorities." *Western Political Quarterly* 45 (1992):895–920.

Fields, Wayne. *Union of Words: A History of Presidential Eloquence*. New York: The Free Press, 1996.

"Fight Flares over Line-Item Veto." *Congressional Quarterly Weekly Report*, 13 March 1993, 589–591.

Fishel, Jeff. *Presidents & Promises: From Campaign Pledge to Presidential Performance*. Washington, DC: CQ Press, 1985.

Fisher, Louis. *Constitutional Conflicts Between the President and Congress*. Lawrence: University Press of Kansas, 1991.

Ford, Gerald R. *Public Papers of the Presidents of the United States: Gerald R. Ford, 1974–1977*, 6 vols. Washington, DC: GPO, 1977.

Gilberg, Sheldon, Chaim Eyal, Maxwell McCombs, and David Nicholas. "The State of the Union Address and the Press Agenda." *Journalism Quarterly* 57 (1980):584–588.

Greenstein, Fred I. *The Presidential Difference: Leadership Style from FDR to Clinton*. New York: Free Press, 2000.

Grossman, Michael, Martha Joynt Kumar, and Francis E. Rourke. "Second-Term Presidencies: The Aging of Administrations." In *The Presidency and the Political System*, 6th ed., ed. Michael Nelson. Washington, DC: CQ Press, 2000.

Hager, Barry M. "Carter Proposes Civil Service Reform." *Congressional Quarterly Weekly Report*, 4 March 1978, 562.

Hager, George. "House Approves Supplemental After Line-Item Veto Fight." *Congressional Quarterly Weekly Report*, 1 August 1992, 2259.

———. "Carper's Compromise." *Congressional Quarterly Weekly Report*, 10 October 1992, 3136.

Hamilton, Alexander, James Madison, and John Jay. *The Federalist Papers*, ed. Garry Wills. New York: Bantam, 1982.

Hargrove, Erwin. *The President as Leader: Appealing to the Better Angels of our Nature*. Lawrence: University Press of Kansas, 1998.

Hart, Roderick P. *The Sound of Leadership: Presidential Communication in the Modern Age*. Chicago: University of Chicago Press, 1987.

Hill, Kim Quaile. "The Policy Agendas of the President and the Mass Public: A Research Validation and Extension." *American Journal of Political Science* 42 (1998):1328–1335.

Hinckley, Barbara. *The Symbolic Presidency: How Presidents Portray Themselves*. New York: Routledge, 1990.

Israel, Fred L., ed. *The State of the Union Messages of the Presidents, 1790–1966*, 3 vols. New York: Chelsea House, 1966.

Jacobson, Gary C. "The Bush Presidency and the American Electorate." *Presidential Studies Quarterly* 33 (December 2003):701–731.

Jacoby, Mary. "White House, Democratic Leaders Support Rep. Stenholms' 'Expedited Rescission' Idea." *Roll Call*, 11 March 1993.

———. "After a Rude Surprise, Democrats Regroup for Second Try at Modified Line-Item Veto." *Roll Call*, 8 April 1993.

———. "Unlikely Coalition of Blacks, Republicans Keeps the Line-Item Veto Bill Bottled Up; Vote on Rule Put Off Twice; Maybe Wednesday?" *Roll Call*, 26 April 1993.

———. "Will Sen. Byrd's Line-Item Veto Cover Tax Bills? A Scenario Begins to Take Shape." *Roll Call*, 6 May 1993.

———. "Modified Line-Item Veto Is Looking More Shaky in Senate, Thanks to Byrd and GOP." *Roll Call*, 13 May 1993.

———. "Sen. Byrd's Series of Floor Speeches Links Ancient Roman Wars With Line-Item Veto." *Roll Call*, 17 June 1993.

———. "Senators Suggest 'Gang of 3' for GOP." *Roll Call*, 14 March 1996.

Jefferson, Thomas. "Opinion on the Constitutionality of a National Bank" (1791). Avalon Project at Yale University Law School [online]. Available from http://www.yale.edu/lawweb/avalon/amerdoc/bank-tj.htm. [27 December 2004].

Jefferson, Thomas. "Draft on an Amendment to the Constitution" (1803). Avalon

Project at Yale University Law School [online]. Available from http://www. yale.edu/lawweb/avalon/amerdoc/jeffdraf.htm. [27 December 2004]

Johnson, Lyndon B. *Public Papers of the Presidents of the United States*: *Lyndon B. Johnson, 1963–1969*. 10 vols. Washington, DC: GPO, 1969.

Johnson, Thomas J., and Wayne Wanta with John T. Byrd and Cindy Lee. "Exploring FDR's Relationship with the Press: A Historical Agenda-Setting Study." *Political Communication* 12 (1995):157–172.

Jones, Charles O. *Every Second Year: Congressional Behavior and the Two-Year Term*. Washington, DC: Brookings Institution, 1967.

Katz, Jeffrey. "Senate Anticipates Veto, Passes Program Cuts." *Congressional Quarterly Weekly Report* 53, no. 38 (30 September 1995):3003.

Kennedy, George A. Introduction to *On Rhetoric,* by Aristotle. New York: Oxford University Press, 1991.

Kennedy, John F. *Public Papers of the Presidents of the United States*: *John F. Kennedy, 1961–1963*. 3 vols. Washington, DC: GPO, 1963.

Kernell, Samuel. *Going Public: New Strategies of Presidential Leadership,* 3rd ed. Washington, DC: CQ Press, 1997.

Kessel, John H. "The Parameters of Presidential Politics." *Social Science Quarterly* 55 (1974):8–24.

———. "The Seasons of Presidential Politics." *Social Science Quarterly* 58 (1977):418–435.

Kingdon, John W. *Agendas, Alternatives, and Public Policies,* 2nd ed. New York: HarperCollins, 1995.

Kondracke, Morton M. "Clinton's National Service Could Beat JFK's Peace Corps." *Roll Call,* 4 July 1994.

"LBJ Election Law Proposals Surprise, Delight Reformers." *Congressional Quarterly Weekly Report,* 21 January 1966, 246–247.

"Legislative History of P.L. 104-130." Available from LexisNexis Congressional [online]. Bethesda: Maryland: Congressional Information Service, 1996.

Lewis, David. "The Two Rhetorical Presidencies: An Analysis of Televised Presidential Speeches, 1947–1991." *American Politics Quarterly* 25 (1997):380–395.

Light, Paul C. *The President's Agenda: Domestic Policy Choice from Kennedy to Clinton,* 3rd ed. Baltimore: Johns Hopkins University Press, 1999.

Lim, Elvin. "Five Trends in Presidential Rhetoric: An Analysis of Rhetoric from George Washington to Bill Clinton." *Presidential Studies Quarterly* 32 (2002):328–366.

Lowi, Theodore J. *The Personal President: Power Invested, Promise Unfulfilled.* Ithaca, NY: Cornell University Press, 1985.

———. "Four Systems of Policy, Politics, and Choice." *Public Administration Review* 32 (1972):299.

Malbin, Michael J. "Rhetoric and Leadership: A Look Backward at the Carter National Energy Plan." In *Both Ends of the Avenue: The Presidency, the Executive Branch, and Congress in the 1980s,* ed. Anthony King. Washington, DC: American Enterprise Institute, 1983.

Mayhew, David R. *Congress: The Electoral Connection.* New Haven, CT: Yale University Press, 1974.

McMurtry, Virginia A. "Item Veto and Expanded Impoundment Proposals." Issue Brief IB89148. Washington, DC: Congressional Research Service, 2001. Available from http://www.ncseonline.org/nle/crsreports/government/gov-2.cfm [15 November 2004].

Medhurst, Martin J., ed. *Beyond the Rhetorical Presidency.* College Station: Texas A&M University, 1996.

Mezey, Michael. *Congress, the President, and Public Policy.* Boulder, CO: Westview Press, 1989.

Moen, Matthew C. "The Political Agenda of Ronald Reagan: A Content Analysis of the State of the Union Messages." *Presidential Studies Quarterly* 18 (1988):775–785.

Mueller, John E. *War, Presidents, and Public Opinion.* New York: John Wiley & Sons, 1973.

Neale, Thomas H. "The President's State of the Union Message: Frequently Asked Questions." Report for Congress RS20021. Washington, DC: Congressional Research Service, Library of Congress, 2003. Available from http://www.senate .gov/reference/resources/pdf/RS20021.pdf [April 28, 2004].

Nelson, Michael. "Bill Clinton and the Politics of Second Terms." *Presidential Studies Quarterly* 29 (1998).

———, ed. *The Presidency and the Political System,* 6th ed. Washington, DC: CQ Press, 2000.

———, ed. *The Presidency and the Political System,* 7th ed. Washington, DC: CQ Press, 2003.

Neustadt, Richard E. *Presidential Power and the Modern Presidents,* Rev. ed. New York: Free Press, 1990.

———. "Presidency and Legislation: Planning the President's Program." *American Political Science Review* 39 (1955):1015.

Nixon, Richard M. *Public Papers of the Presidents of the United States: Richard M. Nixon, 1969–1974,* 8 vols. Washington, DC: GPO, 1974.

Oliver, Willard M. "The Pied Piper of Crime in America: An Analysis of the Presidents' and Public's Agenda on Crime." *Criminal Justice Policy Review* 13 (2002):139–155.

Peterson, Mark A. *Legislating Together: The White House and Capitol Hill from Eisenhower to Reagan.* Cambridge: Harvard University Press, 1990.

Peterson, Paul E. "The President's Dominance in Foreign Policy Making." *Political Science Quarterly* 109 (1994):215–234.

Pomper, Gerald M. *Elections in America: Control and Influence in Democratic Politics.* New York: Dodd, Mead & Co., 1968.

Pomper, Gerald M., with Susan S. Lederman. *Elections in America,* 2nd ed. New York: Longman, 1980.

Prothro, James W. "Verbal Shifts in the American Presidency: A Content Analysis," *American Political Science Review* 50 (September 1956):726–739.

Pytte, Alyson. "Fairness Doctrine, Dial-a-Porn Coupled on House Measure." *Congressional Quarterly Weekly Report,* 7 October 1989, 2629.

Ragsdale, Lyn. "The Politics of Presidential Speechmaking, 1949–1980," *American Political Science Review* 78 (December 1984):971–984.

———. *Vital Statistics on the Presidency.* Washington, DC: CQ Press, 1996.

———. *Vital Statistics on the Presidency: Washington to Clinton.* Rev. ed. Washington, DC: CQ Press, 1998.

Reagan, Ronald W. *Public Papers of the Presidents of the United States: Ronald W. Reagan, 1981–1988.* 15 vols. Washington, DC: GPO, 1989.

Redman, Eric. *The Dance of Legislation.* New York: Simon and Schuster, 1973.

Register of Debates in Congress. 14 vols. Washington, DC: Gales & Seaton, 1825–1837.

Rossiter, Clinton. *The American Presidency.* New York: Harcourt, Brace and Company, 1956.

Rothman, Robert. "1985 Budget: $8 Billion Total Cost Expected: Planning Funds Requested for Manned Space Station." *Congressional Quarterly Weekly Report*, 4 February 1984, 192.

———. "NASA Authorization Approved: Manned Space Station Wins House Panel's Endorsement." *Congressional Quarterly Weekly Report*, 17 March 1984, 614.

———. "Space Station Funds Included: House Committee Authorizes $7.5 Billion for NASA Programs." *Congressional Quarterly Weekly Report*, 24 March 1984, 670.

———. "NASA Authorization, Landsat Sale." *Congressional Quarterly Weekly Report*, 12 May 1984, 1151.

———. "$14 Billion Approved for HUD." *Congressional Quarterly Weekly Report*, 19 May 1984, 1199.

———. "EPA, Veterans Included: House Passes $58.4 Billion HUD/Agency Bill." *Congressional Quarterly Weekly Report*, 2 June 1984, 1327.

———. "Trims $2.4 Billion from House Bill: Panel Votes $56.1 Billion for HUD, Agencies." *Congressional Quarterly Weekly Report*, 9 June 1984, 1393.

———. "HUD Appropriations Cleared for President." *Congressional Quarterly Weekly Report*, 30 June 1984, 1588.

———. "President Signs NASA Authorization Measure." *Congressional Quarterly Weekly Report*, 28 July 1984, 1865.

Rudalevige, Andrew. *Managing the President's Program: Presidential Leadership and Legislative Policy Formation*. Princeton, NJ: Princeton University Press, 2002.

Schlesinger, Arthur M., Jr. *The Coming of the New Deal*. New York: Houghton Mifflin, 1959.

———. "Annual Messages of the Presidents: Major Themes of American History." In *The State of the Union Messages of the Presidents 1790–1966*, ed. Fred A. Israel. New York: Chelsea, 1966.

"Section Notes: Senate Action Stalled on Transportation Bill." *Congressional Quarterly Weekly Report*, 11 November 1989, 3054.

Skowronek, Stephen. *The Politics Presidents Make: Leadership from John Adams to Bill Clinton*. Cambridge: Harvard University Press, 1997.

Smith, Craig Allen, and Kathy B. Smith. "Presidential Values and Public Priorities: Recurrent Patterns in Addresses to the Nation, 1963–1984." *Presidential Studies Quarterly* 15 (1985):743–753.

Solomon, Burt. "Clinton's 'Transcendent Legacy'?" *National Journal* 27 (1995):2235.

Spitzer, Robert J. *The Presidential Veto: Touchstone of the American Presidency*. Albany: State University of New York Press, 1988.

———. "The Item Veto Dispute and the Secular Crisis of the Presidency." *Presidential Studies Quarterly* 28, no. 4 (1998):799–805.

Stevens, C. Ellis. *Sources of the Constitution of the United States*. New York: Macmillan and Co, 1894.

Stid, Daniel D. *The President as Statesman: Woodrow Wilson and the Constitution*. Lawrence: University of Kansas Press, 1998.

Storing, Herbert J., ed. *The Complete Anti-Federalist*. 7 vols. Chicago: University of Chicago Press, 1981.

Sykes, Patricia Lee. "The President as Legislator: A 'Superepresenator.'" *Presidential Studies Quarterly* 19 (1989):313.

Taylor, Andrew. "Line-Item Veto Bill Becomes Law." *Congressional Quarterly Weekly Report*, 13 April 1996, 984.

————. "Judge Voids Line-Item Veto Law; Backers Look to High Court." *Congressional Quarterly Weekly Report*, 12 April 1997, 833–834.

————. "Few in Congress Grieve as Justices Give Line-Item Veto the Ax." *Congressional Quarterly Weekly Report*, 27 June 1998, 1747.

Teten, Ryan L. "Evolution of the Modern Rhetorical Presidency: Presidential Presentation and Development of the State of the Union Addresses." *Presidential Studies Quarterly* 33 (2003):333–346.

"Toward a More Responsible Two-Party System: A Report of the Committee on Political Parties, American Political Science Association." *American Political Science Review* 44 (1950).

Towle, Michael J. *Out of Touch: The Presidency and Public Opinion.* College Station: Texas A&M University Press, 2004.

Truman, Harry S. *Public Papers of the Presidents of the United States: Harry S Truman, 1945–1953.* 8 vols. Washington, DC: GPO, 1963–1965.

Tulis, Jeffrey K. *The Rhetorical Presidency.* Princeton: Princeton University Press, 1987.

————. "The Two Constitutional Presidencies." In *The Presidency and the Political System,* 7th ed., ed. Michael Nelson. Washington, DC: CQ Press, 2003.

US Senate. *The Constitution of the United States of America: Analysis and Interpretation.* 103rd Cong., 1st Sess., 1992, S. Doc. 91.

"Vets Job Preference Rule Hurts Women, Minorities." *Congressional Quarterly Weekly Report*, 15 July 1978, 1780.

Waldrop, M. Mitchell. "The Selling of the Space Station; All the Washington Heavyweights Voted 'Nay' on the Space Station, but Reagan Voted 'Aye'; the 'Ayes' Had It." *Science* 223 (1984):793.

Wanta, Wayne, Mary Ann Stephenson, Judy VanSlyke Turk, and Maxwell E. McCombs. "How President's State of the Union Talk Influenced News Media Agendas." *Journalism Quarterly* 66 (1989):537–541.

Waterman, Richard W., Hank C. Jenkins-Smith, and Carol L. Silva. "The Expectations Gap Thesis: Public Attitudes Toward an Incumbent President." *Journal of Politics* 61 (1999):944–966.

Wayne, Stephen J. *The Legislative Presidency.* New York: Harper & Row, 1978.

West, Darrell M. *The Rise and Fall of the Media Establishment.* Boston: Bedford/St. Martin's Press, 2001.

Wilson, Woodrow. *Constitutional Government in the United States.* New York: Columbia University Press, 1961.

Wlezien, Christopher. "The Politics of Impoundment." *Political Research Quarterly* 42 (1994):59–84.

Wood, B. Dan. "Presidential Rhetoric and Economic Leadership." *Presidential Studies Quarterly* 34 (September 2004):573–606.

Zevin, B. O., ed. *Nothing to Fear: The Selected Addresses of Franklin Delano Roosevelt.* New York: Houghton Mifflin, 1946.

Index

About the Book

The State of the Union address is no ordinary speech. It is a fundamental statement of how a president approaches current policy debates and has the distinction of being the one presidential address that US citizens are most likely to tune in to hear each year. Donna Hoffman and Alison Howard document the political significance and legislative impact—or often, lack of impact—of this most visible of presidential communications.

Exploring how and why the State of the Union address came to be a key tool in the exercise of presidential power, the authors outline the ways presidents use it to gain attention, to communicate with target audiences, and to make specific policy proposals. Their richly textured analysis offers a penetrating look at the complex relationship between contemporary presidential leadership and Congressional lawmaking.

Donna R. Hoffman is assistant professor of political science at the University of Northern Iowa. **Alison D. Howard** is adjunct instructor of political science at Dominican University of California.